MznLnx

Missing Links Exam Preps

Exam Prep for

Essentials of Geology

Marshak, 2nd Edition

The MznLnx Exam Prep is your link from the textbook and lecture to your exams.
The MznLnx Exam Preps are unauthorized and comprehensive reviews of your textbooks.

All material provided by MznLnx and Rico Publications (c) 2010
Textbook publishers and textbook authors do not particpate in or contribute to these reviews.

MznLnx

Rico Publications

Exam Prep for Essentials of Geology
2nd Edition
Marshak

Publisher: Raymond Houge	*Product Manager:* Dave Mason
Assistant Editor: Michael Rouger	*Editorial Assitant:* Rachel Guzmanji
Text and Cover Designer: Lisa Buckner	*Pedagogy:* Debra Long
Marketing Manager: Sara Swagger	*Cover Image:* Jim Reed/Getty Images
Project Manager, Editorial Production: Jerry Emerson	*Text and Cover Printer:* City Printing, Inc.
Art Director: Vernon Lowerui	*Compositor:* Media Mix, Inc.

(c) 2010 Rico Publications

ALL RIGHTS RESERVED. No part of this work covered by the copyright may be reproduced or used in any form or by an means--graphic, electronic, or mechanical, including photocopying, recording, taping, Web distribution, information storage, and retrieval systems, or in any other manner--without the written permission of the publisher.

Printed in the United States
ISBN:

For more information about our products, contact us at:
Dave.Mason@RicoPublications.com

For permission to use material from this text or product, submit a request online to:
Dave.Mason@RicoPublications.com

Contents

CHAPTER 1
The Earth in Context — 1

CHAPTER 2
The Way the Earth Works: Plate Tectonics — 12

CHAPTER 3
Patterns in Nature: Minerals — 22

CHAPTER 4
Up from the Inferno: Magma and Igneous Rocks — 33

CHAPTER 5
A Surface Veneer: Sediments, Soils, and Sedimentary Rocks — 43

CHAPTER 6
Metamorphism: A Process of Change — 57

CHAPTER 7
The Wrath of Vulcan: Volcanic Eruptions — 70

CHAPTER 8
A Violent Pulse: Earthquakes — 82

CHAPTER 9
Crags, Cracks, and Crumples: Crustal Deformation and Mountain Building — 95

CHAPTER 10
Deep Time: How Old Is Old? — 109

CHAPTER 11
A Biography of Earth — 115

CHAPTER 12
Riches in Rock: Energy and Mineral Resources — 129

CHAPTER 13
Unsafe Ground: Landslides and Other Mass Movements — 141

CHAPTER 14
Streams and Associated Flooding: The Geology of Running Water — 147

CHAPTER 15
Restless Realm: Oceans and Coasts — 155

CHAPTER 16
A Hidden Reserve: Groundwater — 166

CHAPTER 17
Dry Regions: The Geology of Deserts — 173

CHAPTER 18
Amazing Ice: Glaciers and Ice Ages — 183

CHAPTER 19
Global Change in the Earth System — 197

ANSWER KEY — 205

TO THE STUDENT

COMPREHENSIVE

The *MznLnx* Exam Prep series is designed to help you pass your exams. Editors at MznLnx review your textbooks and then prepare these practice exams to help you master the textbook material. Unlike study guides, workbooks, and practice tests provided by the texbook publisher and textbook authors, *MznLnx* gives you **all** of the material in each chapter in exam form, not just samples, so you can be sure to nail your exam.

MECHANICAL

The MznLnx Exam Prep series creates exams that will help you learn the subject matter as well as test you on your understanding. Each question is designed to help you master the concept. Just working through the exams, you gain an understanding of the subject--its a simple mechanical process that produces success.

INTEGRATED STUDY GUIDE AND REVIEW

MznLnx is not just a set of exams designed to test you, its also a comprehensive review of the subject content. Each exam question is also a review of the concept, making sure that you will get the answer correct without having to go to other sources of material. You learn as you go! Its the easiest way to pass an exam.

HUMOR

Studying can be tedious and dry. MznLnx's instructional design includes moderate humor within the exam questions on occassion, to break the tedium and revitalize the brain

Chapter 1. The Earth in Context 1

1. A _____ is a large, slow-moving mass of ice, formed from compacted layers of snow, that slowly deforms and flows in response to gravity and high pressure.

_____ ice is the largest reservoir of fresh water on Earth, and second only to oceans as the largest reservoir of total water.

- a. Little Ice Age
- b. Keeling Curve
- c. Pacific Decadal Oscillation
- d. Glacier

2. A _____ is a mountain rising from the ocean seafloor that does not reach to the water's surface (sea level), and thus is not an island. These are typically formed from extinct volcanoes, that rise abruptly and are usually found rising from a seafloor of 1,000-4,000 meters depth. They are defined by oceanographers as independent features that rise to at least 1,000 meters above the seafloor.
- a. 1703 Genroku earthquake
- b. 1700 Cascadia earthquake
- c. 1509 Istanbul earthquake
- d. Seamount

3. The _____ is a chronologic schema (or idealized model) relating stratigraphy to time that is used by geologists, paleontologists and other earth scientists to describe the timing and relationships between events that have occurred during the history of the Earth. The table of geologic time spans presented here agrees with the dates and nomenclature proposed by the International Commission on Stratigraphy, and uses the standard color codes of the United States Geological Survey.

Evidence from radiometric dating indicates that the Earth is about 4.570 billion years old.

- a. 1700 Cascadia earthquake
- b. 1703 Genroku earthquake
- c. 1509 Istanbul earthquake
- d. Geologic time scale

4. _____ is the solid-state recrystallization of pre-existing rocks due to changes in physical and chemical conditions, primarily heat, pressure, and the introduction of chemically active fluids. Both mineralogical, chemical and crystallographic changes can occur during this process.

Three types of _____ exist: dynamic, contact and regional.

- a. Reading Prong
- b. Compression
- c. Detritus
- d. Metamorphism

5. The _____ was a mountain-building event that affected western North America from Canada to the north to Mexico to the south. This orogeny was the result of convergent boundary tectonism between approximately 140 million years (Ma) ago, and 50 Ma. This orogeny was produced by the collision of the oceanic Farallon Plate and Kula Plate, predecessors of the Pacific Plate, and their subduction underneath the continental North American Plate. The _____ was preceded by several other mountain-building events including the Nevadan orogeny, the Sonoman orogeny, and the Antler orogeny, and partially overlapped in time and space with the Laramide orogeny.
- a. Pan-African orogeny
- b. Sevier orogeny
- c. Kaikoura Orogeny
- d. Trans-Hudson orogeny

6. _____ refers to natural mountain building, and may be studied as a tectonic structural event, (b) as a geographical event, and (c) a chronological event. Orogenic events (a) cause distinctive structural phenomena and related tectonic activity, (b) affect certain regions of rocks and crust, and (c) happen within a specific period of time.

Chapter 1. The Earth in Context

a. Orogenesis
b. Antler orogeny
c. Alice Springs Orogeny
d. Orogeny

7. _____ are rare geological features that are only known to form in the bedrock beneath meteorite impact craters or underground nuclear explosions. They are evidence that the rock has been subjected to a shock with pressures in the range of 2-30 GPa.

_____ have a distinctively conical shape that radiates from the top of the cones repeating cone-on-cone in large and small scales in the same sample.

a. 1700 Cascadia earthquake
b. 1509 Istanbul earthquake
c. Shatter cones
d. 1703 Genroku earthquake

8. A _____ is an opening in a planet's surface or crust, which allows hot, molten rock, ash, and gases to escape from below the surface. Volcanic activity involving the extrusion of rock tends to form mountains or features like mountains over a period of time.

a. 1700 Cascadia earthquake
b. 1509 Istanbul earthquake
c. 1703 Genroku earthquake
d. Volcano

9. A _____ is a deep active seismic area in a subduction zone. Differential motion along the zone produces deep-seated earthquakes, the foci of which may be as deep as about 700 kilometres (435 miles.) They develop beneath volcanic island arcs and continental margins above active subduction zones.

a. Pyroclastic flow
b. Pit crater
c. Lava
d. Wadati-Benioff zone

10. The _____ is the level at which the ground water pressure is equal to atmospheric pressure. It may be conveniently visualized as the 'surface' of the ground water in a given vicinity. It usually coincides with the phreatic surface, but can be many feet above it. As water infiltrates through pore spaces in the soil, it first passes through the zone of aeration, where the soil is unsaturated. At increasing depths water fills in more spaces, until the zone of saturation is reached. The relatively horizontal plane atop this zone constitutes the _____.

a. Crosshole sonic logging
b. Rock bolt
c. Shaft construction
d. Water table

11. The _____ is a cosmological model of the initial conditions and subsequent development of the universe. It is supported by the most comprehensive and accurate explanations from current scientific evidence and observation. As used by cosmologists, the term _____ generally refers to the idea that the universe has expanded from a primordial hot and dense initial condition at some finite time in the past, and continues to expand to this day.

a. 1700 Cascadia earthquake
b. 1703 Genroku earthquake
c. 1509 Istanbul earthquake
d. Big bang

12. A _____ is a natural formation (or landform) where a rock arch forms, with a natural passageway through underneath. Most natural arches form as a narrow ridge, walled by cliffs, become narrower from erosion, with a softer rock stratum under the cliff-forming stratum gradually eroding out until the rock shelters thus formed meet underneath the ridge, thus forming the arch. They commonly form where cliffs are subject to erosion from the sea, rivers or weathering (sub-aerial processes); the processes 'find' weaknesses in rocks and work on them, making them bigger until they break through.

Chapter 1. The Earth in Context

   a. 1509 Istanbul earthquake
   b. 1703 Genroku earthquake
   c. 1700 Cascadia earthquake
   d. Natural arch

13. In mineralogy and crystallography, a _____ is a unique arrangement of atoms in a crystal. A _____ is composed of a motif, a set of atoms arranged in a particular way, and a lattice. Motifs are located upon the points of a lattice, which is an array of points repeating periodically in three dimensions.
   a. 1700 Cascadia earthquake
   b. 1509 Istanbul earthquake
   c. 1703 Genroku earthquake
   d. Crystal structure

14. _____, is the process of coastal sediments returning to the visible portion of a beach or foreshore following a submersion event. A sustainable beach or foreshore often goes through a cycle of submersion during rough weather then _____ during calmer periods. If a coastline is not in a healthy sustainable condition, then erosion can be more serious and _____ does not fully restore the original volume of the visible beach or foreshore leading to permanent beach or foreshore loss.
   a. AL 129-1
   b. AL 333
   c. AASHTO Soil Classification System
   d. Accretion

15. Geologically, a _____ is a long, narrow inlet with steep sides, created in a valley carved by glacial activity.

The seeds of a _____ are laid when a glacier cuts a U-shaped valley through abrasion of the surrounding bedrock by the sediment it carries. Many such valleys were formed during the recent ice age.

   a. 1700 Cascadia earthquake
   b. 1703 Genroku earthquake
   c. 1509 Istanbul earthquake
   d. Fjord

16. _____ describes the large scale motions of Earth's lithosphere. The theory encompasses the older concepts of continental drift, developed during the first decades of the 20th century by Alfred Wegener, and seafloor spreading, understood during the 1960s.

The outermost part of the Earth's interior is made up of two layers: the lithosphere and the asthenosphere.

   a. Continental crust
   b. Thrust fault
   c. Plate tectonics
   d. Forearc

17. A _____ column (or _____) is a column of rising air in the lower altitudes of the Earth's atmosphere. They are created by the uneven heating of the Earth's surface from solar radiation, and an example of convection. The Sun warms the ground, which in turn warms the air directly above it.
   a. 1703 Genroku earthquake
   b. 1700 Cascadia earthquake
   c. 1509 Istanbul earthquake
   d. Thermal

18. The _____ was an ocean that existed in the Neoproterozoic and Paleozoic eras of the geologic timescale (between 600 and 400 million years ago.) The _____ was situated in the southern hemisphere, between the paleocontinents of Laurentia, Baltica and Avalonia. The ocean disappeared with the Caledonian, Taconic and Acadian orogenies, when these three continents joined to form one big landmass called Laurussia.

a. Iapetus Ocean
b. AL 333
c. AASHTO Soil Classification System
d. AL 129-1

19. _____ is a common extrusive volcanic rock. It is usually grey to black and fine-grained due to rapid cooling of lava at the surface of a planet. It may be porphyritic containing larger crystals in a fine matrix, or vesicular, or frothy scoria.
   a. Basalt
   b. 1703 Genroku earthquake
   c. 1509 Istanbul earthquake
   d. 1700 Cascadia earthquake

20.

A widely accepted theory of planet formation, the so-called _____ hypothesis of Viktor Safronov, states that planets form out of dust grains that collide and stick to form larger and larger bodies. When the bodies reach sizes of approximately one kilometer, then they can attract each other directly through their mutual gravity, aiding further growth into moon-sized protoplanets enormously.

   a. 1703 Genroku earthquake
   b. 1700 Cascadia earthquake
   c. 1509 Istanbul earthquake
   d. Planetesimal

21. An _____ is the result of a sudden release of energy in the Earth's crust that creates seismic waves. They are recorded with a seismometer or the related and mostly obsolete Richter magnitude, with a magnitude 3 or lower _____ being mostly imperceptible and magnitude 7 causing serious damage over large areas.
   a. AASHTO Soil Classification System
   b. AL 333
   c. AL 129-1
   d. Earthquake

22. The _____ is the rigid outermost shell of a rocky planet.

In the Earth, the _____ includes the crust and the uppermost mantle, which constitute the hard and rigid outer layer of the planet. The _____ is underlain by the asthenosphere, the weaker, hotter, and deeper part of the upper mantle.

   a. Gorda Ridge
   b. Lithosphere
   c. Juan de Fuca Ridge
   d. Continental drift

23. The _____ Eon is the current eon in the geologic timescale, and the one during which abundant animal life has existed. It covers roughly 545 million years and goes back to the time when diverse hard-shelled animals first appeared.
   a. 1509 Istanbul earthquake
   b. 1703 Genroku earthquake
   c. 1700 Cascadia earthquake
   d. Phanerozoic

24. The _____ is the epoch from 1.8 million to 11550 years BP covering the world's recent period of repeated glaciations. The _____ epoch follows the Pliocene epoch and is followed by the Holocene epoch. The _____ is the third epoch of the Neogene period or 6th epoch of the Cenozoic Era. The end of the _____ corresponds with the retreat of the last continental glacier. It also corresponds with the end of the Paleolithic age used in archaeology.
   a. Sicilian Stage
   b. Tyrrhenian
   c. Late Pleistocene
   d. Pleistocene

25. The _____ is a geological eon representing a period before the first abundant complex life on Earth. The _____ extended from 2500 Ma to 542.0 >± 1.0 Ma (million years ago), and is the most recent part of the old, informally named 'e;Precambrian'e; time.

The Proterozoic consists of 3 geologic eras, from oldest to youngest:

- Paleoproterozoic
- Mesoproterozoic
- Neoproterozoic

The well-identified events were:

- The transition to an oxygenated atmosphere during the Mesoproterozoic.
- Several glaciations, including the hypothesized Snowball Earth during the Cryogenian period in the late Neoproterozoic.
- The Ediacaran Period (635 to 542 Ma) which is characterized by the evolution of abundant soft-bodied multicellular organisms.

The geoloic record of the Proterozoic is much better than that for the preceding Archean. In contrast to the deep-water deposits of the Archean, the Proterozoic features many strata that were laid down in extensive shallow epicontinental seas; furthermore, many of these rocks are less metamorphosed than Archean-age ones, and plenty are unaltered.

a. 1509 Istanbul earthquake
b. 1703 Genroku earthquake
c. 1700 Cascadia earthquake
d. Proterozoic Eon

26. _____ is water located beneath the ground surface in soil pore spaces and in the fractures of lithologic formations. A unit of rock or an unconsolidated deposit is called an aquifer when it can yield a usable quantity of water. The depth at which soil pore spaces or fractures and voids in rock become completely saturated with water is called the water table.

a. Depression focused recharge
b. Groundwater
c. 1509 Istanbul earthquake
d. 1700 Cascadia earthquake

27. The general term '_____' or, more precisely, 'glacial age' denotes a geological period of long-term reduction in the temperature of the Earth's surface and atmosphere, resulting in an expansion of continental ice sheets, polar ice sheets and alpine glaciers. Within a long-term _____, individual pulses of extra cold climate are termed 'glaciations'. Glaciologically, _____ implies the presence of extensive ice sheets in the northern and southern hemispheres; by this definition we are still in an _____

a. Ice age
b. AL 333
c. AL 129-1
d. AASHTO Soil Classification System

28. _____, originally Gondwanaland, is the name given to a southern precursor-supercontinent and then as a remnant separated from Laurasia 180-200 million years ago during the breakup of the Pangaea supercontinent that existed about 500 to 200 Ma ago into two large segments. While the corresponding northern hemisphere continent Laurasia moved further north, the nearly equal in area _____ included most of the landmasses in today's southern hemisphere, including Antarctica, South America, Africa, Madagascar, Australia-New Guinea, and New Zealand, as well as Arabia and the Indian subcontinent, which have now moved into the Northern Hemisphere.
   a. Laurasia
   b. 1509 Istanbul earthquake
   c. 1700 Cascadia earthquake
   d. Gondwana

29. The _____ is a geologic period and system, the second of six of the Paleozoic era, and covers the time between 488.3>±1.7 to 443.7>±1.5 million years ago (ICS, 2004.) It follows the Cambrian period and is followed by the Silurian period. The _____ was defined by Charles Lapworth in 1879, to resolve a dispute between followers of Adam Sedgwick and Roderick Murchison, who were placing the same rock beds in northern Wales into the Cambrian and Silurian periods respectively.
   a. AL 129-1
   b. AASHTO Soil Classification System
   c. AL 333
   d. Ordovician

30. The _____ is the extended perimeter of each continent and associated coastal plain, and was part of the continent during the glacial periods, but is undersea during interglacial periods such as the current epoch by relatively shallow seas (known as shelf seas) and gulfs.

The continental rise is below the slope, but landward of the abyssal plains. Its gradient is intermediate between the slope and the shelf, on the order of 0.5-1°.

   a. 1703 Genroku earthquake
   b. Continental shelf
   c. 1509 Istanbul earthquake
   d. 1700 Cascadia earthquake

31. The _____ or Appalachian orogeny is one of the geological mountain-forming events (orogeny) that formed the Appalachian Mountains and Allegheny Mountains. The term and spelling 'Alleghany Orogeny' (sic) originally proposed by H.P. Woodward (1957, 1958) is preferred usage. Approximately 350 million to 300 million years ago, in the Carboniferous period, the combined continents of Europe and Africa (Gondwana) collided with North America to form the supercontinent of Pangaea.
   a. Alleghenian orogeny
   b. Antler orogeny
   c. Alice Springs Orogeny
   d. Alpine orogeny

32. A _____ is an elongated whale-shaped hill formed by glacial action. Its long axis is parallel with the movement of the ice, with the blunter end facing into the glacial movement. They may be more than 45 m (150 ft) high and more than 0.8 km (1/2 mile) long, and are often in _____ fields of similarly shaped, sized and oriented hills. They usually have layers indicating that the material was repeatedly added to a core, which may be of rock or glacial till.
   a. Sandur
   b. Monadnock
   c. 1509 Istanbul earthquake
   d. Drumlin

33. _____ are the preserved remains or traces of animals, plants, and other organisms from the remote past. The totality of _____, both discovered and undiscovered, and their placement in fossiliferous rock formations and sedimentary layers (strata) is known as the fossil record. The study of _____ across geological time, how they were formed, and the evolutionary relationships between taxa (phylogeny) are some of the most important functions of the science of paleontology.
   a. 1509 Istanbul earthquake
   b. Fossils
   c. 1700 Cascadia earthquake
   d. 1703 Genroku earthquake

34. _____ is a common and widely occurring type of intrusive, felsic, igneous rock. _____ has a medium to coarse texture, occasionally with some individual crystals larger than the groundmass forming a rock known as porphyry. Granites can be pink to dark gray or even black, depending on their chemistry and mineralogy.
   a. 1700 Cascadia earthquake
   b. Granite
   c. 1509 Istanbul earthquake
   d. 1703 Genroku earthquake

35. _____ is one of the three main rock types (the others being sedimentary and metamorphic rock.) _____ is formed by magma (molten rock) being cooled and becoming solid . They may form with or without crystallization, either below the surface as intrusive (plutonic) rocks or on the surface as extrusive (volcanic) rocks. They make up approximately 95% of the upper part of the Earth's crust, but their great abundance is hidden on the Earth's surface by a relatively thin but widespread layer of sedimentary and metamorphic rocks.
   a. AASHTO Soil Classification System
   b. AL 129-1
   c. AL 333
   d. Igneous rock

36. _____ is molten rock that is found beneath the surface of the Earth, and may also exist on other terrestrial planets. Besides molten rock, _____ may also contain suspended crystals and gas bubbles. _____ often collects in a _____ chamber inside a volcano. _____ is capable of intrusion into adjacent rocks, extrusion onto the surface as lava, and explosive ejection as tephra to form pyroclastic rock.
   a. Laccolith
   b. Rock cycle
   c. Magma
   d. Volcanic rock

37. A _____ is a chemical reaction that takes place during the geological process of metamorphism in an amalgamate of minerals that helps determine the final stable state of the resulting metamorphic rock.
   a. Lithotope
   b. Platform cover
   c. Geostrophic current
   d. Metamorphic reaction

38. _____ is the result of the transformation of an existing rock type, the protolith, in a process called metamorphism, which means 'change in form'. The protolith is subjected to heat and pressure (temperatures greater than 150 to 200 >°C and pressures of 1500 bars) causing profound physical and/or chemical change. The protolith may be sedimentary rock, igneous rock or another older _____.
   a. Sedimentary rock
   b. Migmatite
   c. Metavolcanic rock
   d. Metamorphic rock

39. A _____ is a dense, coarse-grained igneous rock, consisting mostly of the minerals olivine and pyroxene. _____ is ultramafic, as the rock contains less than 45% silica. It is high in magnesium, reflecting the high proportions of magnesium-rich olivine, with appreciable iron.

Chapter 1. The Earth in Context

_____ is the dominant rock of the upper part of the Earth's mantle. The compositions of _____ nodules found in certain basalts and diamond pipes (kimberlites) are of special interest, because they provide samples of the Earth's Mantle roots of continents brought up from depths from about 30 km or so to depths at least as great as about 200 km.

- a. 1703 Genroku earthquake
- b. 1509 Istanbul earthquake
- c. 1700 Cascadia earthquake
- d. Peridotite

40. _____ is any particulate matter that can be transported by fluid flow, and which eventually is deposited.

They are most often transported by water (fluvial processes) transported by wind (aeolian processes) and glaciers. Beach sands and river channel deposits are examples of fluvial transport and deposition, though _____ also often settles out of slow-moving or standing water in lakes and oceans.

- a. Bovey Beds
- b. Brickearth
- c. Sediment
- d. Quicksand

41. _____ is one of the three main rock types (the others being igneous and metamorphic rock.) _____ is formed by deposition and consolidation of mineral and organic material and from precipitation of minerals from solution. The processes that form _____ occur at the surface of the Earth and within bodies of water.
- a. Petrology
- b. Serpentinite
- c. Rock cycle
- d. Sedimentary rock

42. A _____ is a compound containing an anion in which one or more central silicon atoms are surrounded by electronegative ligands. This definition is broad enough to include species such as hexafluorosilicate ('fluorosilicate'), $[SiF_6]^{2-}$, but the _____ species that are encountered most often consist of silicon with oxygen as the ligand. _____ anions, with a negative net electrical charge, must have that charge balanced by other cations to make an electrically neutral compound.
- a. 1703 Genroku earthquake
- b. 1700 Cascadia earthquake
- c. 1509 Istanbul earthquake
- d. Silicate

43. _____ are igneous and meta-igneous rocks with very low silica content (less than 45%), generally >18% MgO, high FeO, low potassium, and are composed of usually greater than 90% mafic minerals (dark colored, high magnesium and iron content.) The Earth's mantle is considered to be composed of _____.
- a. AL 129-1
- b. AASHTO Soil Classification System
- c. Ultramafic rocks
- d. AL 333

44. The _____ was a major ice sheet that covered, during glacial periods of the Quaternary, a large area of North America. This included the following areas:

- Western Montana
- The Idaho Panhandle
- Northern Washington state down to about Seattle and Spokane, Washington
- All of British Columbia
- The southwestern third or so of Yukon territory
- All of the Alaska Panhandle
- South Central Alaska
- The Alaska Peninsula
- Almost all of the continental shelf north of the Strait of Juan de Fuca

The ice sheet covered up to two and a half million square kilometres at the Last Glacial Maximum and probably more than that in some previous periods, when it may have extended into the northeast extremity of Oregon and the Salmon River Mountains in Idaho. It is probable, though, that its northern margin also migrated south due to the influence of starvation caused by very low levels of precipitation.

At its eastern end the _____ merged with the Laurentide ice sheet at the Continental Divide, forming an area of ice that contained one and a half times as much water as the Antarctic ice sheet does today.

   a. Wolstonian Stage   b. Snowball Earth
   c. Cordilleran ice sheet   d. Rock flour

45. The _____ was an ancient oceanic plate, which began subducting under the west coast of the North American Plate-- then located in modern Utah-- as Pangaea broke apart during the Jurassic period. It is named for the Farallon Islands which are located just west of San Francisco, California.

Over time the central part of the _____ was completely subducted under the southwestern part of the North American Plate. The remains of the _____ are the Juan de Fuca, Explorer and Gorda Plates, subducting under the northern part of the North American Plate, the Cocos Plate subducting under Central America and the Nazca Plate subducting under the South American Plate.

   a. Fault trace   b. Farallon Plate
   c. Cocos Plate   d. Rivera Plate

46. In geology, a _____ or _____ line is a planar fracture in rock in which the rock on one side of the fracture has moved with respect to the rock on the other side. Large faults within the Earth's crust are the result of differential or shear motion and active _____ zones are the causal locations of most earthquakes. Earthquakes are caused by energy release during rapid slippage along a _____.

   a. Dali   b. Stack
   c. Fault   d. Combe

47. _____ are the largest glaciers, enormous masses of ice that are not visibly affected by the landscape and that cover the entire surface beneath them, except possibly on the margins where they are thinnest. Antarctica and Greenland are the only places where continental _____ currently exist. These regions contain vast quantities of fresh water.

a. AL 129-1
b. AL 333
c. Ice sheets
d. AASHTO Soil Classification System

48. _____ is a sedimentary rock. It is a natural chemical precipitate of carbonate minerals; typically aragonite, but often recrystallized to, or primarily, calcite.

_____ forms as calcium carbonate is deposited from the water of mineral springs or rivulets that are saturated with dissolved calcium bicarbonate. The spring water from which the calcium carbonate precipitates can be hot, warm or cold. The rate of deposition increases with the temperature of the water, or alternatively, when biotic material accelerates the process of precipitation.

a. 1700 Cascadia earthquake
b. Travertine
c. 1703 Genroku earthquake
d. 1509 Istanbul earthquake

49. The _____ is the layer of igneous, sedimentary, and metamorphic rocks which form the continents and the areas of shallow seabed close to their shores, known as continental shelves. This layer is sometimes called sial due to more felsic, or granitic, bulk composition, which lies in contrast to the oceanic crust, called sima due to its mafic, or basaltic rock. (Based on the change in velocity of seismic waves, it is believed that at a certain depth sial becomes close in its physical properties to sima.

a. Continental crust
b. Tectonic plates
c. Nappe
d. Convergent boundary

50. _____ is the part of Earth's lithosphere that surfaces in the ocean basins. _____ is primarily composed of mafic rocks, or sima. It is thinner than continental crust, or sial, generally less than 10 kilometers thick, however it is denser, having a mean density of about 3.3 grams per cubic centimeter.

a. AL 129-1
b. Oceanic crust
c. AL 333
d. AASHTO Soil Classification System

51. In seismology, _____ are surface seismic waves that cause horizontal shifting of the earth during an earthquake. A.E.H. Love predicted the existence of _____ mathematically in 1911. They form a distinct class, different from other types of seismic waves, such as P-waves and S-waves (both body waves), or Rayleigh waves (another type of surface wave). _____ travel with a slower velocity than P- or S- waves, but faster than Rayleigh waves.

a. Seismic refraction
b. Love waves
c. Mazuku
d. Strainmeter

52. The _____ is the mechanically weak ductily-deforming region of the upper mantle of the Earth. It lies below the lithosphere, at depths between 100 and 200 km (~ 62 and 124 miles) below the surface, but perhaps extending as deep as 400 km (~ 249 miles.)

The _____ is a portion of the upper mantle just below the lithosphere that is involved in plate movements and isostatic adjustments. In spite of its heat, pressures keep it plastic, and it has a relatively low density. Seismic waves pass relatively slowly through the _____, compared to the overlying lithospheric mantle, thus it has been called the low-velocity zone. This was the observation that originally alerted seismologists to its presence and gave some information about its physical properties, as the speed of seismic waves decreases with decreasing rigidity.

a. AASHTO Soil Classification System
b. AL 129-1
c. AL 333
d. Asthenosphere

53. The lithosphere is broken up into what are called _____. In the case of Earth, there are eight major and many minor plates The lithospheric plates ride on the asthenosphere. These plates move in relation to one another at one of three types of plate boundaries: convergent, or collisional boundaries; divergent boundaries, also called spreading centers; and transform boundaries.

a. Copperbelt Province
b. Gorda Ridge
c. Tectonic plates
d. Thrust fault

54. The _____ is part of the Earth's mantle, and is located between the lower mantle and the upper mantle, between a depth of 410 and 660 km. The Earth's mantle, including the _____, consists primarily of peridotite, a course grained, ultramafic, igneous rock.

The mantle was divided into the upper mantle, _____, and lower mantle as a result of sudden seismic-velocity discontinuities at depths of 410 and 660 km.

a. Transition zone
b. Dissolved load
c. Subfossil
d. Teilzone

Chapter 2. The Way the Earth Works: Plate Tectonics

1. _____ was the supercontinent that is theorized to have existed during the Paleozoic and Mesozoic eras about 250 million years ago, before the component continents were separated into their current configuration.

The name was first used by the German originator of the continental drift theory, Alfred Wegener, in the 1920 edition of his book The Origin of Continents and Oceans, in which a postulated supercontinent _____ played a key role.

The single enormous ocean which surrounded Pangaea is known as Panthalassa.

- a. 1703 Genroku earthquake
- b. 1509 Istanbul earthquake
- c. 1700 Cascadia earthquake
- d. Pangea

2. _____ is the movement of the Earth's continents relative to each other. The hypothesis that continents 'drift' was first put forward by Abraham Ortelius in 1596 and was fully developed by Alfred Wegener in 1912. However, it was not until the development of the theory of plate tectonics in the 1960s, that a sufficient geological explanation of that movement was found.
- a. Continental drift
- b. Thrust fault
- c. Plate tectonics
- d. Panthalassa

3. In geology, _____ is transported rock debris overlying the solid bedrock. The term is also sometimes refers to organic debris so-transported. In the largest sense, it refers to the material left behind by retreating continental glaciers.
- a. Platform cover
- b. Patterned ground
- c. Geodiversity
- d. Drift

4. _____ occurs at mid-ocean ridges, where new oceanic crust is formed through volcanic activity and then gradually moves away from the ridge. _____ helps explain continental drift in the theory of plate tectonics.

Earlier theories (e.g., by Alfred Wegener) of continental drift were that continents 'plowed' through the sea. The idea that the seafloor itself moves (and carries the continents with it) as it expands from a central axis was proposed by Harry Hess from Princeton University in the 1960s. The theory is well-accepted now, and the phenomenon is known to be caused by convection currents in the plastic, very weak upper mantle, or asthenosphere.

- a. Diagenesis
- b. Saltation
- c. Seafloor spreading
- d. Deposition

5. In geology, _____ is the process that takes place at convergent boundaries by which one tectonic plate moves under another tectonic plate, sinking into the Earth's mantle, as the plates converge. A _____ zone is an area on Earth where two tectonic plates move towards one another and _____ occurs. Rates of _____ are typically measured in centimeters per year, with the average rate of convergence being approximately 2 to 8 centimeters per year (about the rate a fingernail grows.)
- a. Divergent boundary
- b. Motagua Fault
- c. Forearc
- d. Subduction

6. A _____ is a large, slow-moving mass of ice, formed from compacted layers of snow, that slowly deforms and flows in response to gravity and high pressure.

_____ ice is the largest reservoir of fresh water on Earth, and second only to oceans as the largest reservoir of total water.

   a. Glacier
   c. Little Ice Age
   b. Pacific Decadal Oscillation
   d. Keeling Curve

7. _____ is any particulate matter that can be transported by fluid flow, and which eventually is deposited.

They are most often transported by water (fluvial processes) transported by wind (aeolian processes) and glaciers. Beach sands and river channel deposits are examples of fluvial transport and deposition, though _____ also often settles out of slow-moving or standing water in lakes and oceans.

   a. Bovey Beds
   c. Quicksand
   b. Sediment
   d. Brickearth

8. The _____ is a geological signature, usually a thin band, dated to (65.5 ± 0.3) Ma (million years ago). The boundary marks the end of the Mesozoic era and the beginning of the Cenozoic era, and is associated with the Cretaceous-Tertiary extinction event, a mass extinction.
   a. 1700 Cascadia earthquake
   c. Shiva crater
   b. 1509 Istanbul earthquake
   d. K-T boundary

9. _____ are the preserved remains or traces of animals, plants, and other organisms from the remote past. The totality of _____, both discovered and undiscovered, and their placement in fossiliferous rock formations and sedimentary layers (strata) is known as the fossil record. The study of _____ across geological time, how they were formed, and the evolutionary relationships between taxa (phylogeny) are some of the most important functions of the science of paleontology.
   a. 1703 Genroku earthquake
   c. 1509 Istanbul earthquake
   b. 1700 Cascadia earthquake
   d. Fossils

10. The _____ is an oceanic tectonic plate beneath the Pacific Ocean.

To the north the easterly side is a divergent boundary with the Explorer Plate, the Juan de Fuca Plate and the Gorda Plate forming respectively the Explorer Ridge, the Juan de Fuca Ridge and the Gorda Ridge. In the middle the easterly side is a transform boundary with the North American Plate along the San Andreas Fault and a boundary with the Cocos Plate.

   a. Conway Reef Plate
   c. Somali Plate
   b. Gorda Plate
   d. Pacific Plate

11. _____ is the study of the record of the Earth's magnetic field preserved in various magnetic minerals through time. The study of _____ has demonstrated that the Earth's magnetic field varies substantially in both orientation and intensity through time. <
   a. Stage
   c. Paleomagnetism
   b. Chronozone
   d. Law of superposition

Chapter 2. The Way the Earth Works: Plate Tectonics

12. The _____ is the earliest of three geologic eras of the Phanerozoic eon. The _____ spanned from roughly 542 to 251 million years ago (ICS, 2004), and is subdivided into six geologic periods; from oldest to youngest they are: the Cambrian, Ordovician, Silurian, Devonian, Carboniferous, and Permian.

The _____ covers the time from the first appearance of abundant, soft-shelled fossils to the time when the continents were beginning to be dominated by large, relatively sophisticated reptiles and modern plants. The lower (oldest) boundary was classically set at the first appearance of creatures known as trilobites and archeocyathids.

   a. 1700 Cascadia earthquake
   b. Paleozoic
   c. 1509 Istanbul earthquake
   d. 1703 Genroku earthquake

13. _____ is a sedimentary rock composed largely of the mineral calcite (calcium carbonate: $CaCO_3$.) The deposition of _____ strata is often a by-product and indicator of biological activity in the geologic record. Calcium (along with nitrogen, phosphorus, and potassium) is a key mineral to plant nutrition: soils overlying _____ bedrock tend to be pre-fertilized with calcium.
   a. Limestone
   b. 1700 Cascadia earthquake
   c. 1703 Genroku earthquake
   d. 1509 Istanbul earthquake

14. The _____ is a mid-ocean ridge, a divergent tectonic plate boundary located along the floor of the Atlantic Ocean, and the longest mountain range in the world. It separates the Eurasian Plate and North American Plate in the North Atlantic, and the African Plate from the South American Plate in the South Atlantic. The MAR extends from a junction with the Gakkel Ridge (Mid-Arctic Ridge) northeast of Greenland southward to the Bouvet Triple Junction in the South Atlantic.
   a. 1700 Cascadia earthquake
   b. Mid-Atlantic Ridge
   c. 1703 Genroku earthquake
   d. 1509 Istanbul earthquake

15. A _____ is an underwater mountain range, typically having a valley known as a rift running along its spine, formed by plate tectonics. This type of oceanic ridge is characteristic of what is known as an oceanic spreading center, which is responsible for seafloor spreading. The uplifted sea floor results from convection currents which rise in the mantle as magma at a linear weakness in the oceanic crust, and emerge as lava, creating new crust upon cooling.
   a. Transgression
   b. Seafloor spreading
   c. Permineralization
   d. Mid-ocean ridge

16. In chronostratigraphy, a _____ is a succession of rock strata laid down in an single age on the geologic timescale, which usually represents millions of years of deposition. A given _____ of rock and the corresponding age of time will by convention have the same name, and the same boundaries.
   a. Geologic record
   b. Chronostratigraphy
   c. Relative dating
   d. Stage

17. A _____ is a chain of volcanic islands or mountains formed by plate tectonics as an oceanic tectonic plate subducts under another tectonic plate and produces magma. There are two types of these: oceanic arcs (commonly called island arcs, a type of archipelago) and continental arcs. In the former, oceanic crust subducts beneath other oceanic crust on an adjacent plate, while in the latter case the oceanic crust subducts beneath continental crust. In some situations, a single subduction zone may show both aspects along its length, as part of a plate subducts beneath a continent and part beneath adjacent oceanic crust.

a. Volcanic arc
b. 1509 Istanbul earthquake
c. 1703 Genroku earthquake
d. 1700 Cascadia earthquake

18. _____ is the part of Earth's lithosphere that surfaces in the ocean basins. _____ is primarily composed of mafic rocks, or sima. It is thinner than continental crust, or sial, generally less than 10 kilometers thick, however it is denser, having a mean density of about 3.3 grams per cubic centimeter.
   a. AASHTO Soil Classification System
   b. Oceanic crust
   c. AL 333
   d. AL 129-1

19. A _____ is a mountain rising from the ocean seafloor that does not reach to the water's surface (sea level), and thus is not an island. These are typically formed from extinct volcanoes, that rise abruptly and are usually found rising from a seafloor of 1,000-4,000 meters depth. They are defined by oceanographers as independent features that rise to at least 1,000 meters above the seafloor.
   a. Seamount
   b. 1703 Genroku earthquake
   c. 1700 Cascadia earthquake
   d. 1509 Istanbul earthquake

20. _____ is the geomorphic process by which soil, regolith, and rock move downslope under the force of gravity. Types of _____ include creep, slides, flows, topples, and falls, each with its own characteristic features, and taking place over timescales from seconds to years. _____ occurs on both terrestrial and submarine slopes, and has been observed on Earth, Mars, and Venus.
   a. 1700 Cascadia earthquake
   b. Soil liquefaction
   c. 1509 Istanbul earthquake
   d. Mass wasting

21. The _____ is the mechanically weak ductily-deforming region of the upper mantle of the Earth. It lies below the lithosphere, at depths between 100 and 200 km (~ 62 and 124 miles) below the surface, but perhaps extending as deep as 400 km (~ 249 miles.)

The _____ is a portion of the upper mantle just below the lithosphere that is involved in plate movements and isostatic adjustments. In spite of its heat, pressures keep it plastic, and it has a relatively low density. Seismic waves pass relatively slowly through the _____, compared to the overlying lithospheric mantle, thus it has been called the low-velocity zone. This was the observation that originally alerted seismologists to its presence and gave some information about its physical properties, as the speed of seismic waves decreases with decreasing rigidity.

   a. AL 333
   b. AL 129-1
   c. AASHTO Soil Classification System
   d. Asthenosphere

22. The _____ is the layer of igneous, sedimentary, and metamorphic rocks which form the continents and the areas of shallow seabed close to their shores, known as continental shelves. This layer is sometimes called sial due to more felsic, or granitic, bulk composition, which lies in contrast to the oceanic crust, called sima due to its mafic, or basaltic rock. (Based on the change in velocity of seismic waves, it is believed that at a certain depth sial becomes close in its physical properties to sima.
   a. Tectonic plates
   b. Nappe
   c. Convergent boundary
   d. Continental crust

Chapter 2. The Way the Earth Works: Plate Tectonics

23. The _____ is the extended perimeter of each continent and associated coastal plain, and was part of the continent during the glacial periods, but is undersea during interglacial periods such as the current epoch by relatively shallow seas (known as shelf seas) and gulfs.

The continental rise is below the slope, but landward of the abyssal plains. Its gradient is intermediate between the slope and the shelf, on the order of 0.5-1°.

   a. 1700 Cascadia earthquake   b. Continental shelf
   c. 1703 Genroku earthquake   d. 1509 Istanbul earthquake

24. An _____ is the result of a sudden release of energy in the Earth's crust that creates seismic waves. They are recorded with a seismometer or the related and mostly obsolete Richter magnitude, with a magnitude 3 or lower _____ being mostly imperceptible and magnitude 7 causing serious damage over large areas.
   a. Earthquake   b. AASHTO Soil Classification System
   c. AL 333   d. AL 129-1

25. The _____ is the rigid outermost shell of a rocky planet.

In the Earth, the _____ includes the crust and the uppermost mantle, which constitute the hard and rigid outer layer of the planet. The _____ is underlain by the asthenosphere, the weaker, hotter, and deeper part of the upper mantle.

   a. Lithosphere   b. Continental drift
   c. Gorda Ridge   d. Juan de Fuca Ridge

26. The lithosphere is broken up into what are called _____. In the case of Earth, there are eight major and many minor plates The lithospheric plates ride on the asthenosphere. These plates move in relation to one another at one of three types of plate boundaries: convergent, or collisional boundaries; divergent boundaries, also called spreading centers; and transform boundaries.
   a. Tectonic plates   b. Copperbelt Province
   c. Gorda Ridge   d. Thrust fault

27. The _____ was an ancient oceanic plate, which began subducting under the west coast of the North American Plate-- then located in modern Utah-- as Pangaea broke apart during the Jurassic period. It is named for the Farallon Islands which are located just west of San Francisco, California.

Over time the central part of the _____ was completely subducted under the southwestern part of the North American Plate. The remains of the _____ are the Juan de Fuca, Explorer and Gorda Plates, subducting under the northern part of the North American Plate, the Cocos Plate subducting under Central America and the Nazca Plate subducting under the South American Plate.

   a. Rivera Plate   b. Fault trace
   c. Cocos Plate   d. Farallon Plate

Chapter 2. The Way the Earth Works: Plate Tectonics

28. In geology, a _____ or _____ line is a planar fracture in rock in which the rock on one side of the fracture has moved with respect to the rock on the other side. Large faults within the Earth's crust are the result of differential or shear motion and active _____ zones are the causal locations of most earthquakes. Earthquakes are caused by energy release during rapid slippage along a _____.
   a. Stack
   b. Combe
   c. Dali
   d. Fault

29. The _____ Eon is the current eon in the geologic timescale, and the one during which abundant animal life has existed. It covers roughly 545 million years and goes back to the time when diverse hard-shelled animals first appeared.
   a. 1509 Istanbul earthquake
   b. 1703 Genroku earthquake
   c. 1700 Cascadia earthquake
   d. Phanerozoic

30. The _____ is a geological eon representing a period before the first abundant complex life on Earth. The _____ extended from 2500 Ma to 542.0 >± 1.0 Ma (million years ago), and is the most recent part of the old, informally named 'e;Precambrian'e; time.

The Proterozoic consists of 3 geologic eras, from oldest to youngest:

- Paleoproterozoic
- Mesoproterozoic
- Neoproterozoic

The well-identified events were:

- The transition to an oxygenated atmosphere during the Mesoproterozoic.
- Several glaciations, including the hypothesized Snowball Earth during the Cryogenian period in the late Neoproterozoic.
- The Ediacaran Period (635 to 542 Ma) which is characterized by the evolution of abundant soft-bodied multicellular organisms.

The geoloic record of the Proterozoic is much better than that for the preceding Archean. In contrast to the deep-water deposits of the Archean, the Proterozoic features many strata that were laid down in extensive shallow epicontinental seas; furthermore, many of these rocks are less metamorphosed than Archean-age ones, and plenty are unaltered.

   a. 1700 Cascadia earthquake
   b. 1509 Istanbul earthquake
   c. 1703 Genroku earthquake
   d. Proterozoic Eon

31. In plate tectonics, a _____ is a linear feature that exists between two tectonic plates that are moving away from each other. These areas can form in the middle of continents but eventually form ocean basins. Divergent boundaries within continents initially produce rifts which produce rift valleys. Therefore, most active divergent plate boundaries are between oceanic plates and are often called mid-oceanic ridges. Divergent boundaries also form Volcanic Islands which occur when the plates move apart to produce gaps which molten lava rises to fill. Thus creating a shield volcano which would eventually build up to become a volcanic island.

a. Nappe
b. Divergent boundary
c. Subduction
d. Tectonic plates

32. _____ is molten rock that is found beneath the surface of the Earth, and may also exist on other terrestrial planets. Besides molten rock, _____ may also contain suspended crystals and gas bubbles. _____ often collects in a _____ chamber inside a volcano. _____ is capable of intrusion into adjacent rocks, extrusion onto the surface as lava, and explosive ejection as tephra to form pyroclastic rock.
   a. Laccolith
   b. Rock cycle
   c. Volcanic rock
   d. Magma

33. The _____, usually referred to as the Moho, is the boundary between the Earth's crust and the mantle. The Moho serves to separate both oceanic crust and continental crust from underlying mantle. The Moho mostly lies entirely within the lithosphere; only beneath mid-ocean ridges does it define the lithosphere-asthenosphere boundary.
   a. Mohorovičić discontinuity
   b. Gorda Ridge
   c. Panthalassa
   d. Copperbelt Province

34. _____ is a sedimentary rock. It is a natural chemical precipitate of carbonate minerals; typically aragonite, but often recrystallized to, or primarily, calcite.

_____ forms as calcium carbonate is deposited from the water of mineral springs or rivulets that are saturated with dissolved calcium bicarbonate. The spring water from which the calcium carbonate precipitates can be hot, warm or cold. The rate of deposition increases with the temperature of the water, or alternatively, when biotic material accelerates the process of precipitation.

   a. 1509 Istanbul earthquake
   b. Travertine
   c. 1703 Genroku earthquake
   d. 1700 Cascadia earthquake

35. A _____ is a deep active seismic area in a subduction zone. Differential motion along the zone produces deep-seated earthquakes, the foci of which may be as deep as about 700 kilometres (435 miles.) They develop beneath volcanic island arcs and continental margins above active subduction zones.
   a. Lava
   b. Wadati-Benioff zone
   c. Pit crater
   d. Pyroclastic flow

36. An _____ or accretionary prism is formed from sediments that are accreted onto the non-subducting tectonic plate at a convergent plate boundary. Most of the material in the _____ consists of marine sediments scraped off from the downgoing slab of oceanic crust but in some cases includes the erosional products of volcanic island arcs formed on the overriding plate.

The internal structure of an _____ is similar to that found in a thin-skinned foreland thrust belt.

   a. Accretionary wedge
   b. AL 333
   c. AASHTO Soil Classification System
   d. AL 129-1

37. A _____ is a depression in the sea floor located between a subduction zone and an associated volcanic arc. It is typically filled with sediments from the adjacent landmass and the island arc in addition to trapped oceanic crustal material. The oceanic crustal fragments may be obducted as ophiolites onto the continent during terrane accretion.

a. Lithosphere
b. Subduction
c. Continental crust
d. Forearc

38. The _____ is a tectonic plate covering most of North America, Greenland and part of Siberia. It extends eastward to the Mid-Atlantic Ridge and westward to the Chersky Range in eastern Siberia. The plate includes both continental and oceanic crust. The interior of the main continental landmass includes an extensive granitic core called a craton. Along most of the edges of this craton are fragments of crustal material called terranes, accreted to the craton by tectonic actions over the long span of geologic time. It is believed that much of North America west of the Rockies is composed of such terranes.
   a. Burma Plate
   b. Philippine Sea Plate
   c. Kermadec Plate
   d. North American Plate

39. The _____ is a continental transform fault that runs a length of roughly 800 miles (1,300 km) through California in the United States. The fault's motion is right-lateral strike-slip (horizontal motion.) It forms the tectonic boundary between the Pacific Plate and the North American Plate.
   a. 1703 Genroku earthquake
   b. 1509 Istanbul earthquake
   c. 1700 Cascadia earthquake
   d. San Andreas Fault

40. In geology, a _____ is a location on the Earth's surface that has experienced active volcanism for a long period of time.

J. Tuzo Wilson came up with the idea in 1963 that volcanic chains like the Hawaiian Islands result from the slow movement of a tectonic plate across a 'fixed' _____ deep beneath the surface of the planet.

   a. 1700 Cascadia earthquake
   b. 1509 Istanbul earthquake
   c. 1703 Genroku earthquake
   d. Hotspot

41. A _____ is an upwelling of abnormally hot rock within the Earth's mantle. As the heads of mantle plumes can partly melt when they reach shallow depths, they are thought to be the cause of volcanic centers known as hotspots and probably also to have caused flood basalts. It is a secondary way that Earth loses heat, much less important in this regard than is heat loss at plate margins.
   a. Seismic refraction
   b. Mazuku
   c. Strainmeter
   d. Mantle plume

42. _____ is a geologic term for a type of topography characterized by a series of separate and parallel mountain ranges with broad valleys interposed, extending over a more or less wide area. It is typified by the topography found in the Great Basin in the western United States, which is part of a larger regional topography known as the _____ Province. _____ topography results from crustal extension.
   a. Zechstein
   b. Basin and Range
   c. Tidal scour
   d. Rill

43. The _____ is a large geologic province which includes parts of the southwestern United States and northwestern Mexico, typified by basin and range topography.

The topography of the _____ is a result of crustal extension within this part of the North American Plate. The cause of this extension is as yet not fully understood, although several hypotheses have been offered. The crust here has been stretched up to 100% of its original width. In fact, the crust underneath the _____, especially under the Great Basin, is some of the thinnest in the world.

  a. Yilgarn Craton
  b. Canadian Shield
  c. Quaternary
  d. Basin and Range Province

44. The _____, also known as the local magnitude (M_L) scale, assigns a single number to quantify the amount of seismic energy released by an earthquake. It is a base-10 logarithmic scale obtained by calculating the logarithm of the combined horizontal amplitude of the largest displacement from zero on a Wood-Anderson torsion seismometer output. So, for example, an earthquake that measures 5.0 on the Richter scale has a shaking amplitude 10 times larger than one that measures 4.0.
  a. China Seismic Intensity Scale
  b. Moment magnitude scale
  c. Richter magnitude scale
  d. Medvedev-Sponheuer-Karnik scale

45. In geology, a _____ is a place where the Earth's crust and lithosphere are being pulled apart and is an example of extensional tectonics.

Typical _____ features are a central linear downdropped fault segment, called a graben, with parallel normal faulting and _____-flank uplifts on either side forming a _____ valley, where the _____ remains above sea level. The axis of the _____ area commonly contains volcanic rocks and active volcanism is a part of many, but not all active _____ systems.

  a. 1700 Cascadia earthquake
  b. Rift
  c. 1703 Genroku earthquake
  d. 1509 Istanbul earthquake

46. A _____ is an opening in a planet's surface or crust, which allows hot, molten rock, ash, and gases to escape from below the surface. Volcanic activity involving the extrusion of rock tends to form mountains or features like mountains over a period of time.
  a. Volcano
  b. 1703 Genroku earthquake
  c. 1700 Cascadia earthquake
  d. 1509 Istanbul earthquake

47. The _____ was a mountain-building event that affected western North America from Canada to the north to Mexico to the south. This orogeny was the result of convergent boundary tectonism between approximately 140 million years (Ma) ago, and 50 Ma. This orogeny was produced by the collision of the oceanic Farallon Plate and Kula Plate, predecessors of the Pacific Plate, and their subduction underneath the continental North American Plate. The _____ was preceded by several other mountain-building events including the Nevadan orogeny, the Sonoman orogeny, and the Antler orogeny, and partially overlapped in time and space with the Laramide orogeny.
  a. Kaikoura Orogeny
  b. Sevier orogeny
  c. Trans-Hudson orogeny
  d. Pan-African orogeny

Chapter 2. The Way the Earth Works: Plate Tectonics

48. The general term '_____' or, more precisely, 'glacial age' denotes a geological period of long-term reduction in the temperature of the Earth's surface and atmosphere, resulting in an expansion of continental ice sheets, polar ice sheets and alpine glaciers. Within a long-term _____, individual pulses of extra cold climate are termed 'glaciations'. Glaciologically, _____ implies the presence of extensive ice sheets in the northern and southern hemispheres; by this definition we are still in an _____

   a. AASHTO Soil Classification System   b. AL 129-1
   c. AL 333   d. Ice age

49. _____ refers to natural mountain building, and may be studied as a tectonic structural event, (b) as a geographical event, and (c) a chronological event. Orogenic events (a) cause distinctive structural phenomena and related tectonic activity, (b) affect certain regions of rocks and crust, and (c) happen within a specific period of time.

   a. Alice Springs Orogeny   b. Antler orogeny
   c. Orogenesis   d. Orogeny

50. Study of geological _____ is related to the study of structural geology, rock microstructure or rock texture and fault mechanics.

_____ is the response of a rock to deformation usually by compressive stress and forms particular textures. _____ can be homogeneous or non-homogeneous, and may be pure _____ or simple _____.

   a. Crenulation   b. Sag pond
   c. Shear   d. Molasse basin

Chapter 3. Patterns in Nature: Minerals

1. The _____ is a geologic period and system, the second of six of the Paleozoic era, and covers the time between 488.3>±1.7 to 443.7>±1.5 million years ago (ICS, 2004.) It follows the Cambrian period and is followed by the Silurian period. The _____ was defined by Charles Lapworth in 1879, to resolve a dispute between followers of Adam Sedgwick and Roderick Murchison, who were placing the same rock beds in northern Wales into the Cambrian and Silurian periods respectively.
   a. AASHTO Soil Classification System
   b. AL 129-1
   c. AL 333
   d. Ordovician

2. _____ is iron magnesium chromium oxide: $(Fe, Mg)Cr_2O_4$. It is an oxide mineral belonging to the spinel group. Magnesium can substitute for iron in variable amounts; also, aluminium and ferric iron commonly substitute for chromium.

   _____ is found in peridotite from the Earth's mantle. It also occurs in layered ultramafic intrusive rocks. In addition, it is found in metamorphic rocks such as some serpentinites. Ore deposits of _____ form as early magmatic differentiates.

   a. 1700 Cascadia earthquake
   b. 1703 Genroku earthquake
   c. 1509 Istanbul earthquake
   d. Chromite

3. _____ refers to natural mountain building, and may be studied as a tectonic structural event, (b) as a geographical event, and (c) a chronological event. Orogenic events (a) cause distinctive structural phenomena and related tectonic activity, (b) affect certain regions of rocks and crust, and (c) happen within a specific period of time.
   a. Antler orogeny
   b. Alice Springs Orogeny
   c. Orogenesis
   d. Orogeny

4. The mineral _____ is a magnesium iron silicate with the formula $(Mg,Fe)_2SiO_4$. It is one of the most common minerals on Earth, and has also been identified in meteorites and on the Moon, Mars, and comet Wild 2.

   The ratio of magnesium and iron varies between the two endmembers of the solid solution series: forsterite (Mg-endmember) and fayalite (Fe-endmember.)

   a. AL 129-1
   b. AASHTO Soil Classification System
   c. AL 333
   d. Olivine

5. An _____ is a type of rock that contains minerals such as gemstones and metals that can be extracted through mining and refined for use. Samples of _____ in the form of exceptionally beautiful crystals, exotic layering visible when sectioned or polished or metallic presentations such as large nuggets or crystalline formations of metals such as gold or copper may command a value far beyond their value as mere _____ or raw metal for subsequent reduction to utilitarian purposes.

   The grade or concentration of an _____ mineral, or metal, as well as its form of occurrence, will directly affect the costs associated with mining the _____.

   a. Ore genesis
   b. AL 129-1
   c. AASHTO Soil Classification System
   d. Ore

6. _____ is an important tectosilicate mineral which forms igneous rock. The name is from the Greek for 'straight fracture,' because its two cleavage planes are at right angles to each other. An alternate name is alkali feldspar.

Chapter 3. Patterns in Nature: Minerals 23

_____ is a common constituent of most granites and other felsic igneous rocks and often forms huge crystals and masses in pegmatite.

- a. AASHTO Soil Classification System
- b. Orthoclase
- c. AL 333
- d. AL 129-1

7. _____ is a sedimentary rock composed largely of the mineral calcite (calcium carbonate: $CaCO_3$.) The deposition of _____ strata is often a by-product and indicator of biological activity in the geologic record. Calcium (along with nitrogen, phosphorus, and potassium) is a key mineral to plant nutrition: soils overlying _____ bedrock tend to be pre-fertilized with calcium.
- a. 1703 Genroku earthquake
- b. 1700 Cascadia earthquake
- c. Limestone
- d. 1509 Istanbul earthquake

8. _____ are type of elastic wave, also called seismic waves, that can travel through gases, elastic solids and liquids, including the Earth. _____ can be produced by earthquakes and recorded by seismometers.
- a. P-waves
- b. 1703 Genroku earthquake
- c. 1509 Istanbul earthquake
- d. 1700 Cascadia earthquake

9. _____ is a common extrusive volcanic rock. It is usually grey to black and fine-grained due to rapid cooling of lava at the surface of a planet. It may be porphyritic containing larger crystals in a fine matrix, or vesicular, or frothy scoria.
- a. 1509 Istanbul earthquake
- b. 1700 Cascadia earthquake
- c. 1703 Genroku earthquake
- d. Basalt

10. A _____, sometimes called a composite volcano, is a tall, conical volcano with many layers (strata) of hardened lava, tephra, and volcanic ash. They are characterized by a steep profile and periodic, explosive eruptions. The lava that flows from a _____ tends to be viscous; it cools and hardens before spreading far.
- a. Mount Baker
- b. Broken Top
- c. Stratovolcano
- d. Mount Overlord

11. _____ are the preserved remains or traces of animals, plants, and other organisms from the remote past. The totality of _____, both discovered and undiscovered, and their placement in fossiliferous rock formations and sedimentary layers (strata) is known as the fossil record. The study of _____ across geological time, how they were formed, and the evolutionary relationships between taxa (phylogeny) are some of the most important functions of the science of paleontology.
- a. 1509 Istanbul earthquake
- b. Fossils
- c. 1703 Genroku earthquake
- d. 1700 Cascadia earthquake

12. _____ is the electromagnetic interaction between delocalized electrons, called conduction electrons, and the metallic nuclei within metals. Understood as the sharing of 'free' electrons among a lattice of positively-charged ions (cations), _____ is sometimes compared with that of molten salts; however, this simplistic view holds true for very few metals. In a more quantum-mechanical view, the conduction electrons divide their density equally over all atoms that function as neutral (non-charged) entities.
- a. 1700 Cascadia earthquake
- b. Metallic bonding
- c. 1703 Genroku earthquake
- d. 1509 Istanbul earthquake

13. _____ is the second most abundant mineral in the Earth's continental crust. It is made up of a framework of silicon-oxygen tetrahedra SiO_4, with each silicon shared between two oxygens to give the overall formula SiO_2. _____ has a hardness of 7 on the Mohs scale and a density of 2.65 g/cmÂ³.

  a. 1700 Cascadia earthquake
  b. 1509 Istanbul earthquake
  c. Quartz
  d. 1703 Genroku earthquake

14. A _____ is an area in which an S-Wave (secondary seismic wave) is not detected due to it not being able to pass through the outer core of the earth due to it being liquid. When an earthquake occurs, seismographs near the epicenter, out to about 90° distance, are able to record both Primary and Secondary waves, but those at a greater distance no longer detect the S-wave. This is because shear waves cannot pass through liquids.

  a. Tornillo event
  b. Maximum magnitude
  c. Receiver function
  d. Shadow zone

15. A _____ is an opening in a planet's surface or crust, which allows hot, molten rock, ash, and gases to escape from below the surface. Volcanic activity involving the extrusion of rock tends to form mountains or features like mountains over a period of time.

  a. 1700 Cascadia earthquake
  b. 1703 Genroku earthquake
  c. Volcano
  d. 1509 Istanbul earthquake

16. A _____ is an extent of land where water from rain or snow melt drains downhill into a body of water, such as a river, lake, reservoir, estuary, wetland, sea or ocean. The _____ includes both the streams and rivers that convey the water as well as the land surfaces from which water drains into those channels, and is separated from adjacent basins by a drainage divide.

The _____ acts like a funnel, collecting all the water within the area covered by the basin and channelling it into a waterway.

  a. 1703 Genroku earthquake
  b. 1700 Cascadia earthquake
  c. Drainage basin
  d. 1509 Istanbul earthquake

17. A _____ is a large, slow-moving mass of ice, formed from compacted layers of snow, that slowly deforms and flows in response to gravity and high pressure.

_____ ice is the largest reservoir of fresh water on Earth, and second only to oceans as the largest reservoir of total water.

  a. Glacier
  b. Little Ice Age
  c. Keeling Curve
  d. Pacific Decadal Oscillation

18. The _____ is a geological eon representing a period before the first abundant complex life on Earth. The _____ extended from 2500 Ma to 542.0 >± 1.0 Ma (million years ago), and is the most recent part of the old, informally named 'e;Precambrian'e; time.

Chapter 3. Patterns in Nature: Minerals 25

The Proterozoic consists of 3 geologic eras, from oldest to youngest:

- Paleoproterozoic
- Mesoproterozoic
- Neoproterozoic

The well-identified events were:

- The transition to an oxygenated atmosphere during the Mesoproterozoic.
- Several glaciations, including the hypothesized Snowball Earth during the Cryogenian period in the late Neoproterozoic.
- The Ediacaran Period (635 to 542 Ma) which is characterized by the evolution of abundant soft-bodied multicellular organisms.

The geoloic record of the Proterozoic is much better than that for the preceding Archean. In contrast to the deep-water deposits of the Archean, the Proterozoic features many strata that were laid down in extensive shallow epicontinental seas; furthermore, many of these rocks are less metamorphosed than Archean-age ones, and plenty are unaltered.

a. Proterozoic Eon
c. 1509 Istanbul earthquake
b. 1703 Genroku earthquake
d. 1700 Cascadia earthquake

19. In mineralogy and crystallography, a _____ is a unique arrangement of atoms in a crystal. A _____ is composed of a motif, a set of atoms arranged in a particular way, and a lattice. Motifs are located upon the points of a lattice, which is an array of points repeating periodically in three dimensions.

a. Crystal structure
c. 1703 Genroku earthquake
b. 1509 Istanbul earthquake
d. 1700 Cascadia earthquake

20. A type of seismic wave, the _____, secondary wave or shear wave (sometimes called an elastic _____) is one of the two main types of elastic body waves, so named because they move through the body of an object, unlike surface waves.

The _____ move as a shear or transverse wave, so motion is perpendicular to the direction of wave propagation: S-waves, like waves in a rope, as opposed to waves moving through a slinky, the P-wave. The wave moves through elastic media, and the main restoring force comes from shear effects.

a. 1700 Cascadia earthquake
c. S-wave
b. 1703 Genroku earthquake
d. 1509 Istanbul earthquake

21. The _____ is the epoch from 1.8 million to 11550 years BP covering the world's recent period of repeated glaciations. The _____ epoch follows the Pliocene epoch and is followed by the Holocene epoch. The _____ is the third epoch of the Neogene period or 6th epoch of the Cenozoic Era. The end of the _____ corresponds with the retreat of the last continental glacier. It also corresponds with the end of the Paleolithic age used in archaeology.

Chapter 3. Patterns in Nature: Minerals

    a. Tyrrhenian   b. Sicilian Stage
    c. Late Pleistocene   d. Pleistocene

22. The general term '_____' or, more precisely, 'glacial age' denotes a geological period of long-term reduction in the temperature of the Earth's surface and atmosphere, resulting in an expansion of continental ice sheets, polar ice sheets and alpine glaciers. Within a long-term _____, individual pulses of extra cold climate are termed 'glaciations'. Glaciologically, _____ implies the presence of extensive ice sheets in the northern and southern hemispheres; by this definition we are still in an _____

    a. Ice age   b. AL 129-1
    c. AL 333   d. AASHTO Soil Classification System

23. _____ is a technique used to date materials, usually based on a comparison between the observed abundance of a naturally occurring radioactive isotope and its decay products, using known decay rates. It is the principal source of information about the absolute age of rocks and other geological features, including the age of the Earth itself, and can be used to date a wide range of natural and man-made materials. Together with stratigraphic principles, _____ methods are used in geochronology to establish the geological time scale.

    a. Paleomagnetism   b. Radiometric dating
    c. Chronozone   d. Global Standard Stratigraphic Age

24. In seismology, _____ are surface seismic waves that cause horizontal shifting of the earth during an earthquake. A.E.H. Love predicted the existence of _____ mathematically in 1911. They form a distinct class, different from other types of seismic waves, such as P-waves and S-waves (both body waves), or Rayleigh waves (another type of surface wave). _____ travel with a slower velocity than P- or S- waves, but faster than Rayleigh waves.

    a. Strainmeter   b. Seismic refraction
    c. Mazuku   d. Love waves

25. An _____ is the result of a sudden release of energy in the Earth's crust that creates seismic waves. They are recorded with a seismometer or the related and mostly obsolete Richter magnitude, with a magnitude 3 or lower _____ being mostly imperceptible and magnitude 7 causing serious damage over large areas.

    a. AASHTO Soil Classification System   b. AL 129-1
    c. AL 333   d. Earthquake

26. The _____ of a mineral is the color of the powder produced when it is dragged across an unweathered surface. Unlike the apparent color of a mineral, which for most minerals can vary considerably, the trail of finely ground powder generally has a more consistent characteristic color, and is thus an important diagnostic tool in mineral identification. If no _____ seems to be made, the mineral's _____ is said to be white or colorless.

    a. Nodule   b. Submersion
    c. Cohesion   d. Streak

27. _____, in structural geology and related disciplines, describes the tendency of a rock to break along preferred planes of weakness.

Rocks deformed under very low to low metamorphic grade often develop planes along which the rock can easily be split. Slates are an example of a rock with a penetrative _____ caused partly by the realignment of phyllosilicate minerals with increasing flattening strain.

Chapter 3. Patterns in Nature: Minerals

27

a. Combe
b. Cleavage
c. Compaction
d. Drainage system

28. _____ is molten rock expelled by a volcano during eruption. When first expelled from a volcanic vent, it is a liquid at temperatures from 700 >°C to 1,200 >°C (1,300 >°F to 2,200 >°F.) Although _____ is quite viscous, with about 100,000 times the viscosity of water, it can flow great distances before cooling and solidifying, because of both its thixotropic and shear thinning properties.
   a. Supervolcano
   b. Pit crater
   c. Volcanic ash
   d. Lava

29. _____ is defined as the ratio of the density of a given solid or liquid substance to the density of water at a specific temperature and pressure, typically at 4 >°C (39 >°F) and 1 atm (760.00 mmHg) , making it a dimensionless quantity Substances with a _____ greater than one are denser than water, and so (ignoring surface tension effects) will sink in it, and those with a _____ of less than one are less dense than water, and so will float in it. _____ is a special case of, or in some usages synonymous with, relative density, with the latter term often preferred in modern scientific writing.
   a. 1703 Genroku earthquake
   b. 1700 Cascadia earthquake
   c. 1509 Istanbul earthquake
   d. Specific gravity

30. The _____ is a geological signature, usually a thin band, dated to (65.5 ± 0.3) Ma (million years ago). The boundary marks the end of the Mesozoic era and the beginning of the Cenozoic era, and is associated with the Cretaceous-Tertiary extinction event, a mass extinction.
   a. 1700 Cascadia earthquake
   b. Shiva crater
   c. 1509 Istanbul earthquake
   d. K-T boundary

31. _____ defines an important group of generally dark-colored rock-forming inosilicate minerals, composed of double chain SiO_4 tetrahedra, linked at the vertices and generally containing ions of iron and/or magnesium in their structures. They crystallize into two crystal systems, monoclinic and orthorhombic. In chemical composition and general characteristics they are similar to the pyroxenes. They are minerals of either igneous or metamorphic origin; in the former case occurring as constituents (hornblende) of igneous rocks, such as granite, diorite, andesite and others. Those of metamorphic origin include examples such as those developed in limestones by contact metamorphism (tremolite) and those formed by the alteration of other ferromagnesian minerals (hornblende).
   a. AASHTO Soil Classification System
   b. AL 129-1
   c. AL 333
   d. Amphibole

32. _____ is molten rock that is found beneath the surface of the Earth, and may also exist on other terrestrial planets. Besides molten rock, _____ may also contain suspended crystals and gas bubbles. _____ often collects in a _____ chamber inside a volcano. _____ is capable of intrusion into adjacent rocks, extrusion onto the surface as lava, and explosive ejection as tephra to form pyroclastic rock.
   a. Volcanic rock
   b. Magma
   c. Laccolith
   d. Rock cycle

33. A _____ is a compound containing an anion in which one or more central silicon atoms are surrounded by electronegative ligands. This definition is broad enough to include species such as hexafluorosilicate ('fluorosilicate'), $[SiF_6]^{2-}$, but the _____ species that are encountered most often consist of silicon with oxygen as the ligand. _____ anions, with a negative net electrical charge, must have that charge balanced by other cations to make an electrically neutral compound.

a. 1703 Genroku earthquake
b. 1509 Istanbul earthquake
c. 1700 Cascadia earthquake
d. Silicate

34. In chemistry, a _____ is a salt or ester of carbonic acid.

To test for the presence of the _____ anion in a salt, the addition of dilute mineral acid (e.g. hydrochloric acid) will yield carbon dioxide gas.

_____-containing salts are industrially and mineralogically ubiquitous.

a. 1509 Istanbul earthquake
b. 1703 Genroku earthquake
c. 1700 Cascadia earthquake
d. Carbonate

35. _____ are a group of rock-forming tectosilicate minerals which make up as much as 60% of the Earth's crust.

_____ crystallize from magma in both intrusive and extrusive igneous rocks, as veins, and are also present in many types of metamorphic rock. Rock formed entirely of plagioclase feldspar is known as anorthosite.

a. 1509 Istanbul earthquake
b. Feldspars
c. 1700 Cascadia earthquake
d. 1703 Genroku earthquake

36. A _____ is a mountain rising from the ocean seafloor that does not reach to the water's surface (sea level), and thus is not an island. These are typically formed from extinct volcanoes, that rise abruptly and are usually found rising from a seafloor of 1,000-4,000 meters depth. They are defined by oceanographers as independent features that rise to at least 1,000 meters above the seafloor.

a. 1703 Genroku earthquake
b. 1509 Istanbul earthquake
c. 1700 Cascadia earthquake
d. Seamount

37. The _____, also known as the local magnitude (M_L) scale, assigns a single number to quantify the amount of seismic energy released by an earthquake. It is a base-10 logarithmic scale obtained by calculating the logarithm of the combined horizontal amplitude of the largest displacement from zero on a Wood-Anderson torsion seismometer output. So, for example, an earthquake that measures 5.0 on the Richter scale has a shaking amplitude 10 times larger than one that measures 4.0.

a. Medvedev-Sponheuer-Karnik scale
b. China Seismic Intensity Scale
c. Moment magnitude scale
d. Richter magnitude scale

38. _____ is a type of potassic volcanic rock best known for sometimes containing diamonds. It is named after the town of Kimberley in South Africa, where the discovery of an 83.5 carats (16.7 g) diamond in 1871 spawned a diamond rush, eventually creating the Big Hole.

_____ occurs in the Earth's crust in vertical structures known as _____ pipes.

a. Kimberlite
b. 1700 Cascadia earthquake
c. 1703 Genroku earthquake
d. 1509 Istanbul earthquake

Chapter 3. Patterns in Nature: Minerals 29

39. In geology, a _____ is a place where the Earth's crust and lithosphere are being pulled apart and is an example of extensional tectonics.

Typical _____ features are a central linear downdropped fault segment, called a graben, with parallel normal faulting and _____-flank uplifts on either side forming a _____ valley, where the _____ remains above sea level. The axis of the _____ area commonly contains volcanic rocks and active volcanism is a part of many, but not all active _____ systems.

  a. 1703 Genroku earthquake
  c. 1509 Istanbul earthquake
  b. 1700 Cascadia earthquake
  d. Rift

40. In geology, _____ is the process that takes place at convergent boundaries by which one tectonic plate moves under another tectonic plate, sinking into the Earth's mantle, as the plates converge. A _____ zone is an area on Earth where two tectonic plates move towards one another and _____ occurs. Rates of _____ are typically measured in centimeters per year, with the average rate of convergence being approximately 2 to 8 centimeters per year (about the rate a fingernail grows.)

  a. Divergent boundary
  c. Motagua Fault
  b. Subduction
  d. Forearc

41. _____ is a crystalline form of aluminium oxide (>α-Al_2O_3) and is one of the rock-forming minerals. It is naturally clear, but can have different colors when impurities are present. Transparent specimens are used as gems, called ruby if red, while all other colors are called sapphire.

  a. Corundum
  c. 1703 Genroku earthquake
  b. 1509 Istanbul earthquake
  d. 1700 Cascadia earthquake

42. A _____ or gem is a piece of attractive mineral, which -- when cut and polished -- is used to make jewelry or other adornments. However certain rocks, and organic materials are not minerals, but are still used for jewelry, and are therefore often considered to be gemstones as well. Most gemstones are hard, but some soft minerals are used in jewelry because of their lustre or other physical properties that have aesthetic value.

  a. 1703 Genroku earthquake
  c. 1509 Istanbul earthquake
  b. 1700 Cascadia earthquake
  d. Gemstone

43. A _____, in biogeography, is an isthmus or wider land connection between otherwise separate areas, which allows terrestrial animals and plants to cross over and colonise new lands. They can be created by marine regression, in which sea levels fall, exposing shallow, previously submerged sections of continental shelf; or when new land is created by plate tectonics; or occasionally when the sea floor rises due to post-glacial rebound after an ice age.

  a. 1703 Genroku earthquake
  c. 1509 Istanbul earthquake
  b. Land bridge
  d. 1700 Cascadia earthquake

44. A _____ is an elongated whale-shaped hill formed by glacial action. Its long axis is parallel with the movement of the ice, with the blunter end facing into the glacial movement. They may be more than 45 m (150 ft) high and more than 0.8 km (1/2 mile) long, and are often in _____ fields of similarly shaped, sized and oriented hills. They usually have layers indicating that the material was repeatedly added to a core, which may be of rock or glacial till.

  a. Sandur
  c. 1509 Istanbul earthquake
  b. Monadnock
  d. Drumlin

30   *Chapter 3. Patterns in Nature: Minerals*

45. In geology, a _____ or _____ line is a planar fracture in rock in which the rock on one side of the fracture has moved with respect to the rock on the other side. Large faults within the Earth's crust are the result of differential or shear motion and active _____ zones are the causal locations of most earthquakes. Earthquakes are caused by energy release during rapid slippage along a _____.
   a. Stack
   c. Combe
   b. Dali
   d. Fault

46. _____, originally Gondwanaland, is the name given to a southern precursor-supercontinent and then as a remnant separated from Laurasia 180-200 million years ago during the breakup of the Pangaea supercontinent that existed about 500 to 200 Ma ago into two large segments. While the corresponding northern hemisphere continent Laurasia moved further north, the nearly equal in area _____ included most of the landmasses in today's southern hemisphere, including Antarctica, South America, Africa, Madagascar, Australia-New Guinea, and New Zealand, as well as Arabia and the Indian subcontinent, which have now moved into the Northern Hemisphere.
   a. 1509 Istanbul earthquake
   c. Laurasia
   b. 1700 Cascadia earthquake
   d. Gondwana

47. The _____ is a continental transform fault that runs a length of roughly 800 miles (1,300 km) through California in the United States. The fault's motion is right-lateral strike-slip (horizontal motion.) It forms the tectonic boundary between the Pacific Plate and the North American Plate.
   a. 1509 Istanbul earthquake
   c. 1703 Genroku earthquake
   b. 1700 Cascadia earthquake
   d. San Andreas Fault

48. _____ rocks are composed of fragments of pre-existing rock. The term is most commonly, but not uniquely, applied to sedimentary rocks.

   _____ metamorphic rocks include breccias formed in faults, as well as some protomylonite and pseudotachylite.

   a. 1700 Cascadia earthquake
   c. 1703 Genroku earthquake
   b. 1509 Istanbul earthquake
   d. Clastic

49. _____ are composed of fragments of pre-existing rock. The term is most commonly, but not uniquely, applied to sedimentary rocks.
   a. Clastic rocks
   c. 1700 Cascadia earthquake
   b. 1703 Genroku earthquake
   d. 1509 Istanbul earthquake

50. _____ is a sedimentary rock composed mainly of sand-size mineral or rock grains. Most _____ is composed of quartz and/or feldspar because these are the most common minerals in the Earth's crust. Like sand, _____ may be any color, but the most common colors are tan, brown, yellow, red, gray and white.
   a. Dolostone
   c. Lithification
   b. Porcellanite
   d. Sandstone

51. In geology a _____ is the smallest division of a geologic formation or stratigraphic rock series marked by well-defined divisional planes (bedding planes) separating it from layers above and below. A _____ is the smallest lithostratigraphic unit, usually ranging in thickness from a centimeter to several meters and distinguishable from beds above and below it. Beds can be differentiated in various ways, including rock or mineral type and particle size.

Chapter 3. Patterns in Nature: Minerals

a. Cyclostratigraphy
b. Bed
c. Biozones
d. Sequence stratigraphy

52. In stratigraphy, _____ is the native consolidated rock underlying the surface of a terrestrial planet, usually the Earth. Above the _____ is usually an area of broken and weathered unconsolidated rock in the basal subsoil. The top of the _____ is known as rockhead and identifying this, via excavations, drilling or geophysical methods, is an important task in most civil engineering projects.
 a. Polystrate
 b. Bedrock
 c. Sequence stratigraphy
 d. Biozones

53. _____ is a common and widely occurring type of intrusive, felsic, igneous rock. _____ has a medium to coarse texture, occasionally with some individual crystals larger than the groundmass forming a rock known as porphyry. Granites can be pink to dark gray or even black, depending on their chemistry and mineralogy.
 a. 1509 Istanbul earthquake
 b. 1700 Cascadia earthquake
 c. 1703 Genroku earthquake
 d. Granite

54. _____ is the result of the transformation of an existing rock type, the protolith, in a process called metamorphism, which means 'change in form'. The protolith is subjected to heat and pressure (temperatures greater than 150 to 200 >°C and pressures of 1500 bars) causing profound physical and/or chemical change. The protolith may be sedimentary rock, igneous rock or another older _____.
 a. Migmatite
 b. Metavolcanic rock
 c. Sedimentary rock
 d. Metamorphic rock

55. _____ is a geological term referring to the appearance of bedrock or superficial deposits exposed at the surface of the Earth. In most places the bedrock or superficial deposits are covered by a mantle of soil and vegetation and cannot be seen or examined closely. However in places where the overlying cover is removed through erosion, the rock may be exposed, or crop out.
 a. AL 333
 b. Outcrop
 c. AASHTO Soil Classification System
 d. AL 129-1

56. Geologically, a _____ is a long, narrow inlet with steep sides, created in a valley carved by glacial activity.

The seeds of a _____ are laid when a glacier cuts a U-shaped valley through abrasion of the surrounding bedrock by the sediment it carries. Many such valleys were formed during the recent ice age.

 a. 1703 Genroku earthquake
 b. 1509 Istanbul earthquake
 c. 1700 Cascadia earthquake
 d. Fjord

57. _____ is one of the three main rock types (the others being sedimentary and metamorphic rock.) _____ is formed by magma (molten rock) being cooled and becoming solid . They may form with or without crystallization, either below the surface as intrusive (plutonic) rocks or on the surface as extrusive (volcanic) rocks. They make up approximately 95% of the upper part of the Earth's crust, but their great abundance is hidden on the Earth's surface by a relatively thin but widespread layer of sedimentary and metamorphic rocks.
 a. AASHTO Soil Classification System
 b. AL 333
 c. AL 129-1
 d. Igneous rock

32 *Chapter 3. Patterns in Nature: Minerals*

58. _____ is the solid-state recrystallization of pre-existing rocks due to changes in physical and chemical conditions, primarily heat, pressure, and the introduction of chemically active fluids. Both mineralogical, chemical and crystallographic changes can occur during this process.

Three types of _____ exist: dynamic, contact and regional.

- a. Detritus
- b. Compression
- c. Metamorphism
- d. Reading Prong

59. A _____ is a chemical reaction that takes place during the geological process of metamorphism in an amalgamate of minerals that helps determine the final stable state of the resulting metamorphic rock.
- a. Geostrophic current
- b. Lithotope
- c. Metamorphic reaction
- d. Platform cover

60. _____ is one of the three main rock types (the others being igneous and metamorphic rock.) _____ is formed by deposition and consolidation of mineral and organic material and from precipitation of minerals from solution. The processes that form _____ occur at the surface of the Earth and within bodies of water.
- a. Rock cycle
- b. Sedimentary rock
- c. Serpentinite
- d. Petrology

61. _____ describes the large scale motions of Earth's lithosphere. The theory encompasses the older concepts of continental drift, developed during the first decades of the 20th century by Alfred Wegener, and seafloor spreading, understood during the 1960s.

The outermost part of the Earth's interior is made up of two layers: the lithosphere and the asthenosphere.

- a. Plate tectonics
- b. Continental crust
- c. Thrust fault
- d. Forearc

62. A _____ column (or _____) is a column of rising air in the lower altitudes of the Earth's atmosphere. They are created by the uneven heating of the Earth's surface from solar radiation, and an example of convection. The Sun warms the ground, which in turn warms the air directly above it.
- a. 1509 Istanbul earthquake
- b. 1700 Cascadia earthquake
- c. Thermal
- d. 1703 Genroku earthquake

63. _____ is the study of the record of the Earth's magnetic field preserved in various magnetic minerals through time. The study of _____ has demonstrated that the Earth's magnetic field varies substantially in both orientation and intensity through time. <
- a. Paleomagnetism
- b. Chronozone
- c. Law of superposition
- d. Stage

Chapter 4. Up from the Inferno: Magma and Igneous Rocks

1. _____ is a measure of the resistance of a fluid which is being deformed by either shear stress or extensional stress. In everyday terms (and for fluids only), _____ is 'thickness'. Thus, water is 'thin', having a lower _____, while honey is 'thick' having a higher _____.
   a. Tensile stress
   b. Viscosity
   c. Shear stress
   d. Thixotropy

2. A _____ is an opening in a planet's surface or crust, which allows hot, molten rock, ash, and gases to escape from below the surface. Volcanic activity involving the extrusion of rock tends to form mountains or features like mountains over a period of time.
   a. Volcano
   b. 1509 Istanbul earthquake
   c. 1703 Genroku earthquake
   d. 1700 Cascadia earthquake

3. A _____ is a mountain rising from the ocean seafloor that does not reach to the water's surface (sea level), and thus is not an island. These are typically formed from extinct volcanoes, that rise abruptly and are usually found rising from a seafloor of 1,000-4,000 meters depth. They are defined by oceanographers as independent features that rise to at least 1,000 meters above the seafloor.
   a. 1703 Genroku earthquake
   b. 1700 Cascadia earthquake
   c. 1509 Istanbul earthquake
   d. Seamount

4. In mineralogy and crystallography, a _____ is a unique arrangement of atoms in a crystal. A _____ is composed of a motif, a set of atoms arranged in a particular way, and a lattice. Motifs are located upon the points of a lattice, which is an array of points repeating periodically in three dimensions.
   a. Crystal structure
   b. 1703 Genroku earthquake
   c. 1509 Istanbul earthquake
   d. 1700 Cascadia earthquake

5. Geologically, a _____ is a long, narrow inlet with steep sides, created in a valley carved by glacial activity.

   The seeds of a _____ are laid when a glacier cuts a U-shaped valley through abrasion of the surrounding bedrock by the sediment it carries. Many such valleys were formed during the recent ice age.

   a. 1700 Cascadia earthquake
   b. 1509 Istanbul earthquake
   c. 1703 Genroku earthquake
   d. Fjord

6. _____ is one of the three main rock types (the others being sedimentary and metamorphic rock.) _____ is formed by magma (molten rock) being cooled and becoming solid . They may form with or without crystallization, either below the surface as intrusive (plutonic) rocks or on the surface as extrusive (volcanic) rocks. They make up approximately 95% of the upper part of the Earth's crust, but their great abundance is hidden on the Earth's surface by a relatively thin but widespread layer of sedimentary and metamorphic rocks.
   a. Igneous rock
   b. AASHTO Soil Classification System
   c. AL 333
   d. AL 129-1

7. _____ is molten rock expelled by a volcano during eruption. When first expelled from a volcanic vent, it is a liquid at temperatures from 700 >°C to 1,200 >°C (1,300 >°F to 2,200 >°F.) Although _____ is quite viscous, with about 100,000 times the viscosity of water, it can flow great distances before cooling and solidifying, because of both its thixotropic and shear thinning properties.

34   *Chapter 4. Up from the Inferno: Magma and Igneous Rocks*

    a. Pit crater   b. Supervolcano
    c. Volcanic ash   d. Lava

8. _____ is the solid-state recrystallization of pre-existing rocks due to changes in physical and chemical conditions, primarily heat, pressure, and the introduction of chemically active fluids. Both mineralogical, chemical and crystallographic changes can occur during this process.

Three types of _____ exist: dynamic, contact and regional.

    a. Compression   b. Metamorphism
    c. Reading Prong   d. Detritus

9. _____ are type of elastic wave, also called seismic waves, that can travel through gases, elastic solids and liquids, including the Earth. _____ can be produced by earthquakes and recorded by seismometers.
    a. 1703 Genroku earthquake   b. P-waves
    c. 1509 Istanbul earthquake   d. 1700 Cascadia earthquake

10. The _____ is an active transform fault, located between the North American Plate and the Pacific Plate, Canada's equivalent of the San Andreas Fault. The _____ forms a triple junction on its south with the Cascadia subduction zone and the Explorer Ridge (the Queen Charlotte Triple Junction.) The fault is named for Queen Charlotte Island which lies just north of the triple junction.
    a. 1700 Cascadia earthquake   b. Queen Charlotte fault
    c. 1509 Istanbul earthquake   d. 1703 Genroku earthquake

11. In geology, a _____ or _____ line is a planar fracture in rock in which the rock on one side of the fracture has moved with respect to the rock on the other side. Large faults within the Earth's crust are the result of differential or shear motion and active _____ zones are the causal locations of most earthquakes. Earthquakes are caused by energy release during rapid slippage along a _____.
    a. Combe   b. Stack
    c. Dali   d. Fault

12. A _____ is an area in which an S-Wave (secondary seismic wave) is not detected due to it not being able to pass through the outer core of the earth due to it being liquid. When an earthquake occurs, seismographs near the epicenter, out to about 90° distance, are able to record both Primary and Secondary waves, but those at a greater distance no longer detect the S-wave. This is because shear waves cannot pass through liquids.
    a. Receiver function   b. Maximum magnitude
    c. Tornillo event   d. Shadow zone

13. _____ consists of small tephra, which are bits of pulverized rock and glass created by volcanic eruptions, less than 2 millimetres (0.079 in) in diameter. There are three mechanisms of _____ formation: gas release under decompression causing magmatic eruptions; thermal contraction from chilling on contact with water causing phreatomagmatic eruptions and ejection of entrained particles during steam eruptions causing phreatic eruptions. The violent nature of volcanic eruptions involving steam results in the magma and solid rock surrounding the vent being torn into particles of clay to sand size.

a. Volcanic ash b. Supervolcano
c. Cinder d. Lava

14. _____ is a term used in geology to refer to silicate minerals, magma, and rocks which are enriched in the lighter elements such as silicon, oxygen, aluminium, sodium, and potassium. _____ minerals are usually light in color and have specific gravities less than 3. Common _____ minerals include quartz, muscovite, orthoclase, and the sodium-rich plagioclase feldspars.
   a. Laccolith b. Magma
   c. Tephra d. Felsic

15. A _____ is a geological phenomenon which includes a wide range of ground movement, such as rock falls, deep failure of slopes and shallow debris flows, which can occur in offshore, coastal and onshore environments. Although the action of gravity is the primary driving force for a _____ to occur, there are other contributing factors affecting the original slope stability. Typically, pre-conditional factors build up specific sub-surface conditions that make the area/slope prone to failure, whereas the actual _____ often requires a trigger before being released.
   a. Landslide b. 1509 Istanbul earthquake
   c. Mass wasting d. 1700 Cascadia earthquake

16. _____ is an adjective describing a silicate mineral or rock that is rich in magnesium and iron; the term was derived by contracting 'magnesium' and 'ferric'. Most _____ minerals are dark in color and the specific gravity is greater than 3. Common rock-forming _____ minerals include olivine, pyroxene, amphibole, and biotite.

_____ lava, before cooling, has a low viscosity, in comparison to felsic lava, due to the lower silica content in _____ magma. Water and other volatiles can more easily and gradually escape from _____ lava, so eruptions of volcanoes made of _____ lavas are less explosively violent than felsic lava eruptions.

   a. 1509 Istanbul earthquake b. 1703 Genroku earthquake
   c. 1700 Cascadia earthquake d. Mafic

17. _____ is molten rock that is found beneath the surface of the Earth, and may also exist on other terrestrial planets. Besides molten rock, _____ may also contain suspended crystals and gas bubbles. _____ often collects in a _____ chamber inside a volcano. _____ is capable of intrusion into adjacent rocks, extrusion onto the surface as lava, and explosive ejection as tephra to form pyroclastic rock.
   a. Rock cycle b. Magma
   c. Laccolith d. Volcanic rock

18. _____ is a process of melting that takes place in the Earth's mantle. The melting temperatures are unlikely high enough to melt the entire source rock, and only portions of or some of the minerals they contain melt.
   a. Volcanic blocks b. Partial melting
   c. Raton hotspot d. Submarine eruption

19. The _____ is a geological signature, usually a thin band, dated to (65.5 ± 0.3) Ma (million years ago). The boundary marks the end of the Mesozoic era and the beginning of the Cenozoic era, and is associated with the Cretaceous-Tertiary extinction event, a mass extinction.

a. Shiva crater
c. K-T boundary
b. 1509 Istanbul earthquake
d. 1700 Cascadia earthquake

20. _____ is the (natural or artificial) process of formation of solid crystals precipitating from a solution, melt or more rarely deposited directly from a gas. _____ is also a chemical solid-liquid separation technique, in which mass transfer of a solute from the liquid solution to a pure solid crystalline phase occurs.

The _____ process consists of two major events, nucleation and crystal growth.

a. 1703 Genroku earthquake
c. Crystallization
b. 1700 Cascadia earthquake
d. 1509 Istanbul earthquake

21. A _____ is a large emplacement of igneous intrusive rock that forms from cooled magma deep in the Earth's crust. they are almost always made mostly of felsic or intermediate rock-types, such as granite, quartz monzonite, or diorite

Although they may appear uniform, batholiths are in fact structures with complex histories and compositions.

a. Great Dyke
c. Tuff
b. Flood basalt
d. Batholith

22. _____ is a geological term meaning the rock native to an area. It is similar and in many cases interchangeable with the terms basement and wall rocks.

The term is used to denote the usual strata of a region in relation to the rock which is being discussed or observed.

a. Lopolith
c. Tuff
b. Country rock
d. Coldwell Complex

23. A _____ or dyke in geology is a type of sheet intrusion referring to any geologic body that cuts discordantly across

- planar wall rock structures, such as bedding or foliation
- massive rock formations, like igneous/magmatic intrusions and salt diapirs.

They can therefore be either intrusive or sedimentary in origin.

An intrusive _____ is an igneous body with a very high aspect ratio, which means that its thickness is usually much smaller than the other two dimensions. Thickness can vary from sub-centimeter scale to many meters and the lateral dimensions can extend over many kilometers. A _____ is an intrusion into an opening cross-cutting fissure, shouldering aside other pre-existing layers or bodies of rock; this implies that a _____ is always younger than the rocks that contain it.

a. Schmidt hammer
c. Pneumatolysis
b. Geopetal
d. Dike

Chapter 4. Up from the Inferno: Magma and Igneous Rocks

24. A _____ is an igneous intrusion (or concordant pluton) that has been injected between two layers of sedimentary rock. The pressure of the magma is high enough that the overlying strata are forced upward, giving the _____ a dome or mushroom-like form with a generally planar base.

They tend to form at relatively shallow depths and are typically formed by relatively viscous magmas, such as those that crystallize to diorite, granodiorite, and granite. Cooling underground takes place slowly, giving time for larger crystals to form in the cooling magma. The surface rock above the _____ often erodes away completely, leaving the core mound of igneous rock.

a. Laccolith
c. Serpentinite
b. Rock cycle
d. Volcanic rock

25. A _____ in geology is an intrusive igneous rock body that crystallized from a magma slowly cooling below the surface of the Earth. Plutons include batholiths, dikes, sills, laccoliths, lopoliths, and other igneous bodies. In practice, '_____' usually refers to a distinctive mass of igneous rock, typically kilometers in dimension, without a tabular shape like those of dikes and sills.

a. Metamorphic zone
c. Pluton
b. Migmatite
d. Vesicular texture

26. A _____ is a natural depression or hole in the surface topography caused by the removal of soil or bedrock, often both, by water. They may vary in size from less than a meter to several hundred meters both in diameter and depth, and vary in form from soil-lined bowls to bedrock-edged chasms. They may be formed gradually or suddenly, and are found worldwide.

a. Sinkhole
c. 1509 Istanbul earthquake
b. 1703 Genroku earthquake
d. 1700 Cascadia earthquake

27. _____ is a process accommodating the ascent of magmatic bodies from their sources in the mantle (geology) or lower crust to the surface. The process involves the mechanical disintegration of the surrounding country/host rock, typically through fracturing due to pressure increases associated with thermal expansion of the host rock in proximity of the interface with the melt. Once fractures are formed, melt and/or volatiles will typically invade, widening the fracture and promoting the foundering of host rock blocks (i.e. stoped blocks.)

a. Stoping
c. Wave pounding
b. Transgression
d. Spheroidal weathering

28. _____ is the rock that constitutes the wall of an area undergoing geologic activity. Examples are the rock along the neck of a volcano, on the edge of a pluton that is being emplaced, along a fault plane, enclosing a mineral deposit, or where a vein or dike is being emplaced.

In volcanoes, _____ can often become broken off of the wall and incoporated into the erupted volcanic rock.

a. 1703 Genroku earthquake
c. Wall rock
b. 1700 Cascadia earthquake
d. 1509 Istanbul earthquake

Chapter 4. Up from the Inferno: Magma and Igneous Rocks

29. A _____ is a rock fragment which becomes enveloped in a larger rock during the latter's development and hardening. In geology, the term _____ is almost exclusively used to describe inclusions in igneous rock during magma emplacement and eruption. Xenoliths may be engulfed along the margins of a magma chamber, torn loose from the walls of an erupting lava conduit or explosive diatreme or picked up along the base of a flowing lava on Earth's surface.
- a. 1703 Genroku earthquake
- b. 1700 Cascadia earthquake
- c. 1509 Istanbul earthquake
- d. Xenolith

30. _____, (Navajo: >Ts>é Bit'a'>í, 'rock with wings' or 'winged rock') is a rock formation rising nearly 1,800 feet (550 m) above the high-desert plain on the Navajo Nation and in San Juan County, New Mexico.

_____ is composed of fractured volcanic breccia and black dikes of igneous rock called 'minette'. It is the erosional remnant of the throat of a volcano, and the volcanic breccia formed in a diatreme. The exposed rock probably was originally formed 2,500-3000 feet (750-1,000 meters) below the earth's surface, but it was exposed after millions of years of erosion. Wall-like sheets of minette, known as dikes, radiate away from the central formation. Radiometric age determinations of the minette establish that these volcanic rocks solidified about 27 million years ago.

- a. 1509 Istanbul earthquake
- b. 1700 Cascadia earthquake
- c. Shiprock
- d. 1703 Genroku earthquake

31. A _____ is a volcanic landform created when magma hardens within a vent on an active volcano. When forming, a _____ can cause an extreme build-up of pressure if volatile-charged magma is trapped beneath it, and this can sometimes lead to an explosive eruption. If a plug is preserved, erosion may remove the surrounding rock while the erosion-resistant plug remains, producing a distinctive landform.
- a. 1703 Genroku earthquake
- b. 1700 Cascadia earthquake
- c. 1509 Istanbul earthquake
- d. Volcanic plug

32. In geology, a _____ is a location on the Earth's surface that has experienced active volcanism for a long period of time.

J. Tuzo Wilson came up with the idea in 1963 that volcanic chains like the Hawaiian Islands result from the slow movement of a tectonic plate across a 'fixed' _____ deep beneath the surface of the planet.

- a. 1703 Genroku earthquake
- b. 1700 Cascadia earthquake
- c. 1509 Istanbul earthquake
- d. Hotspot

33. A _____ is a chain of volcanic islands or mountains formed by plate tectonics as an oceanic tectonic plate subducts under another tectonic plate and produces magma. There are two types of these: oceanic arcs (commonly called island arcs, a type of archipelago) and continental arcs. In the former, oceanic crust subducts beneath other oceanic crust on an adjacent plate, while in the latter case the oceanic crust subducts beneath continental crust. In some situations, a single subduction zone may show both aspects along its length, as part of a plate subducts beneath a continent and part beneath adjacent oceanic crust.
- a. 1700 Cascadia earthquake
- b. 1509 Istanbul earthquake
- c. 1703 Genroku earthquake
- d. Volcanic arc

Chapter 4. Up from the Inferno: Magma and Igneous Rocks 39

34. _____ is a common and widely occurring type of intrusive, felsic, igneous rock. _____ has a medium to coarse texture, occasionally with some individual crystals larger than the groundmass forming a rock known as porphyry. Granites can be pink to dark gray or even black, depending on their chemistry and mineralogy.
- a. 1703 Genroku earthquake
- b. 1509 Istanbul earthquake
- c. 1700 Cascadia earthquake
- d. Granite

35. The _____ Era, is the most recent of the three classic geological eras and covers the period from 65.5 million years ago to the present. It is marked by the Cretaceous-Tertiary extinction event at the end of the Cretaceous that saw the demise of the last non-avian dinosaurs and the end of the Mesozoic Era. The _____ era is ongoing.
- a. 1700 Cascadia earthquake
- b. 1703 Genroku earthquake
- c. 1509 Istanbul earthquake
- d. Cenozoic

36. A _____ is a large, slow-moving mass of ice, formed from compacted layers of snow, that slowly deforms and flows in response to gravity and high pressure.

_____ ice is the largest reservoir of fresh water on Earth, and second only to oceans as the largest reservoir of total water.

- a. Pacific Decadal Oscillation
- b. Little Ice Age
- c. Glacier
- d. Keeling Curve

37. The _____ Era is one of three geologic eras of the Phanerozoic eon. The division of time into eras dates back to Giovanni Arduino, in the 18th century, although his original name for the era now called the '_____' was 'Secondary' (making the modern era the 'Tertiary'.)

The _____ was a time of tectonic, climatic and evolutionary activity. The continents gradually shifted from a state of connectedness into their present configuration; the drifting provided for speciation and other important evolutionary developments.

- a. Mesozoic
- b. 1703 Genroku earthquake
- c. 1509 Istanbul earthquake
- d. 1700 Cascadia earthquake

38. The _____ is the earliest of three geologic eras of the Phanerozoic eon. The _____ spanned from roughly 542 to 251 million years ago (ICS, 2004), and is subdivided into six geologic periods; from oldest to youngest they are: the Cambrian, Ordovician, Silurian, Devonian, Carboniferous, and Permian.

The _____ covers the time from the first appearance of abundant, soft-shelled fossils to the time when the continents were beginning to be dominated by large, relatively sophisticated reptiles and modern plants. The lower (oldest) boundary was classically set at the first appearance of creatures known as trilobites and archeocyathids.

- a. 1703 Genroku earthquake
- b. Paleozoic
- c. 1509 Istanbul earthquake
- d. 1700 Cascadia earthquake

39. The _____ is a geological eon representing a period before the first abundant complex life on Earth. The _____ extended from 2500 Ma to 542.0 >± 1.0 Ma (million years ago), and is the most recent part of the old, informally named 'e;Precambrian'e; time.

The Proterozoic consists of 3 geologic eras, from oldest to youngest:

- Paleoproterozoic
- Mesoproterozoic
- Neoproterozoic

The well-identified events were:

- The transition to an oxygenated atmosphere during the Mesoproterozoic.
- Several glaciations, including the hypothesized Snowball Earth during the Cryogenian period in the late Neoproterozoic.
- The Ediacaran Period (635 to 542 Ma) which is characterized by the evolution of abundant soft-bodied multicellular organisms.

The geoloic record of the Proterozoic is much better than that for the preceding Archean. In contrast to the deep-water deposits of the Archean, the Proterozoic features many strata that were laid down in extensive shallow epicontinental seas; furthermore, many of these rocks are less metamorphosed than Archean-age ones, and plenty are unaltered.

a. 1703 Genroku earthquake
b. 1700 Cascadia earthquake
c. Proterozoic Eon
d. 1509 Istanbul earthquake

40. _____ is a name given to certain typically dark-coloured igneous rocks which are so fine-grained that their component mineral crystals are not detected by the unaided eye. This texture results from rapid cooling in volcanic or hypabyssal environments.

They are commonly porphyritic, having large crystals embedded in the fine groundmass or matrix.

a. AL 333
b. AL 129-1
c. AASHTO Soil Classification System
d. Aphanite

41. _____ is a naturally occurring glass formed as an extrusive igneous rock. It is produced when felsic lava extruded from a volcano cools without crystal growth. _____ is commonly found within the margins of rhyolitic lava flows known as _____ flows, where the chemical composition (high silica content) induces a high viscosity and polymerization degree of the lava.

a. AL 333
b. AASHTO Soil Classification System
c. Obsidian
d. AL 129-1

42. _____ is a textural term for a volcanic rock that is a solidified frothy lava typically created when super-heated, highly pressurized rock is violently ejected from a volcano. It can be formed when lava and water are mixed. This unusual formation is due to the simultaneous actions of rapid cooling and rapid depressurization.

Chapter 4. Up from the Inferno: Magma and Igneous Rocks 41

a. Pyroclastic flow
b. Lapilli
c. Cinder
d. Pumice

43. _____ is an igneous, volcanic (extrusive) rock, of felsic (silicon-rich) composition. It may have any texture from aphanitic to porphyritic. The mineral assemblage is usually quartz, alkali feldspar and plagioclase. Biotite and hornblende are common accessory minerals.

_____ can be considered as the extrusive equivalent to the plutonic granite rock, and consequently, outcroppings of it often bear a resemblance to granite. Due to their high content of silica and low iron and magnesium contents, _____ melts are highly polymerized and form highly viscous lavas.

a. 1703 Genroku earthquake
b. 1700 Cascadia earthquake
c. 1509 Istanbul earthquake
d. Rhyolite

44. _____ is a naturally occurring granular material composed of finely divided rock and mineral particles.

As the term is used by geologists, _____ particles range in diameter from 0.0625 (or $>^1\!\!/_{16}$ mm, or 62.5 micrometers) to 2 millimeters. An individual particle in this range size is termed a _____ grain.

a. Sand
b. 1509 Istanbul earthquake
c. 1703 Genroku earthquake
d. 1700 Cascadia earthquake

45. _____ is a type of rock consisting of consolidated volcanic ash ejected from vents during a volcanic eruption. _____ is sometimes called tufa, particularly when used as construction material, although tufa also refers to a quite different rock.

The products of a volcanic eruption are volcanic gases, lava, steam, and tephra. Magma is blown apart when it interacts violently with volcanic gases and steam. Solid material produced and thrown into the air by such volcanic eruptions is called tephra, regardless of composition or fragment size. If the resulting pieces of ejecta are small enough, the material is called volcanic ash, defined as such particles less than 2 mm in diameter, sand-sized or smaller.

a. Pyroclastic rocks
b. Country rock
c. Tuff
d. Coldwell Complex

46. _____ is a rock composed of angular fragments of minerals or rocks in a matrix (cementing material), that may be similar or different in composition to the fragments. A _____ may have a variety of different origins, as indicated by the named types including sedimentary _____, tectonic _____, igneous _____, impact _____ and hydrothermal _____.

Sedimentary breccias are a type of clastic sedimentary rock which are composed of angular to subangular, randomly oriented clasts of other sedimentary rocks.

a. 1509 Istanbul earthquake
b. Fault breccia
c. Breccia
d. Ventifacts

47. _____ are clastic rocks composed solely or primarily of volcanic materials. Where the volcanic material has been transported and reworked through mechanical action, such as by wind or water, these rocks are termed volcaniclastic. Commonly associated with explosive volcanic activity - such as Plinian or krakatoan eruption styles, or phreatomagmatic eruptions - pyroclastic deposits are commonly formed from airborne ash, lapilli and bombs or blocks ejected from the volcano itself, mixed in with shattered country rock.
   a. Scoria
   b. Tuff
   c. Charnockite
   d. Pyroclastic rocks

48. _____ is a textural term for macrovesicular volcanic rock. It is commonly, but not exclusively, basaltic or andesitic in composition. _____ is light as a result of numerous macroscopic ellipsoidal vesicles, but most _____ has a specific gravity greater than 1, and sinks in water.
   a. Scoria
   b. Coldwell Complex
   c. Welded tuff
   d. Lopolith

49. _____ is a volcanic rock texture characterised by, or containing many vesicles. The texture is often found in extrusive aphanitic igneous rock. The vesicles are small cavities formed by the expansion of bubbles of gas or steam during the solidification of the rock.
   a. Laccolith
   b. Magma
   c. Migmatite
   d. Vesicular texture

Chapter 5. A Surface Veneer: Sediments, Soils, and Sedimentary Rocks

1. The _____, usually referred to as the Moho, is the boundary between the Earth's crust and the mantle. The Moho serves to separate both oceanic crust and continental crust from underlying mantle. The Moho mostly lies entirely within the lithosphere; only beneath mid-ocean ridges does it define the lithosphere-asthenosphere boundary.
   a. Mohorovičić discontinuity
   b. Copperbelt Province
   c. Panthalassa
   d. Gorda Ridge

2. The _____ is a geological eon representing a period before the first abundant complex life on Earth. The _____ extended from 2500 Ma to 542.0 >± 1.0 Ma (million years ago), and is the most recent part of the old, informally named 'e;Precambrian'e; time.

   The Proterozoic consists of 3 geologic eras, from oldest to youngest:

   - Paleoproterozoic
   - Mesoproterozoic
   - Neoproterozoic

   The well-identified events were:

   - The transition to an oxygenated atmosphere during the Mesoproterozoic.
   - Several glaciations, including the hypothesized Snowball Earth during the Cryogenian period in the late Neoproterozoic.
   - The Ediacaran Period (635 to 542 Ma) which is characterized by the evolution of abundant soft-bodied multicellular organisms.

   The geoloic record of the Proterozoic is much better than that for the preceding Archean. In contrast to the deep-water deposits of the Archean, the Proterozoic features many strata that were laid down in extensive shallow epicontinental seas; furthermore, many of these rocks are less metamorphosed than Archean-age ones, and plenty are unaltered.

   a. 1509 Istanbul earthquake
   b. Proterozoic Eon
   c. 1703 Genroku earthquake
   d. 1700 Cascadia earthquake

3. Two important classifications of weathering processes exist -- physical and _____. Mechanical or physical weathering involves the breakdown of rocks and soils through direct contact with atmospheric conditions, such as heat, water, ice and pressure. The second classification, _____, involves the direct effect of atmospheric chemicals or biologically produced chemicals (also known as biological weathering) in the breakdown of rocks, soils and minerals.
   a. 1509 Istanbul earthquake
   b. Weathering
   c. Physical weathering
   d. Chemical weathering

4. _____ is the part of Earth's lithosphere that surfaces in the ocean basins. _____ is primarily composed of mafic rocks, or sima. It is thinner than continental crust, or sial, generally less than 10 kilometers thick, however it is denser, having a mean density of about 3.3 grams per cubic centimeter.
   a. AL 333
   b. AL 129-1
   c. AASHTO Soil Classification System
   d. Oceanic crust

Chapter 5. A Surface Veneer: Sediments, Soils, and Sedimentary Rocks

5. Two important classifications of weathering processes exist -- _____ and chemical weathering. Mechanical or _____ involves the breakdown of rocks and soils through direct contact with atmospheric conditions, such as heat, water, ice and pressure. The second classification, chemical weathering, involves the direct effect of atmospheric chemicals or biologically produced chemicals (also known as biological weathering) in the breakdown of rocks, soils and minerals.
   a. Weathering
   b. Frost disintegration
   c. Physical weathering
   d. 1509 Istanbul earthquake

6. _____ is any particulate matter that can be transported by fluid flow, and which eventually is deposited.

They are most often transported by water (fluvial processes) transported by wind (aeolian processes) and glaciers. Beach sands and river channel deposits are examples of fluvial transport and deposition, though _____ also often settles out of slow-moving or standing water in lakes and oceans.

   a. Quicksand
   b. Bovey Beds
   c. Brickearth
   d. Sediment

7. _____ is one of the three main rock types (the others being igneous and metamorphic rock.) _____ is formed by deposition and consolidation of mineral and organic material and from precipitation of minerals from solution. The processes that form _____ occur at the surface of the Earth and within bodies of water.
   a. Rock cycle
   b. Petrology
   c. Serpentinite
   d. Sedimentary rock

8. _____ is the naturally occurring, unconsolidated or loose covering on the Earth's surface. _____ is composed of particles of broken rock that have been altered by chemical, biological and environmental processes including weathering and erosion. _____ is different from its parent rock(s) source(s), altered by interactions between the lithosphere, hydrosphere, atmosphere, and the biosphere.
   a. 1509 Istanbul earthquake
   b. Topsoil
   c. Slump
   d. Soil

9. _____ is the decomposition of Earth rocks, soils and their minerals through direct contact with the planet's atmosphere. _____ occurs in situ, or 'with no movement', and thus should not be confused with erosion, which involves the movement of rocks and minerals by agents such as water, ice, wind and gravity.

Two important classifications of _____ processes exist -- physical and chemical _____.

   a. Weathering
   b. Physical weathering
   c. 1509 Istanbul earthquake
   d. Frost disintegration

10. The _____ is a geological signature, usually a thin band, dated to (65.5 ± 0.3) Ma (million years ago). The boundary marks the end of the Mesozoic era and the beginning of the Cenozoic era, and is associated with the Cretaceous-Tertiary extinction event, a mass extinction.
   a. K-T boundary
   b. 1700 Cascadia earthquake
   c. Shiva crater
   d. 1509 Istanbul earthquake

11. The _____ is the level at which the ground water pressure is equal to atmospheric pressure. It may be conveniently visualized as the 'surface' of the ground water in a given vicinity. It usually coincides with the phreatic surface, but can be many feet above it. As water infiltrates through pore spaces in the soil, it first passes through the zone of aeration, where the soil is unsaturated. At increasing depths water fills in more spaces, until the zone of saturation is reached. The relatively horizontal plane atop this zone constitutes the _____.
   a. Rock bolt
   b. Crosshole sonic logging
   c. Shaft construction
   d. Water table

12. An _____ is a fan-shaped deposit formed where a fast flowing stream flattens, slows, and spreads typically at the exit of a canyon onto a flatter plain. A convergence of neighboring fans into a single apron of deposits against a slope is called a bajada, or compound _____.
   a. AL 129-1
   b. Alluvial fan
   c. AL 333
   d. AASHTO Soil Classification System

13. _____ or sheet joints are surface-parallel fracture systems in rock often leading to erosion of concentric slabs.
   a. AL 129-1
   b. AL 333
   c. AASHTO Soil Classification System
   d. Exfoliation joints

14. _____ are the preserved remains or traces of animals, plants, and other organisms from the remote past. The totality of _____, both discovered and undiscovered, and their placement in fossiliferous rock formations and sedimentary layers (strata) is known as the fossil record. The study of _____ across geological time, how they were formed, and the evolutionary relationships between taxa (phylogeny) are some of the most important functions of the science of paleontology.
   a. 1509 Istanbul earthquake
   b. 1700 Cascadia earthquake
   c. 1703 Genroku earthquake
   d. Fossils

15. _____ can also be called frost shattering or frost-wedging. This type of weathering is common in mountain areas where the temperature is around freezing point. Frost induced weathering, although often attributed to the expansion of freezing water captured in cracks, is generally independent of the water-to-ice expansion. It has long been known that moist soils expand or frost heave upon freezing as a result of water migrating along from unfrozen areas via thin films to collect at growing ice lenses. This same phenomena occurs within pore spaces of rocks.
   a. Physical weathering
   b. 1509 Istanbul earthquake
   c. Weathering
   d. Frost disintegration

16. _____ describes the large scale motions of Earth's lithosphere. The theory encompasses the older concepts of continental drift, developed during the first decades of the 20th century by Alfred Wegener, and seafloor spreading, understood during the 1960s.

The outermost part of the Earth's interior is made up of two layers: the lithosphere and the asthenosphere.

   a. Thrust fault
   b. Forearc
   c. Continental crust
   d. Plate tectonics

17. _____ is a term given to an accumulation of broken rock fragments at the base of crags, mountain cliffs, or valley shoulders. Landforms associated with these materials are sometimes called _____ slopes or talus piles. These deposits typically have a concave upwards form, while the maximum inclination of such deposits corresponds to the angle of repose of the mean debris size.
   a. 1700 Cascadia earthquake
   b. 1703 Genroku earthquake
   c. 1509 Istanbul earthquake
   d. Scree

18. A _____ column (or _____) is a column of rising air in the lower altitudes of the Earth's atmosphere. They are created by the uneven heating of the Earth's surface from solar radiation, and an example of convection. The Sun warms the ground, which in turn warms the air directly above it.
   a. 1509 Istanbul earthquake
   b. 1700 Cascadia earthquake
   c. 1703 Genroku earthquake
   d. Thermal

19. A _____ is a mountain rising from the ocean seafloor that does not reach to the water's surface (sea level), and thus is not an island. These are typically formed from extinct volcanoes, that rise abruptly and are usually found rising from a seafloor of 1,000-4,000 meters depth. They are defined by oceanographers as independent features that rise to at least 1,000 meters above the seafloor.
   a. 1509 Istanbul earthquake
   b. 1700 Cascadia earthquake
   c. 1703 Genroku earthquake
   d. Seamount

20. _____ is a sedimentary rock. It is a natural chemical precipitate of carbonate minerals; typically aragonite, but often recrystallized to, or primarily, calcite.

_____ forms as calcium carbonate is deposited from the water of mineral springs or rivulets that are saturated with dissolved calcium bicarbonate. The spring water from which the calcium carbonate precipitates can be hot, warm or cold. The rate of deposition increases with the temperature of the water, or alternatively, when biotic material accelerates the process of precipitation.

   a. Travertine
   b. 1509 Istanbul earthquake
   c. 1703 Genroku earthquake
   d. 1700 Cascadia earthquake

21. _____ is the process by which soil is created. It is the major topic of the science of pedology, whose other aspects include the soil morphology, classification (taxonomy) of soils, and their distribution in nature, present and past (soil geography and paleopedology).
   a. Pedogenesis
   b. Laterite
   c. Soil structure
   d. Podsol

22. A _____ is a specific layer in the soil which measures parallel to the soil surface and possesses physical characteristics which differ from the layers above and beneath. Horizon formation is a function of a range of geological, chemical, and biological processes and occurs over long time periods. Soils vary in the degree to which horizons are expressed.
   a. Soil horizon
   b. Laterite
   c. Vertisol
   d. Mollisols

23. _____, in structural geology and related disciplines, describes the tendency of a rock to break along preferred planes of weakness.

Chapter 5. A Surface Veneer: Sediments, Soils, and Sedimentary Rocks 47

Rocks deformed under very low to low metamorphic grade often develop planes along which the rock can easily be split. Slates are an example of a rock with a penetrative _____ caused partly by the realignement of phyllosilicate minerals with increasing flattening strain.

a. Drainage system
c. Combe
b. Compaction
d. Cleavage

24. _____ is a surface formation in hot and wet tropical areas which is enriched in iron and aluminium and develops by intensive and long lasting weathering of the underlying parent rock. Nearly all kinds of rocks can be deeply decomposed by the action of high rainfall and elevated temperatures. The percolating rain water causes dissolution of primary rock minerals and decrease of easily soluble elements as sodium, potassium, calcium, magnesium and silicon.

a. Podsol
c. Soil structure
b. Paleosol
d. Laterite

25. The _____ or the Dirty Thirties was a period of severe dust storms causing major ecological and agricultural damage to American and Canadian prairie lands from 1930 to 1936 (in some areas until 1940.) The phenomenon was caused by severe drought coupled with decades of extensive farming without crop rotation or other techniques to prevent erosion. Deep plowing of the virgin topsoil of the Great Plains had killed the natural grasses that normally kept the soil in place and trapped moisture even during periods of drought and high winds.

a. 1700 Cascadia earthquake
c. Dust Bowl
b. 1703 Genroku earthquake
d. 1509 Istanbul earthquake

26. The _____ is a geologic period and system, the second of six of the Paleozoic era, and covers the time between 488.3>±1.7 to 443.7>±1.5 million years ago (ICS, 2004.) It follows the Cambrian period and is followed by the Silurian period. The _____ was defined by Charles Lapworth in 1879, to resolve a dispute between followers of Adam Sedgwick and Roderick Murchison, who were placing the same rock beds in northern Wales into the Cambrian and Silurian periods respectively.

a. AL 129-1
c. Ordovician
b. AASHTO Soil Classification System
d. AL 333

27. _____ rocks are composed of fragments of pre-existing rock. The term is most commonly, but not uniquely, applied to sedimentary rocks.

_____ metamorphic rocks include breccias formed in faults, as well as some protomylonite and pseudotachylite.

a. 1509 Istanbul earthquake
c. 1703 Genroku earthquake
b. 1700 Cascadia earthquake
d. Clastic

28. _____ is the removal of solids (sediment, soil, rock and other particles) in the natural environment. It usually occurs due to transport by wind, water, or ice; by down-slope creep of soil and other material under the force of gravity; or by living organisms, such as burrowing animals, in the case of bioerosion.

_____ is distinguished from weathering, which is the process of chemical or physical breakdown of the minerals in the rocks, although the two processes may occur concurrently.

a. AL 333	b. AASHTO Soil Classification System
c. AL 129-1	d. Erosion

29. In geology, a _____ or _____ line is a planar fracture in rock in which the rock on one side of the fracture has moved with respect to the rock on the other side. Large faults within the Earth's crust are the result of differential or shear motion and active _____ zones are the causal locations of most earthquakes. Earthquakes are caused by energy release during rapid slippage along a _____.

a. Dali	b. Combe
c. Fault	d. Stack

30. The _____ is a continental transform fault that runs a length of roughly 800 miles (1,300 km) through California in the United States. The fault's motion is right-lateral strike-slip (horizontal motion.) It forms the tectonic boundary between the Pacific Plate and the North American Plate.

a. San Andreas Fault	b. 1509 Istanbul earthquake
c. 1703 Genroku earthquake	d. 1700 Cascadia earthquake

31. _____ is the geological process by which material is added to a landform or land mass. Fluids such as wind and water, as well as sediment gravity flows, transport previously eroded sediment, which, at the loss of enough kinetic energy in the fluid, is deposited, building up layers of sediment.

_____ occurs when the forces responsible for sediment transportation are no longer sufficient to overcome the forces of particle weight and friction, which resist motion.

a. Downcutting	b. Diagenesis
c. Deposition	d. Headward erosion

32. _____ is a geological term used to describe particles of rock derived from pre-existing rock through processes of weathering and erosion. Thesel particles can consist of lithic fragments (particles of recognisable rock), or of monomineralic fragments (mineral grains.) These particles are often transported through sedimentary processes into depositional systems such as riverbeds, lakes or the ocean forming sedimentary successions.

a. Perched coastline	b. Geomechanics
c. Medical geology	d. Detritus

33. An _____ is the result of a sudden release of energy in the Earth's crust that creates seismic waves. They are recorded with a seismometer or the related and mostly obsolete Richter magnitude, with a magnitude 3 or lower _____ being mostly imperceptible and magnitude 7 causing serious damage over large areas.

a. AL 333	b. AASHTO Soil Classification System
c. AL 129-1	d. Earthquake

34. _____ is the process in which sediments compact under pressure, expel connate fluids, and gradually become solid rock. Essentially, _____ is a process of porosity destruction through compaction and cementation. _____ includes all the processes which convert unconsolidated sediments into sedimentary rocks.

a. Jasperoid	b. Dolomite
c. Metasediment	d. Lithification

Chapter 5. A Surface Veneer: Sediments, Soils, and Sedimentary Rocks

35. The lithosphere is broken up into what are called _____. In the case of Earth, there are eight major and many minor plates The lithospheric plates ride on the asthenosphere. These plates move in relation to one another at one of three types of plate boundaries: convergent, or collisional boundaries; divergent boundaries, also called spreading centers; and transform boundaries.
   a. Copperbelt Province
   b. Thrust fault
   c. Gorda Ridge
   d. Tectonic plates

36. _____ is a sedimentary rock composed mainly of sand-size mineral or rock grains. Most _____ is composed of quartz and/or feldspar because these are the most common minerals in the Earth's crust. Like sand, _____ may be any color, but the most common colors are tan, brown, yellow, red, gray and white.
   a. Lithification
   b. Dolostone
   c. Porcellanite
   d. Sandstone

37. The _____ was a mountain-building event that affected western North America from Canada to the north to Mexico to the south. This orogeny was the result of convergent boundary tectonism between approximately 140 million years (Ma) ago, and 50 Ma. This orogeny was produced by the collision of the oceanic Farallon Plate and Kula Plate, predecessors of the Pacific Plate, and their subduction underneath the continental North American Plate. The _____ was preceded by several other mountain-building events including the Nevadan orogeny, the Sonoman orogeny, and the Antler orogeny, and partially overlapped in time and space with the Laramide orogeny.
   a. Kaikoura Orogeny
   b. Pan-African orogeny
   c. Sevier orogeny
   d. Trans-Hudson orogeny

38. _____ is a rock composed of angular fragments of minerals or rocks in a matrix (cementing material), that may be similar or different in composition to the fragments. A _____ may have a variety of different origins, as indicated by the named types including sedimentary _____, tectonic _____, igneous _____, impact _____ and hydrothermal _____.

Sedimentary breccias are a type of clastic sedimentary rock which are composed of angular to subangular, randomly oriented clasts of other sedimentary rocks.

   a. Ventifacts
   b. Fault breccia
   c. 1509 Istanbul earthquake
   d. Breccia

39. A _____ is a rock consisting of individual stones that have become cemented together. They are sedimentary rocks consisting of rounded fragments and are thus differentiated from breccias, which consist of angular clasts. Both conglomerates and breccias are characterized by clasts larger than sand (>2 mm).
   a. Pelagic sediments
   b. Porcellanite
   c. Conglomerate
   d. Keystone

40. _____ is a fine grained sedimentary rock whose original constituents were clays or muds. Grain size is up to 0.0625 mm with individual grains too small to be distinguished without a microscope. With increased pressure over time the platey clay minerals may become aligned, with the appearance of fissility or parallel layering.
   a. Jasperoid
   b. Diatomaceous earth
   c. Mudstone
   d. Shale

41. _____ refers to natural mountain building, and may be studied as a tectonic structural event, (b) as a geographical event, and (c) a chronological event. Orogenic events (a) cause distinctive structural phenomena and related tectonic activity, (b) affect certain regions of rocks and crust, and (c) happen within a specific period of time.
 a. Alice Springs Orogeny
 b. Orogeny
 c. Antler orogeny
 d. Orogenesis

42. _____ is a fine-grained sedimentary rock whose original constituents were clay minerals or muds. It is characterized by thin laminae breaking with an irregular curving fracture, often splintery and usually parallel to the often-indistinguishable bedding plane. This property is called fissility.
 a. Metasediment
 b. Pelagic sediments
 c. Mudstone
 d. Shale

43. _____ is a soft, white, porous sedimentary rock, a form of limestone composed of the mineral calcite. It forms under relatively deep marine conditions from the gradual accumulation of minute calcite plates shed from micro-organisms called coccolithophores. It is common to find flint and chert nodules embedded in _____.
 a. Chalk
 b. 1509 Istanbul earthquake
 c. 1703 Genroku earthquake
 d. 1700 Cascadia earthquake

44. A _____ is flat or nearly flat land adjacent to a stream or river that experiences occasional or periodic flooding. It includes the floodway, which consists of the stream channel and adjacent areas that carry flood flows, and the flood fringe, which are areas covered by the flood, but which do not experience a strong current.

They generally contain unconsolidated sediments, often extending below the bed of the stream.
 a. 1509 Istanbul earthquake
 b. 1700 Cascadia earthquake
 c. 1703 Genroku earthquake
 d. Floodplain

45. _____ is a sedimentary rock composed largely of the mineral calcite (calcium carbonate: $CaCO_3$.) The deposition of _____ strata is often a by-product and indicator of biological activity in the geologic record. Calcium (along with nitrogen, phosphorus, and potassium) is a key mineral to plant nutrition: soils overlying _____ bedrock tend to be pre-fertilized with calcium.
 a. 1703 Genroku earthquake
 b. 1509 Istanbul earthquake
 c. 1700 Cascadia earthquake
 d. Limestone

46. The chemical compound silicon dioxide, also known as _____ , is an oxide of silicon with a chemical formula of SiO_2 and has been known for its hardness since antiquity. _____ is most commonly found in nature as sand or quartz, as well as in the cell walls of diatoms. It is a principal component of most types of glass and substances such as concrete.
 a. Silica
 b. 1509 Istanbul earthquake
 c. 1703 Genroku earthquake
 d. 1700 Cascadia earthquake

47. The _____ is the epoch from 1.8 million to 11550 years BP covering the world's recent period of repeated glaciations. The _____ epoch follows the Pliocene epoch and is followed by the Holocene epoch. The _____ is the third epoch of the Neogene period or 6th epoch of the Cenozoic Era. The end of the _____ corresponds with the retreat of the last continental glacier. It also corresponds with the end of the Paleolithic age used in archaeology.

a. Late Pleistocene
b. Sicilian Stage
c. Tyrrhenian
d. Pleistocene

48. _____ is a fine-grained silica-rich microcrystalline, cryptocrystalline or microfibrous sedimentary rock that may contain small fossils. It varies greatly in color (from white to black), but most often manifests as gray, brown, grayish brown and light green to rusty red; its color is an expression of trace elements present in the rock, and both red and green are most often related to traces of iron (in its oxidized and reduced forms respectively.)

_____ occurs as oval to irregular nodules in greensand, limestone, chalk, and dolostone formations as a replacement mineral, where it is formed as a result of some type of diagenesis.

a. 1700 Cascadia earthquake
b. 1509 Istanbul earthquake
c. 1703 Genroku earthquake
d. Chert

49. _____ are water-soluble mineral sediments that result from the evaporation of bodies of surficial water. _____ are considered sedimentary rocks.

Although all water bodies on the surface and in aquifers contain dissolved salts, the water must evaporate into the atmosphere for the minerals to precipitate.

a. Evaporites
b. AL 129-1
c. AASHTO Soil Classification System
d. AL 333

50. _____ is an organic-rich fine-grained sedimentary rock. It contains significant amounts of kerogen, a solid mixture of organic chemical compounds from which liquid hydrocarbons can be extracted. Deposits of _____ occur around the world, including major deposits in the United States of America. Estimates of global deposits range from 2.8 trillion to 3.3 trillion barrels >(450 >× 10^9 to 520 >× 10^9 m^3) of recoverable oil.

a. AL 333
b. AASHTO Soil Classification System
c. AL 129-1
d. Oil shale

51. _____ is the second most abundant mineral in the Earth's continental crust . It is made up of a framework of silicon-oxygen tetrahedra SiO_4, with each silicon shared between two oxygens to give the overall formula SiO_2. _____ has a hardness of 7 on the Mohs scale and a density of 2.65 g/cmÂ³.

a. 1700 Cascadia earthquake
b. 1509 Istanbul earthquake
c. 1703 Genroku earthquake
d. Quartz

52. _____ or kerogen oil is a non-conventional oil produced by the destructive distillation of oil shale. This process, a controlled form of pyrolysis, converts the organic matter within the rock (kerogen) into synthetic oil and gas. The resulting oil can be used immediately as a fuel or upgraded to meet refinery feedstock specifications by adding hydrogen and removing impurities such as sulfur and nitrogen.

a. Shale Oil
b. 1509 Istanbul earthquake
c. 1703 Genroku earthquake
d. 1700 Cascadia earthquake

Chapter 5. A Surface Veneer: Sediments, Soils, and Sedimentary Rocks

53. The _____ are a 159 square mile (412 km^2) salt flat in northwestern Utah. The depth of the salt has been recorded at 6 feet (1.8 m) in many areas. A remnant of the ancient Lake Bonneville of glacial times, the salt flats are now public land managed by the Bureau of Land Management.

   a. 1700 Cascadia earthquake   b. 1509 Istanbul earthquake
   c. Bonneville Salt Flats   d. 1703 Genroku earthquake

54. _____ is soil or sediments deposited by a river or other running water. _____ is typically made up of a variety of materials, including fine particles of silt and clay and larger particles of sand and gravel.

Flowing water associated with glaciers may also deposit _____, but deposits directly from ice are not _____.

   a. AL 333   b. AL 129-1
   c. Alluvium   d. AASHTO Soil Classification System

55. A _____, commonly known as a cave formation, is a secondary mineral deposit formed in a cave. They are typically formed in limestone or dolostone solutional caves.

Water seeping through cracks in a cave's surrounding bedrock may dissolve certain compounds, usually calcite and aragonite, or gypsum (calcium sulfate.)

   a. Speleothem   b. 1509 Istanbul earthquake
   c. 1700 Cascadia earthquake   d. 1703 Genroku earthquake

56. _____ is the name of a sedimentary carbonate rock and a mineral, both composed of calcium magnesium carbonate $CaMg_2$ found in crystals.

_____ rock (also dolostone) is composed predominantly of the mineral _____. Limestone that is partially replaced by _____ is referred to as dolomitic limestone, or in old U.S. geologic literature as magnesian limestone.

   a. Metasediment   b. Dolostone
   c. Porcellanite   d. Dolomite

57. _____ or dolomite rock is a sedimentary carbonate rock that contains a high percentage of the mineral dolomite. In old U.S.G.S. publications it was referred to as magnesian limestone. Most _____ formed as a magnesium replacement of limestone or lime mud prior to lithification.

   a. Dolostone   b. Lithification
   c. Pelagic sediments   d. Jasperoid

58. The term _____ is used in geology when one or a stack of originally flat and planar surfaces, such as sedimentary strata, are bent or curved as a result of plastic (i.e. permanent) deformation. Synsedimentary folds are those due to slumping of sedimentary material before it is lithified. Folds in rocks vary in size from microscopic crinkles to mountain-sized folds.

Chapter 5. A Surface Veneer: Sediments, Soils, and Sedimentary Rocks

a. Fold
b. 1703 Genroku earthquake
c. 1700 Cascadia earthquake
d. 1509 Istanbul earthquake

59. _____ is molten rock expelled by a volcano during eruption. When first expelled from a volcanic vent, it is a liquid at temperatures from 700 >°C to 1,200 >°C (1,300 >°F to 2,200 >°F.) Although _____ is quite viscous, with about 100,000 times the viscosity of water, it can flow great distances before cooling and solidifying, because of both its thixotropic and shear thinning properties.

a. Lava
b. Volcanic ash
c. Supervolcano
d. Pit crater

60. A _____ is a natural depression or hole in the surface topography caused by the removal of soil or bedrock, often both, by water. They may vary in size from less than a meter to several hundred meters both in diameter and depth, and vary in form from soil-lined bowls to bedrock-edged chasms. They may be formed gradually or suddenly, and are found worldwide.

a. 1700 Cascadia earthquake
b. 1509 Istanbul earthquake
c. 1703 Genroku earthquake
d. Sinkhole

61. _____ is a type of fossil: it consists of fossil wood where all the organic materials have been replaced with minerals, while retaining the original structure of the wood. The petrifaction process occurs underground, when wood becomes buried under sediment and is initially preserved due to a lack of oxygen. Mineral-rich water flowing through the sediment deposits minerals in the plant's cells and as the plant's lignin and cellulose decay away, a stone mould forms in its place.

a. Glossopteris
b. Pteridospermatophyta
c. 1509 Istanbul earthquake
d. Petrified wood

62. _____ are those structures formed during sediment deposition.

_____ such as cross bedding, graded bedding and ripple marks are utilized in stratigraphic studies to indicate original position of strata in geologically complex terranes.

There are two kinds of flow regimes, which at varying speeds and velocities produce different structures.

a. 1509 Istanbul earthquake
b. 1703 Genroku earthquake
c. Sedimentary structures
d. 1700 Cascadia earthquake

63. In geology a _____ is the smallest division of a geologic formation or stratigraphic rock series marked by well-defined divisional planes (bedding planes) separating it from layers above and below. A _____ is the smallest lithostratigraphic unit, usually ranging in thickness from a centimeter to several meters and distinguishable from beds above and below it. Beds can be differentiated in various ways, including rock or mineral type and particle size.

a. Cyclostratigraphy
b. Sequence stratigraphy
c. Biozones
d. Bed

54   *Chapter 5. A Surface Veneer: Sediments, Soils, and Sedimentary Rocks*

64. In geology, _____ are sedimentary structures that indicate agitation by water (current or waves) or wind. _____ formed by water consist of two basic types:

   1. Current _____ are asymmetrical in profile, with a gentle up-current slope and a steeper down-current slope. The down-current slope depends on the shape of the sediment, with 33>° being typical.
   2. Wave-formed _____ have a symmetrical, almost sinusoidal profile; they indicate an environment with weak currents where water motion is dominated by wave oscillations.

Ripples will not form in sediment larger than course sand.

   a. 1700 Cascadia earthquake
   c. 1703 Genroku earthquake
   b. 1509 Istanbul earthquake
   d. Ripple marks

65. _____, originally Gondwanaland, is the name given to a southern precursor-supercontinent and then as a remnant separated from Laurasia 180-200 million years ago during the breakup of the Pangaea supercontinent that existed about 500 to 200 Ma ago into two large segments. While the corresponding northern hemisphere continent Laurasia moved further north, the nearly equal in area _____ included most of the landmasses in today's southern hemisphere, including Antarctica, South America, Africa, Madagascar, Australia-New Guinea, and New Zealand, as well as Arabia and the Indian subcontinent, which have now moved into the Northern Hemisphere.

   a. Laurasia
   c. 1700 Cascadia earthquake
   b. 1509 Istanbul earthquake
   d. Gondwana

66. The _____ or Appalachian orogeny is one of the geological mountain-forming events (orogeny) that formed the Appalachian Mountains and Allegheny Mountains. The term and spelling 'Alleghany Orogeny' (sic) originally proposed by H.P. Woodward (1957, 1958) is preferred usage. Approximately 350 million to 300 million years ago, in the Carboniferous period, the combined continents of Europe and Africa (Gondwana) collided with North America to form the supercontinent of Pangaea.

   a. Antler orogeny
   c. Alpine orogeny
   b. Alleghenian orogeny
   d. Alice Springs Orogeny

67. _____ was a prehistoric pluvial lake that covered much of North America's Great Basin region. Most of the territory it covered was in present-day Utah, though parts of the lake extended into present-day Idaho and Nevada. Formed about 32,000 years ago, it existed until about 16,800 years ago, when a large portion of the lake was released through the Red Rock Pass in Idaho.

Like most, if not all, of the ice age pluvial lakes of the American West, _____ was a result of the combination of lower temperatures, decreased evaporation, and higher precipitation that then prevailed in the region, perhaps due to a more southerly jet stream than today's. The lake was probably not a singular entity either; geologic evidence suggests that it may have evaporated and reformed as many as 28 times in the last 3 million years.

   a. 1509 Istanbul earthquake
   c. 1703 Genroku earthquake
   b. Lake Bonneville
   d. 1700 Cascadia earthquake

68. _____ is a naturally occurring granular material composed of finely divided rock and mineral particles.

Chapter 5. A Surface Veneer: Sediments, Soils, and Sedimentary Rocks

As the term is used by geologists, _____ particles range in diameter from 0.0625 (or $>^1\!\!/_{16}$ mm, or 62.5 micrometers) to 2 millimeters. An individual particle in this range size is termed a _____ grain.

- a. 1703 Genroku earthquake
- b. 1509 Istanbul earthquake
- c. 1700 Cascadia earthquake
- d. Sand

69. The _____ , usually abbreviated K for its German translation Kreide, is a geologic period and system from circa >145.5 >± 4 to >65.5 >± 0.3 million years ago . In the geologic timescale, the _____ follows on the Jurassic period and is followed by the Paleogene period. It is the youngest period of the Mesozoic era, and at 80 million years long, the longest period of the Phanerozoic eon. The end of the _____ defines the boundary between the Mesozoic and Cenozoic eras.
- a. Hauterivian
- b. Coniacian
- c. Campanian
- d. Cretaceous

70. A _____ is an opening in a planet's surface or crust, which allows hot, molten rock, ash, and gases to escape from below the surface. Volcanic activity involving the extrusion of rock tends to form mountains or features like mountains over a period of time.
- a. 1509 Istanbul earthquake
- b. 1703 Genroku earthquake
- c. 1700 Cascadia earthquake
- d. Volcano

71. In chemistry, a _____ is a salt or ester of carbonic acid.

To test for the presence of the _____ anion in a salt, the addition of dilute mineral acid (e.g. hydrochloric acid) will yield carbon dioxide gas.

_____-containing salts are industrially and mineralogically ubiquitous.

- a. 1703 Genroku earthquake
- b. 1509 Istanbul earthquake
- c. 1700 Cascadia earthquake
- d. Carbonate

72. The _____, also known as the local magnitude (M_L) scale, assigns a single number to quantify the amount of seismic energy released by an earthquake. It is a base-10 logarithmic scale obtained by calculating the logarithm of the combined horizontal amplitude of the largest displacement from zero on a Wood-Anderson torsion seismometer output. So, for example, an earthquake that measures 5.0 on the Richter scale has a shaking amplitude 10 times larger than one that measures 4.0.
- a. Medvedev-Sponheuer-Karnik scale
- b. Richter magnitude scale
- c. China Seismic Intensity Scale
- d. Moment magnitude scale

73. A _____ is a piece of rock that differs from the size and type of rock native to the area in which it rests. They are carried by glacial ice, often over distances of hundreds of kilometres and can range in size from pebbles to large boulders such as Big Rock (16,500 tons) in Alberta.
- a. 1700 Cascadia earthquake
- b. 1703 Genroku earthquake
- c. 1509 Istanbul earthquake
- d. Glacial erratic

Chapter 5. A Surface Veneer: Sediments, Soils, and Sedimentary Rocks

74. In geology, a _____ is a place where the Earth's crust and lithosphere are being pulled apart and is an example of extensional tectonics.

Typical _____ features are a central linear downdropped fault segment, called a graben, with parallel normal faulting and _____-flank uplifts on either side forming a _____ valley, where the _____ remains above sea level. The axis of the _____ area commonly contains volcanic rocks and active volcanism is a part of many, but not all active _____ systems.

   a. 1700 Cascadia earthquake
   b. 1703 Genroku earthquake
   c. 1509 Istanbul earthquake
   d. Rift

75. In geology, engineering, and surveying, _____ is the motion of a surface (usually, the Earth's surface) as it shifts downward relative to a datum such as sea-level. The opposite of _____ is uplift, which results in an increase in elevation. There are several types of _____.

   a. 1700 Cascadia earthquake
   b. Pothole
   c. 1509 Istanbul earthquake
   d. Subsidence

76. In geology and oceanography, _____ is any chemical, physical or biological change undergone by a sediment after its initial deposition and during and after its lithification, exclusive of surface alteration (weathering) and metamorphism. These changes happen at relatively low temperatures and pressures and result in changes to the rock's original mineralogy and texture. The boundary between _____ and metamorphism, which occurs under conditions of higher temperature and pressure, is gradational.

   a. Downcutting
   b. Transgression
   c. Seafloor spreading
   d. Diagenesis

77. _____ is the solid-state recrystallization of pre-existing rocks due to changes in physical and chemical conditions, primarily heat, pressure, and the introduction of chemically active fluids. Both mineralogical, chemical and crystallographic changes can occur during this process.

Three types of _____ exist: dynamic, contact and regional.

   a. Detritus
   b. Metamorphism
   c. Reading Prong
   d. Compression

78. A marine _____ is a geologic event during which sea level rises relative to the land and the shoreline moves toward higher ground, resulting in flooding. They can be caused either by the land sinking or the ocean basins filling with water (or decreasing in capacity.) Transgresssions and regressions may be caused by tectonic events such as orogenies, severe climate change such as ice ages or isostatic adjustments following removal of ice or sediment load.

   a. Stoping
   b. Transgression
   c. Wave pounding
   d. Spheroidal weathering

Chapter 6. Metamorphism: A Process of Change

1. The _____ is an informal name for the supereon comprising the eons of the geologic timescale that came before the current Phanerozoic eon. It spans from the formation of Earth around 4500 Mya (million years ago) to the evolution of abundant macroscopic hard-shelled animals, which marked the beginning of the Cambrian, the first period of the first era of the Phanerozoic eon, some 542 Mya. It is named after the Roman name for Wales - Cambria - where rocks from this age were first studied.

   a. 1509 Istanbul earthquake
   b. 1700 Cascadia earthquake
   c. 1703 Genroku earthquake
   d. Precambrian

2. A _____ is a deep active seismic area in a subduction zone. Differential motion along the zone produces deep-seated earthquakes, the foci of which may be as deep as about 700 kilometres (435 miles.) They develop beneath volcanic island arcs and continental margins above active subduction zones.

   a. Pit crater
   b. Lava
   c. Wadati-Benioff zone
   d. Pyroclastic flow

3. _____ is a geological term meaning the rock native to an area. It is similar and in many cases interchangeable with the terms basement and wall rocks.

   The term is used to denote the usual strata of a region in relation to the rock which is being discussed or observed.

   a. Coldwell Complex
   b. Lopolith
   c. Country rock
   d. Tuff

4. _____ is the solid-state recrystallization of pre-existing rocks due to changes in physical and chemical conditions, primarily heat, pressure, and the introduction of chemically active fluids. Both mineralogical, chemical and crystallographic changes can occur during this process.

   Three types of _____ exist: dynamic, contact and regional.

   a. Reading Prong
   b. Compression
   c. Metamorphism
   d. Detritus

5. A _____ is a chemical reaction that takes place during the geological process of metamorphism in an amalgamate of minerals that helps determine the final stable state of the resulting metamorphic rock.

   a. Lithotope
   b. Platform cover
   c. Geostrophic current
   d. Metamorphic reaction

6. _____ is the result of the transformation of an existing rock type, the protolith, in a process called metamorphism, which means 'change in form'. The protolith is subjected to heat and pressure (temperatures greater than 150 to 200 >°C and pressures of 1500 bars) causing profound physical and/or chemical change. The protolith may be sedimentary rock, igneous rock or another older _____.

   a. Sedimentary rock
   b. Metavolcanic rock
   c. Migmatite
   d. Metamorphic rock

7. _____ is the rock that constitutes the wall of an area undergoing geologic activity. Examples are the rock along the neck of a volcano, on the edge of a pluton that is being emplaced, along a fault plane, enclosing a mineral deposit, or where a vein or dike is being emplaced.

58 *Chapter 6. Metamorphism: A Process of Change*

In volcanoes, _____ can often become broken off of the wall and incoporated into the erupted volcanic rock.

a. 1703 Genroku earthquake
b. 1509 Istanbul earthquake
c. 1700 Cascadia earthquake
d. Wall rock

8. The _____ Era, is the most recent of the three classic geological eras and covers the period from 65.5 million years ago to the present. It is marked by the Cretaceous-Tertiary extinction event at the end of the Cretaceous that saw the demise of the last non-avian dinosaurs and the end of the Mesozoic Era. The _____ era is ongoing.

a. 1509 Istanbul earthquake
b. 1700 Cascadia earthquake
c. 1703 Genroku earthquake
d. Cenozoic

9. The _____ Era is one of three geologic eras of the Phanerozoic eon. The division of time into eras dates back to Giovanni Arduino, in the 18th century, although his original name for the era now called the '_____' was 'Secondary' (making the modern era the 'Tertiary'.)

The _____ was a time of tectonic, climatic and evolutionary activity. The continents gradually shifted from a state of connectedness into their present configuration; the drifting provided for speciation and other important evolutionary developments.

a. Mesozoic
b. 1509 Istanbul earthquake
c. 1703 Genroku earthquake
d. 1700 Cascadia earthquake

10. A _____ is a natural formation (or landform) where a rock arch forms, with a natural passageway through underneath. Most natural arches form as a narrow ridge, walled by cliffs, become narrower from erosion, with a softer rock stratum under the cliff-forming stratum gradually eroding out until the rock shelters thus formed meet underneath the ridge, thus forming the arch. They commonly form where cliffs are subject to erosion from the sea, rivers or weathering (sub-aerial processes); the processes 'find' weaknesses in rocks and work on them, making them bigger until they break through.

a. 1700 Cascadia earthquake
b. 1509 Istanbul earthquake
c. Natural arch
d. 1703 Genroku earthquake

11. The _____ is the earliest of three geologic eras of the Phanerozoic eon. The _____ spanned from roughly 542 to 251 million years ago (ICS, 2004), and is subdivided into six geologic periods; from oldest to youngest they are: the Cambrian, Ordovician, Silurian, Devonian, Carboniferous, and Permian.

The _____ covers the time from the first appearance of abundant, soft-shelled fossils to the time when the continents were beginning to be dominated by large, relatively sophisticated reptiles and modern plants. The lower (oldest) boundary was classically set at the first appearance of creatures known as trilobites and archeocyathids.

a. 1700 Cascadia earthquake
b. 1509 Istanbul earthquake
c. 1703 Genroku earthquake
d. Paleozoic

Chapter 6. Metamorphism: A Process of Change

12. _____ are a type of elastic surface wave that travel on solids. They are produced on the Earth by earthquakes, in which case they are also known as 'ground roll', or by other sources of seismic energy such as an explosion or even a sledgehammer impact. They are also produced in materials by acoustic transducers, and are used in non-destructive testing for detecting defects.
   a. Rayleigh waves
   b. Tornillo event
   c. Maximum magnitude
   d. Seismic waves

13. A _____ is any glacially formed accumulation of unconsolidated glacial debris (soil and rock) which can occur in currently glaciated and formerly glaciated regions, such as those areas acted upon by a past ice age. This debris may have been plucked off the valley floor as a glacier advanced or it may have fallen off the valley walls as a result of frost wedging. Moraines may be composed of silt like glacial flour to large boulders.
   a. 1509 Istanbul earthquake
   b. 1703 Genroku earthquake
   c. Moraine
   d. 1700 Cascadia earthquake

14. In geology, solid-state _____ is a metamorphic process that occurs under situations of intense temperature and pressure where grains, atoms or molecules of a rock or mineral are packed closer together, creating a new crystal structure. The basic composition remains the same. This process can be illustrated by observing how snow recrystallizes to ice without melting.
   a. 1509 Istanbul earthquake
   b. 1700 Cascadia earthquake
   c. Recrystallization
   d. 1703 Genroku earthquake

15. The _____ was a mountain-building event that affected western North America from Canada to the north to Mexico to the south. This orogeny was the result of convergent boundary tectonism between approximately 140 million years (Ma) ago, and 50 Ma. This orogeny was produced by the collision of the oceanic Farallon Plate and Kula Plate, predecessors of the Pacific Plate, and their subduction underneath the continental North American Plate. The _____ was preceded by several other mountain-building events including the Nevadan orogeny, the Sonoman orogeny, and the Antler orogeny, and partially overlapped in time and space with the Laramide orogeny.
   a. Trans-Hudson orogeny
   b. Sevier orogeny
   c. Pan-African orogeny
   d. Kaikoura Orogeny

16. _____ refers to natural mountain building, and may be studied as a tectonic structural event, (b) as a geographical event, and (c) a chronological event. Orogenic events (a) cause distinctive structural phenomena and related tectonic activity, (b) affect certain regions of rocks and crust, and (c) happen within a specific period of time.
   a. Antler orogeny
   b. Alice Springs Orogeny
   c. Orogeny
   d. Orogenesis

17. Study of geological _____ is related to the study of structural geology, rock microstructure or rock texture and fault mechanics.

_____ is the response of a rock to deformation usually by compressive stress and forms particular textures. _____ can be homogeneous or non-homogeneous, and may be pure _____ or simple _____.

   a. Shear
   b. Crenulation
   c. Molasse basin
   d. Sag pond

18. A _____, denoted τ (tau), is defined as a stress which is applied parallel or tangential to a face of a material, as opposed to a normal stress which is applied perpendicularly. In other words, considering that weight is a force, hanging something from a wall creates a _____ on the wall, since the weight of the object is acting parallel to the wall, as opposed to hanging something from the ceiling which creates a normal stress on the ceiling, since the weight is acting perpendicular to the ceiling.

The formula to calculate average _____ is:

$$\tau = \frac{F}{A}$$

where

    τ = the _____
    F = the force applied
    A = the cross sectional area

Beam shear is defined as the internal _____ of a beam caused by the shear force applied to the beam.

    a. Viscosity
    b. Thixotropy
    c. Tensile stress
    d. Shear stress

19. In geology a _____ is the smallest division of a geologic formation or stratigraphic rock series marked by well-defined divisional planes (bedding planes) separating it from layers above and below. A _____ is the smallest lithostratigraphic unit, usually ranging in thickness from a centimeter to several meters and distinguishable from beds above and below it. Beds can be differentiated in various ways, including rock or mineral type and particle size.

    a. Biozones
    b. Cyclostratigraphy
    c. Sequence stratigraphy
    d. Bed

20. _____, in structural geology and related disciplines, describes the tendency of a rock to break along preferred planes of weakness.

Rocks deformed under very low to low metamorphic grade often develop planes along which the rock can easily be split. Slates are an example of a rock with a penetrative _____ caused partly by the realignment of phyllosilicate minerals with increasing flattening strain.

    a. Combe
    b. Drainage system
    c. Compaction
    d. Cleavage

21. _____ is any penetrative planar fabric present in rocks. _____ is common to rocks affected by regional metamorphic compression typical of orogenic belts. Rocks exhibiting _____ include the typical metamorphic rock sequence of slate, phyllite, schist and gneiss.

    a. Hornfels
    b. Porphyroblast
    c. Shock metamorphism
    d. Foliation

Chapter 6. Metamorphism: A Process of Change

22. _____ is the chemical alteration of a rock by hydrothermal and other fluids.

_____ can occur via the action of hydrothermal fluids from an igneous or metamorphic source.

In the igneous environment, _____ creates skarns, greisen, and may affect hornfels in the contact metamorphic aureole adjacent to an intrusive rock mass.

   a. Dalradian
   b. Prehnite-pumpellyite facies
   c. Metasomatism
   d. Geothermobarometry

23. _____ is a fine-grained sedimentary rock whose original constituents were clay minerals or muds. It is characterized by thin laminae breaking with an irregular curving fracture, often splintery and usually parallel to the often-indistinguishable bedding plane. This property is called fissility.
   a. Mudstone
   b. Metasediment
   c. Pelagic sediments
   d. Shale

24. A _____ is a natural depression or hole in the surface topography caused by the removal of soil or bedrock, often both, by water. They may vary in size from less than a meter to several hundred meters both in diameter and depth, and vary in form from soil-lined bowls to bedrock-edged chasms. They may be formed gradually or suddenly, and are found worldwide.
   a. 1703 Genroku earthquake
   b. Sinkhole
   c. 1509 Istanbul earthquake
   d. 1700 Cascadia earthquake

25. _____ is a fine-grained, foliated, homogeneous metamorphic rock derived from an original shale-type sedimentary rock composed of clay or volcanic ash through low grade regional metamorphism. The result is a foliated rock in which the foliation may not correspond to the original sedimentary layering. _____ is frequently grey in colour especially when seen en masse covering roofs.
   a. Hornfels
   b. Greenstone belts
   c. Talc carbonate
   d. Slate

26. The _____ is a geological signature, usually a thin band, dated to (65.5 ± 0.3) Ma (million years ago). The boundary marks the end of the Mesozoic era and the beginning of the Cenozoic era, and is associated with the Cretaceous-Tertiary extinction event, a mass extinction.
   a. K-T boundary
   b. Shiva crater
   c. 1700 Cascadia earthquake
   d. 1509 Istanbul earthquake

27. The _____ is a mid-ocean ridge, a divergent tectonic plate boundary located along the floor of the Atlantic Ocean, and the longest mountain range in the world. It separates the Eurasian Plate and North American Plate in the North Atlantic, and the African Plate from the South American Plate in the South Atlantic. The MAR extends from a junction with the Gakkel Ridge (Mid-Arctic Ridge) northeast of Greenland southward to the Bouvet Triple Junction in the South Atlantic.
   a. 1703 Genroku earthquake
   b. 1700 Cascadia earthquake
   c. Mid-Atlantic Ridge
   d. 1509 Istanbul earthquake

Chapter 6. Metamorphism: A Process of Change

28. _____ are the preserved remains or traces of animals, plants, and other organisms from the remote past. The totality of _____, both discovered and undiscovered, and their placement in fossiliferous rock formations and sedimentary layers (strata) is known as the fossil record. The study of _____ across geological time, how they were formed, and the evolutionary relationships between taxa (phylogeny) are some of the most important functions of the science of paleontology.
   a. 1703 Genroku earthquake
   b. Fossils
   c. 1700 Cascadia earthquake
   d. 1509 Istanbul earthquake

29. _____ is a common and widely distributed type of rock formed by high-grade regional metamorphic processes from pre-existing formations that were originally either igneous or sedimentary rocks. Gneissic rocks are usually medium to coarse foliated and largely recrystallized but do not carry large quantities of micas, chlorite or other platy minerals. Gneisses that are metamorphosed igneous rocks or their equivalent are termed granite gneisses, diorite gneisses, etc.
   a. Gneiss
   b. 1703 Genroku earthquake
   c. 1509 Istanbul earthquake
   d. 1700 Cascadia earthquake

30. _____ is the group designation for a series of contact metamorphic rocks that have been baked and indurated by the heat of intrusive igneous masses and have been rendered massive, hard, splintery, and in some cases exceedingly tough and durable. Most _____ are fine-grained, and while the original rocks may have been more or less fissile owing to the presence of bedding or cleavage planes, this structure is effaced or rendered inoperative in the _____. Though they may show banding, due to bedding, etc., they break across this as readily as along it; in fact, they tend to separate into cubical fragments rather than into thin plates.
   a. Metasomatism
   b. Schist
   c. Talc carbonate
   d. Hornfels

31. _____ is the type of rock which originated from conglomerate after undergoing metamorphism. Conglomerate is easily identifiable by the pebbles or larger clasts in a matrix of sand, silt, or clay. _____ looks similar to conglomerate, besides the distorted stones.
   a. Greenschist
   b. Metasomatism
   c. Porphyroblast
   d. Metaconglomerate

32. _____ is a rock at the frontier between igneous and metamorphic rocks. They can also be known as diatexite.

_____ forms under extreme temperature conditions during prograde metamorphism, where partial melting occurs in pre-existing rocks.

   a. Magma
   b. Metamorphic zone
   c. Petrology
   d. Migmatite

33. _____ is a type of foliated metamorphic rock primarily composed of quartz, sericite mica, and chlorite; the rock represents a gradation in the degree of metamorphism between slate and mica schist. Minute crystals of graphite, sericite, or chlorite impart a silky, sometimes golden sheen to the surfaces of cleavage (or schistosity.) _____ is formed from the continued metamorphism of slate.
   a. 1703 Genroku earthquake
   b. 1700 Cascadia earthquake
   c. Phyllite
   d. 1509 Istanbul earthquake

Chapter 6. Metamorphism: A Process of Change

34. The lithosphere is broken up into what are called _____. In the case of Earth, there are eight major and many minor plates The lithospheric plates ride on the asthenosphere. These plates move in relation to one another at one of three types of plate boundaries: convergent, or collisional boundaries; divergent boundaries, also called spreading centers; and transform boundaries.
    a. Tectonic plates
    b. Thrust fault
    c. Copperbelt Province
    d. Gorda Ridge

35. A _____ is the topographic expression of faulting attributed to the displacement of the land surface by movement along the fault. It can be caused by differential erosion along an old inactive geologic fault (a sort of old rupture) with hard and weak rock, or by a movement on an active fault. In many cases, bluffs form from the upthrown block and can be very steep.
    a. Gravitational erosion
    b. Bradyseism
    c. Rejuvenated
    d. Fault scarp

36. _____ forms a group of medium-grade metamorphic rocks, chiefly notable for the preponderance of lamellar minerals such as micas, chlorite, talc, hornblende, graphite, and others. Quartz often occurs in drawn-out grains to such an extent that a particular form called quartz _____ is produced. By definition, _____ contains more than 50% platy and elongated minerals, often finely interleaved with quartz and feldspar.
    a. Metasomatism
    b. Schist
    c. Metaconglomerate
    d. Granoblastic

37. _____ is a feature of rocks containing platy minerals. Platy minerals include clay minerals and micas, with a long thin shape. When these align, they form a series of planes along which the rock tends to split.
    a. Bediasite
    b. Slaty cleavage
    c. Salt tectonics
    d. Marine clay

38. _____ are type of elastic wave, also called seismic waves, that can travel through gases, elastic solids and liquids, including the Earth. _____ can be produced by earthquakes and recorded by seismometers.
    a. 1700 Cascadia earthquake
    b. 1703 Genroku earthquake
    c. 1509 Istanbul earthquake
    d. P-waves

39. _____ is a hard metamorphic rock which was originally sandstone. Sandstone is converted into _____ through heating and pressure usually related to tectonic compression within orogenic belts. Pure _____ is usually white to grey, though quartzites often occur in various shades of pink and red due to varying amounts of iron oxide .
    a. Quartzite
    b. Foliation
    c. Schist
    d. Metaconglomerate

40. A _____ is an area in which an S-Wave (secondary seismic wave) is not detected due to it not being able to pass through the outer core of the earth due to it being liquid. When an earthquake occurs, seismographs near the epicenter, out to about 90° distance, are able to record both Primary and Secondary waves, but those at a greater distance no longer detect the S-wave. This is because shear waves cannot pass through liquids.
    a. Tornillo event
    b. Maximum magnitude
    c. Receiver function
    d. Shadow zone

41. _____ is a sedimentary rock. It is a natural chemical precipitate of carbonate minerals; typically aragonite, but often recrystallized to, or primarily, calcite.

Chapter 6. Metamorphism: A Process of Change

_____ forms as calcium carbonate is deposited from the water of mineral springs or rivulets that are saturated with dissolved calcium bicarbonate. The spring water from which the calcium carbonate precipitates can be hot, warm or cold. The rate of deposition increases with the temperature of the water, or alternatively, when biotic material accelerates the process of precipitation.

- a. 1703 Genroku earthquake
- b. 1700 Cascadia earthquake
- c. 1509 Istanbul earthquake
- d. Travertine

42. In geology, _____ are a body of rock with specified characteristics. Ideally, a _____ is a distinctive rock unit that forms under certain conditions of sedimentation, reflecting a particular process or environment.

The term _____ was introduced by the Swiss geologist Amanz Gressly in 1838 and was part of his significant contribution to the foundations of modern stratigraphy, [Cross and Homewood (1997)] which replaced the earlier notions of Neptunism.

- a. Granulites
- b. Mylonite
- c. Schist
- d. Facies

43. The _____ are groups of mineral compositions in metamorphic rocks, that are typical for a certain field in pressure-temperature space. Rocks which contain certain minerals can therefore be linked to certain tectonic settings.

The name facies was first used for specific sedimentary environments in sedimentary rocks by Swiss geologist Amanz Gressly in 1838.

- a. Metamorphic facies
- b. Mylonite
- c. Supracrustal rocks
- d. Greenstone belts

44. An _____ is used in geology to determine the degree of metamorphism a rock has experienced. Depending on the original composition of and the pressure and temperature experienced by the protolith (parent rock), chemical reactions between minerals in the solid state produce new minerals. When an _____ is found in a metamorphosed rock, it indicates the minimum pressure and temperature the protolith must have achieved in order for that mineral to form.

- a. AASHTO Soil Classification System
- b. AL 129-1
- c. AL 333
- d. Index mineral

45. In geology, an _____ is a plane of constant metamorphic grade in the field; it separates metamorphic zones of different metamorphic index minerals. On geologic maps focusing on metamorphic terranes (or landscapes underlain by metamorphic rocks), the boundaries between rocks of different metamorphic grade are commonly demarcated by _____ lines. The garnet _____, for example, would mark the first occurrence of garnet in the rocks.

- a. Ostwald ripening
- b. Isograd
- c. Exner equation
- d. Espresso crema effect

46. A _____ is in geology an area where, as a result of metamorphism, the same combination of minerals occur in the bed rocks. These zones occur because most metamorphic minerals are only stable in certain intervals of temperature and pressure.

Chapter 6. Metamorphism: A Process of Change

The temperature and pressure at which the mineralogical composition of a rock equilibrated can vary laterally through a metamorphic terrane.

a. Metamorphic rock
c. Tephra
b. Metamorphic zone
d. Magma

47. _____ describes the large scale motions of Earth's lithosphere. The theory encompasses the older concepts of continental drift, developed during the first decades of the 20th century by Alfred Wegener, and seafloor spreading, understood during the 1960s.

The outermost part of the Earth's interior is made up of two layers: the lithosphere and the asthenosphere.

a. Thrust fault
c. Continental crust
b. Plate tectonics
d. Forearc

48. The _____ Formation is one of the world's most celebrated fossil localities, and is famous for the exceptional preservation of the fossils found within it, in which the soft parts are preserved. It is 505 million years (Middle Cambrian) in age, making it one of the earliest fossil beds to preserve the soft parts of animals. The pre-Cambrian fossil record of animals is sparse and ambiguous.
a. 1509 Istanbul earthquake
c. 1700 Cascadia earthquake
b. Burgess Shale
d. 1703 Genroku earthquake

49. _____ occurs typically around intrusive igneous rocks as a result of the temperature increase caused by the intrusion of magma into cooler country rock. The area surrounding the intrusion (called aureoles) where the _____ effects are present is called the metamorphic aureole. Contact metamorphic rocks are usually known as hornfels.
a. Paralithic
c. Perched coastline
b. Gibraltar Arc
d. Contact metamorphism

50. A _____ in geology is an intrusive igneous rock body that crystallized from a magma slowly cooling below the surface of the Earth. Plutons include batholiths, dikes, sills, laccoliths, lopoliths, and other igneous bodies. In practice, '_____' usually refers to a distinctive mass of igneous rock, typically kilometers in dimension, without a tabular shape like those of dikes and sills.
a. Pluton
c. Vesicular texture
b. Metamorphic zone
d. Migmatite

51. A _____ column (or _____) is a column of rising air in the lower altitudes of the Earth's atmosphere. They are created by the uneven heating of the Earth's surface from solar radiation, and an example of convection. The Sun warms the ground, which in turn warms the air directly above it.
a. 1700 Cascadia earthquake
c. Thermal
b. 1509 Istanbul earthquake
d. 1703 Genroku earthquake

Chapter 6. Metamorphism: A Process of Change

52. The _____ or the Dirty Thirties was a period of severe dust storms causing major ecological and agricultural damage to American and Canadian prairie lands from 1930 to 1936 (in some areas until 1940.) The phenomenon was caused by severe drought coupled with decades of extensive farming without crop rotation or other techniques to prevent erosion. Deep plowing of the virgin topsoil of the Great Plains had killed the natural grasses that normally kept the soil in place and trapped moisture even during periods of drought and high winds.
   a. 1700 Cascadia earthquake
   b. Dust Bowl
   c. 1703 Genroku earthquake
   d. 1509 Istanbul earthquake

53. A _____ is an opening in a planet's surface or crust, which allows hot, molten rock, ash, and gases to escape from below the surface. Volcanic activity involving the extrusion of rock tends to form mountains or features like mountains over a period of time.
   a. 1703 Genroku earthquake
   b. 1509 Istanbul earthquake
   c. 1700 Cascadia earthquake
   d. Volcano

54. The _____ Eon is the current eon in the geologic timescale, and the one during which abundant animal life has existed. It covers roughly 545 million years and goes back to the time when diverse hard-shelled animals first appeared.
   a. 1700 Cascadia earthquake
   b. Phanerozoic
   c. 1703 Genroku earthquake
   d. 1509 Istanbul earthquake

55. The _____ is a geological eon representing a period before the first abundant complex life on Earth. The _____ extended from 2500 Ma to 542.0 >± 1.0 Ma (million years ago), and is the most recent part of the old, informally named 'e;Precambrian'e; time.

The Proterozoic consists of 3 geologic eras, from oldest to youngest:

- Paleoproterozoic
- Mesoproterozoic
- Neoproterozoic

The well-identified events were:

- The transition to an oxygenated atmosphere during the Mesoproterozoic.
- Several glaciations, including the hypothesized Snowball Earth during the Cryogenian period in the late Neoproterozoic.
- The Ediacaran Period (635 to 542 Ma) which is characterized by the evolution of abundant soft-bodied multicellular organisms.

The geoloic record of the Proterozoic is much better than that for the preceding Archean. In contrast to the deep-water deposits of the Archean, the Proterozoic features many strata that were laid down in extensive shallow epicontinental seas; furthermore, many of these rocks are less metamorphosed than Archean-age ones, and plenty are unaltered.

   a. 1509 Istanbul earthquake
   b. 1700 Cascadia earthquake
   c. 1703 Genroku earthquake
   d. Proterozoic Eon

Chapter 6. Metamorphism: A Process of Change

56. _____, (Navajo: >Ts>é Bit'a'>í, 'rock with wings' or 'winged rock') is a rock formation rising nearly 1,800 feet (550 m) above the high-desert plain on the Navajo Nation and in San Juan County, New Mexico.

_____ is composed of fractured volcanic breccia and black dikes of igneous rock called 'minette'. It is the erosional remnant of the throat of a volcano, and the volcanic breccia formed in a diatreme. The exposed rock probably was originally formed 2,500-3000 feet (750-1,000 meters) below the earth's surface, but it was exposed after millions of years of erosion. Wall-like sheets of minette, known as dikes, radiate away from the central formation. Radiometric age determinations of the minette establish that these volcanic rocks solidified about 27 million years ago.

a. 1509 Istanbul earthquake
b. Shiprock
c. 1703 Genroku earthquake
d. 1700 Cascadia earthquake

57. _____ is a rock that forms by the metamorphism of basalt and rocks with similar composition at high pressures and low temperatures, approximately corresponding to a depth of 15 to 30 kilometers and 200 to ~500 degrees Celsius. The blue color of the rock comes from the presence of the mineral glaucophane.

They are typically found within orogenic belts as terranes of lithology in faulted contact with greenschist or rarely eclogite facies rocks.

a. Mylonite
b. Metamorphic facies
c. Talc carbonate
d. Blueschist

58. _____ or impact metamorphism describes the effects of shock-wave related deformation and heating during impact events. The formation of similar features during explosive volcanism is generally discounted due to the lack of metamorphic effects unequivocally associated with explosions and the difficulty in reaching sufficient pressures during such an event.

Planar fractures are parallel sets of multiple planar cracks or cleavages in quartz grains; they develop at the lowest pressures characteristic of shock waves (~5-8 GPa) and a common feature of quartz grains found associated with impact structures.

a. Shock metamorphism
b. Prehnite-pumpellyite facies
c. Facies
d. Geothermobarometry

59. In geology, _____ is the process that takes place at convergent boundaries by which one tectonic plate moves under another tectonic plate, sinking into the Earth's mantle, as the plates converge. A _____ zone is an area on Earth where two tectonic plates move towards one another and _____ occurs. Rates of _____ are typically measured in centimeters per year, with the average rate of convergence being approximately 2 to 8 centimeters per year (about the rate a fingernail grows.)

a. Divergent boundary
b. Forearc
c. Subduction
d. Motagua Fault

60. _____ is a fine-grained, compact rock produced by dynamic crystallization of the constituent minerals resulting in a reduction of the grain size of the rock. It is classified as a metamorphic rock. _____ can have many different mineralogical compositions; it is a classification based on the textural appearance of the rock.

a. Metaconglomerate
b. Shock metamorphism
c. Hornfels
d. Mylonite

61. An _____ is a type of rock that contains minerals such as gemstones and metals that can be extracted through mining and refined for use. Samples of _____ in the form of exceptionally beautiful crystals, exotic layering visible when sectioned or polished or metallic presentations such as large nuggets or crystalline formations of metals such as gold or copper may command a value far beyond their value as mere _____ or raw metal for subsequent reduction to utilitarian purposes.

The grade or concentration of an _____ mineral, or metal, as well as its form of occurrence, will directly affect the costs associated with mining the _____.

a. Ore genesis
b. AASHTO Soil Classification System
c. AL 129-1
d. Ore

62. _____ is the removal of solids (sediment, soil, rock and other particles) in the natural environment. It usually occurs due to transport by wind, water, or ice; by down-slope creep of soil and other material under the force of gravity; or by living organisms, such as burrowing animals, in the case of bioerosion.

_____ is distinguished from weathering, which is the process of chemical or physical breakdown of the minerals in the rocks, although the two processes may occur concurrently.

a. AASHTO Soil Classification System
b. Erosion
c. AL 333
d. AL 129-1

63. The _____ is the level at which the ground water pressure is equal to atmospheric pressure. It may be conveniently visualized as the 'surface' of the ground water in a given vicinity. It usually coincides with the phreatic surface, but can be many feet above it. As water infiltrates through pore spaces in the soil, it first passes through the zone of aeration, where the soil is unsaturated. At increasing depths water fills in more spaces, until the zone of saturation is reached. The relatively horizontal plane atop this zone constitutes the _____.

a. Shaft construction
b. Rock bolt
c. Crosshole sonic logging
d. Water table

64. A _____ is generally a large area of exposed Precambrian crystalline igneous and high-grade metamorphic rocks that form tectonically stable areas. In all cases, the age of these rocks is greater than 570 million years and sometimes dates back 2 to 3.5 billion years. They have been little affected by tectonic events following the end of the Precambrian Era, and are relatively flat regions where mountain building, faulting, and other tectonic processes are greatly diminished compared with the activity that occurs at the margins of the shields and the boundaries between tectonic plates.

a. 1700 Cascadia earthquake
b. 1703 Genroku earthquake
c. 1509 Istanbul earthquake
d. Shield

65. A _____ is an elongated whale-shaped hill formed by glacial action. Its long axis is parallel with the movement of the ice, with the blunter end facing into the glacial movement. They may be more than 45 m (150 ft) high and more than 0.8 km (1/2 mile) long, and are often in _____ fields of similarly shaped, sized and oriented hills. They usually have layers indicating that the material was repeatedly added to a core, which may be of rock or glacial till.

a. Monadnock
b. Sandur
c. Drumlin
d. 1509 Istanbul earthquake

66. Geologically, a _____ is a long, narrow inlet with steep sides, created in a valley carved by glacial activity.

The seeds of a _____ are laid when a glacier cuts a U-shaped valley through abrasion of the surrounding bedrock by the sediment it carries. Many such valleys were formed during the recent ice age.

a. Fjord
b. 1703 Genroku earthquake
c. 1509 Istanbul earthquake
d. 1700 Cascadia earthquake

67. The _____ is a fundamental concept in geology that describes the dynamic transitions through geologic time among the three main rock types: sedimentary, metamorphic, and igneous. Each type of rock is altered or destroyed when it is forced out of its equilibrium conditions. An igneous rock such as basalt may break down and dissolve when exposed to the atmosphere, or melt as it is subducted under a continent.

a. Laccolith
b. Volcanic rock
c. Petrology
d. Rock cycle

68. In chronostratigraphy, a _____ is a succession of rock strata laid down in an single age on the geologic timescale, which usually represents millions of years of deposition. A given _____ of rock and the corresponding age of time will by convention have the same name, and the same boundaries.

a. Stage
b. Chronostratigraphy
c. Relative dating
d. Geologic record

Chapter 7. The Wrath of Vulcan: Volcanic Eruptions

1. A _____ is a mountain rising from the ocean seafloor that does not reach to the water's surface (sea level), and thus is not an island. These are typically formed from extinct volcanoes, that rise abruptly and are usually found rising from a seafloor of 1,000-4,000 meters depth. They are defined by oceanographers as independent features that rise to at least 1,000 meters above the seafloor.
   - a. 1509 Istanbul earthquake
   - b. 1700 Cascadia earthquake
   - c. 1703 Genroku earthquake
   - d. Seamount

2. A _____ is an opening in a planet's surface or crust, which allows hot, molten rock, ash, and gases to escape from below the surface. Volcanic activity involving the extrusion of rock tends to form mountains or features like mountains over a period of time.
   - a. Volcano
   - b. 1700 Cascadia earthquake
   - c. 1703 Genroku earthquake
   - d. 1509 Istanbul earthquake

3. The _____ is an oceanic tectonic plate beneath the Pacific Ocean.

   To the north the easterly side is a divergent boundary with the Explorer Plate, the Juan de Fuca Plate and the Gorda Plate forming respectively the Explorer Ridge, the Juan de Fuca Ridge and the Gorda Ridge. In the middle the easterly side is a transform boundary with the North American Plate along the San Andreas Fault and a boundary with the Cocos Plate.

   - a. Pacific Plate
   - b. Conway Reef Plate
   - c. Somali Plate
   - d. Gorda Plate

4. _____ is an igneous, volcanic rock, of intermediate composition, with aphanitic to porphyritic texture. The mineral assemblage is typically dominated by plagioclase plus pyroxene and/or hornblende. Magnetite, zircon, apatite, ilmenite, biotite, and garnet are common accessory minerals.
   - a. AL 129-1
   - b. AL 333
   - c. AASHTO Soil Classification System
   - d. Andesite

5. _____ is a common extrusive volcanic rock. It is usually grey to black and fine-grained due to rapid cooling of lava at the surface of a planet. It may be porphyritic containing larger crystals in a fine matrix, or vesicular, or frothy scoria.
   - a. 1703 Genroku earthquake
   - b. 1700 Cascadia earthquake
   - c. Basalt
   - d. 1509 Istanbul earthquake

6. _____ is molten rock expelled by a volcano during eruption. When first expelled from a volcanic vent, it is a liquid at temperatures from 700 >°C to 1,200 >°C (1,300 >°F to 2,200 >°F.) Although _____ is quite viscous, with about 100,000 times the viscosity of water, it can flow great distances before cooling and solidifying, because of both its thixotropic and shear thinning properties.
   - a. Supervolcano
   - b. Pit crater
   - c. Volcanic ash
   - d. Lava

7. _____ are natural conduits through which lava travels beneath the surface of a lava flow, expelled by a volcano during an eruption. They can be actively draining lava from a source, or can be extinct, meaning the lava flow has ceased and the rock has cooled and left a long, cave-like channel.

   _____ are formed when an active low-viscosity lava flow develops a continuous and hard crust, which thickens and forms a roof above the still-flowing lava stream.

Chapter 7. The Wrath of Vulcan: Volcanic Eruptions

a. Lava tubes
b. 1703 Genroku earthquake
c. 1509 Istanbul earthquake
d. 1700 Cascadia earthquake

8. _____ is molten rock that is found beneath the surface of the Earth, and may also exist on other terrestrial planets. Besides molten rock, _____ may also contain suspended crystals and gas bubbles. _____ often collects in a _____ chamber inside a volcano. _____ is capable of intrusion into adjacent rocks, extrusion onto the surface as lava, and explosive ejection as tephra to form pyroclastic rock.
   a. Volcanic rock
   b. Laccolith
   c. Rock cycle
   d. Magma

9. _____ is basaltic lava that has a smooth, billowy, undulating, or ropy surface. These surface features are due to the movement of very fluid lava under a congealing surface crust.
   a. Strike-slip faults
   b. Pahoehoe lava
   c. Loihi Seamount
   d. Rockall

10. _____ is an igneous, volcanic (extrusive) rock, of felsic (silicon-rich) composition. It may have any texture from aphanitic to porphyritic. The mineral assemblage is usually quartz, alkali feldspar and plagioclase. Biotite and hornblende are common accessory minerals.

    _____ can be considered as the extrusive equivalent to the plutonic granite rock, and consequently, outcroppings of it often bear a resemblance to granite. Due to their high content of silica and low iron and magnesium contents, _____ melts are highly polymerized and form highly viscous lavas.
    a. 1700 Cascadia earthquake
    b. Rhyolite
    c. 1703 Genroku earthquake
    d. 1509 Istanbul earthquake

11. _____ is a measure of the resistance of a fluid which is being deformed by either shear stress or extensional stress. In everyday terms (and for fluids only), _____ is 'thickness'. Thus, water is 'thin', having a lower _____, while honey is 'thick' having a higher _____.
    a. Thixotropy
    b. Viscosity
    c. Tensile stress
    d. Shear stress

12. _____ is the largest volcano on earth in terms of area covered and one of five volcanoes that form the Island of Hawaii in the U.S. state of Hawai>Ê»i in the Pacific Ocean. It is an active shield volcano, with a volume estimated at approximately 18,000 cubic miles (75,000 kmÂ³), although its peak is about 120 feet (37 m) lower than that of its neighbor, Mauna Kea. The Hawaiian name '_____' means 'Long Mountain'.
    a. 1700 Cascadia earthquake
    b. 1703 Genroku earthquake
    c. 1509 Istanbul earthquake
    d. Mauna Loa

13. _____ are type of elastic wave, also called seismic waves, that can travel through gases, elastic solids and liquids, including the Earth. _____ can be produced by earthquakes and recorded by seismometers.
    a. 1700 Cascadia earthquake
    b. 1509 Istanbul earthquake
    c. 1703 Genroku earthquake
    d. P-waves

14. Geologically, a _____ is a long, narrow inlet with steep sides, created in a valley carved by glacial activity.

The seeds of a _____ are laid when a glacier cuts a U-shaped valley through abrasion of the surrounding bedrock by the sediment it carries. Many such valleys were formed during the recent ice age.

a. 1700 Cascadia earthquake
c. 1703 Genroku earthquake
b. 1509 Istanbul earthquake
d. Fjord

15. _____ is a size classification term for tephra, which is material that falls out of the air during a volcanic eruption. They are in some senses similar to ooids or pisoids in calcareous sediments.

By definition _____ range in size from 2 mm to 64 mm in diameter. A pyroclastic particle greater than 64 mm in diameter is correctly known as a volcanic bomb when molten, or a volcanic block when solid.

a. Pyroclastic flow
c. Pit crater
b. Lava
d. Lapilli

16. _____ is a textural term for a volcanic rock that is a solidified frothy lava typically created when super-heated, highly pressurized rock is violently ejected from a volcano. It can be formed when lava and water are mixed. This unusual formation is due to the simultaneous actions of rapid cooling and rapid depressurization.

a. Cinder
c. Lapilli
b. Pumice
d. Pyroclastic flow

17. A _____ is a common and devastating result of some explosive volcanic eruptions. The flows are fast-moving currents of hot gas and rock (collectively known as tephra), which travel away from the volcano at speeds generally as great as 700 km/hr (450 mi/h.) The gas can reach temperatures of about 1,000 >°C (1,830 >°F). The flows normally hug the ground and travel downhill, or spread laterally under gravity. Their speed depends upon the density of the current, the volcanic output rate, and the gradient of the slope.

a. Supervolcano
c. Lava
b. Pit crater
d. Pyroclastic flow

18. _____ is a naturally occurring granular material composed of finely divided rock and mineral particles.

As the term is used by geologists, _____ particles range in diameter from 0.0625 (or $>^1\!/_{16}$ mm, or 62.5 micrometers) to 2 millimeters. An individual particle in this range size is termed a _____ grain.

a. 1509 Istanbul earthquake
c. 1703 Genroku earthquake
b. 1700 Cascadia earthquake
d. Sand

19. _____ is a textural term for macrovesicular volcanic rock. It is commonly, but not exclusively, basaltic or andesitic in composition. _____ is light as a result of numerous macroscopic ellipsoidal vesicles, but most _____ has a specific gravity greater than 1, and sinks in water.

a. Welded tuff
c. Coldwell Complex
b. Scoria
d. Lopolith

Chapter 7. The Wrath of Vulcan: Volcanic Eruptions

20. A _____ is an area in which an S-Wave (secondary seismic wave) is not detected due to it not being able to pass through the outer core of the earth due to it being liquid. When an earthquake occurs, seismographs near the epicenter, out to about 90° distance, are able to record both Primary and Secondary waves, but those at a greater distance no longer detect the S-wave. This is because shear waves cannot pass through liquids.
   a. Shadow zone
   b. Receiver function
   c. Maximum magnitude
   d. Tornillo event

21. _____ is air-fall material produced by a volcanic eruption regardless of composition or fragment size. _____ is typically rhyolitic in composition, as most explosive volcanoes are the product of the more viscous felsic or high silica magmas.

Volcanologists also refer to airborne fragments as pyroclasts.

   a. Migmatite
   b. Metamorphic zone
   c. Rock cycle
   d. Tephra

22. _____ is a type of rock consisting of consolidated volcanic ash ejected from vents during a volcanic eruption. _____ is sometimes called tufa, particularly when used as construction material, although tufa also refers to a quite different rock.

The products of a volcanic eruption are volcanic gases, lava, steam, and tephra. Magma is blown apart when it interacts violently with volcanic gases and steam. Solid material produced and thrown into the air by such volcanic eruptions is called tephra, regardless of composition or fragment size. If the resulting pieces of ejecta are small enough, the material is called volcanic ash, defined as such particles less than 2 mm in diameter, sand-sized or smaller.

   a. Pyroclastic rocks
   b. Country rock
   c. Coldwell Complex
   d. Tuff

23. _____ consists of small tephra, which are bits of pulverized rock and glass created by volcanic eruptions, less than 2 millimetres (0.079 in) in diameter. There are three mechanisms of _____ formation: gas release under decompression causing magmatic eruptions; thermal contraction from chilling on contact with water causing phreatomagmatic eruptions and ejection of entrained particles during steam eruptions causing phreatic eruptions. The violent nature of volcanic eruptions involving steam results in the magma and solid rock surrounding the vent being torn into particles of clay to sand size.
   a. Lava
   b. Cinder
   c. Volcanic ash
   d. Supervolcano

24. A _____ is a type of mudflow or landslide composed of pyroclastic material and water that flows down from a volcano, typically along a river valley. The term '_____' originated in the Javanese language of Indonesia. They can be best described as volcanic mudflows. They may not necessarily be caused by volcanic activity, but at the very least do originate from some type of volcanism.
   a. 1509 Istanbul earthquake
   b. 1700 Cascadia earthquake
   c. 1703 Genroku earthquake
   d. Lahar

Chapter 7. The Wrath of Vulcan: Volcanic Eruptions

25. A _____ is a fast moving mass of unconsolidated, saturated debris that looks like flowing concrete. They differentiate from a mudflow by terms of the viscosity of the flow. Flows can carry clasts ranging in size from clay particles to boulders, and also often contains a large amount of woody debris.
   a. Predator trap
   b. Geohazard
   c. Cryoseism
   d. Debris flow

26. _____ is a volcanic rock texture characterised by, or containing many vesicles. The texture is often found in extrusive aphanitic igneous rock. The vesicles are small cavities formed by the expansion of bubbles of gas or steam during the solidification of the rock.
   a. Vesicular texture
   b. Migmatite
   c. Magma
   d. Laccolith

27. A _____ is a cauldron-like volcanic feature usually formed by the collapse of land following a volcanic eruption such as the one at Yellowstone National Park. They are sometimes confused with volcanic craters.
   a. 1703 Genroku earthquake
   b. 1509 Istanbul earthquake
   c. Caldera
   d. 1700 Cascadia earthquake

28. _____, in structural geology and related disciplines, describes the tendency of a rock to break along preferred planes of weakness.

Rocks deformed under very low to low metamorphic grade often develop planes along which the rock can easily be split. Slates are an example of a rock with a penetrative _____ caused partly by the realignment of phyllosilicate minerals with increasing flattening strain.

   a. Combe
   b. Drainage system
   c. Compaction
   d. Cleavage

29. A _____ is generally a large area of exposed Precambrian crystalline igneous and high-grade metamorphic rocks that form tectonically stable areas. In all cases, the age of these rocks is greater than 570 million years and sometimes dates back 2 to 3.5 billion years. They have been little affected by tectonic events following the end of the Precambrian Era, and are relatively flat regions where mountain building, faulting, and other tectonic processes are greatly diminished compared with the activity that occurs at the margins of the shields and the boundaries between tectonic plates.
   a. 1700 Cascadia earthquake
   b. 1509 Istanbul earthquake
   c. 1703 Genroku earthquake
   d. Shield

30. A _____ is a large volcano with shallow-sloping sides.

They are formed by lava flows of low viscosity - lava that flows easily. Consequently, a volcanic mountain having a broad profile is built up over time by flow after flow of relatively fluid basaltic lava issuing from vents or fissures on the surface of the volcano

   a. 1703 Genroku earthquake
   b. Shield volcano
   c. 1509 Istanbul earthquake
   d. 1700 Cascadia earthquake

31. A _____ is a pyroclastic material. They are extrusive igneous rocks, and are similar to pumice, which has so many cavities and is such low-density that it can float on water.

Chapter 7. The Wrath of Vulcan: Volcanic Eruptions

a. Wadati-Benioff zone
b. Pyroclastic flow
c. Pit crater
d. Cinder

32. A _____ or scoria cone is a steep conical hill of volcanic fragments that accumulate around and downwind from a volcanic vent. The rock fragments, often called cinders or scoria, are glassy and contain numerous gas bubbles 'frozen' into place as magma exploded into the air and then cooled quickly. Cinder cones range in size from tens to hundreds of meters tall.

a. 1509 Istanbul earthquake
b. 1703 Genroku earthquake
c. Cinder cone
d. 1700 Cascadia earthquake

33. A _____ or dyke in geology is a type of sheet intrusion referring to any geologic body that cuts discordantly across

- planar wall rock structures, such as bedding or foliation
- massive rock formations, like igneous/magmatic intrusions and salt diapirs.

They can therefore be either intrusive or sedimentary in origin.

An intrusive _____ is an igneous body with a very high aspect ratio, which means that its thickness is usually much smaller than the other two dimensions. Thickness can vary from sub-centimeter scale to many meters and the lateral dimensions can extend over many kilometers. A _____ is an intrusion into an opening cross-cutting fissure, shouldering aside other pre-existing layers or bodies of rock; this implies that a _____ is always younger than the rocks that contain it.

a. Dike
b. Geopetal
c. Schmidt hammer
d. Pneumatolysis

34. A type of seismic wave, the _____, secondary wave or shear wave (sometimes called an elastic _____) is one of the two main types of elastic body waves, so named because they move through the body of an object, unlike surface waves.

The _____ move as a shear or transverse wave, so motion is perpendicular to the direction of wave propagation: S-waves, like waves in a rope, as opposed to waves moving through a slinky, the P-wave. The wave moves through elastic media, and the main restoring force comes from shear effects.

a. 1700 Cascadia earthquake
b. 1509 Istanbul earthquake
c. 1703 Genroku earthquake
d. S-wave

35. In geology, an _____ is a body of igneous rock that has crystallized from molten magma below the surface of the Earth. Bodies of magma that solidify underground before they reach the surface of the earth are called plutons the Roman god of the underworld. Correspondingly, rocks of this kind are also referred to as igneous plutonic rocks or igneous intrusive rocks.

a. AL 129-1
b. AASHTO Soil Classification System
c. AL 333
d. Intrusion

36. A _____ is an igneous intrusion (or concordant pluton) that has been injected between two layers of sedimentary rock. The pressure of the magma is high enough that the overlying strata are forced upward, giving the _____ a dome or mushroom-like form with a generally planar base.

They tend to form at relatively shallow depths and are typically formed by relatively viscous magmas, such as those that crystallize to diorite, granodiorite, and granite. Cooling underground takes place slowly, giving time for larger crystals to form in the cooling magma. The surface rock above the _____ often erodes away completely, leaving the core mound of igneous rock.

a. Volcanic rock
b. Rock cycle
c. Serpentinite
d. Laccolith

37. _____ is the solid-state recrystallization of pre-existing rocks due to changes in physical and chemical conditions, primarily heat, pressure, and the introduction of chemically active fluids. Both mineralogical, chemical and crystallographic changes can occur during this process.

Three types of _____ exist: dynamic, contact and regional.

a. Metamorphism
b. Detritus
c. Compression
d. Reading Prong

38. A _____ in geology is an intrusive igneous rock body that crystallized from a magma slowly cooling below the surface of the Earth. Plutons include batholiths, dikes, sills, laccoliths, lopoliths, and other igneous bodies. In practice, '_____' usually refers to a distinctive mass of igneous rock, typically kilometers in dimension, without a tabular shape like those of dikes and sills.

a. Metamorphic zone
b. Vesicular texture
c. Pluton
d. Migmatite

39. The _____ Period is the last geological period of the Neoproterozoic Era and of the Proterozoic Eon, immediately preceding the Cambrian Period, the first period of the Paleozoic Era and of the Phanerozoic Eon. Its status as an official geological period was ratified in 2004 by the International Union of Geological Sciences (IUGS), making it the first new geological period declared in 120 years. The type section is in the Flinders Ranges in South Australia.

a. Ediacaran
b. AL 333
c. AASHTO Soil Classification System
d. AL 129-1

40. A _____, sometimes called a composite volcano, is a tall, conical volcano with many layers (strata) of hardened lava, tephra, and volcanic ash. They are characterized by a steep profile and periodic, explosive eruptions. The lava that flows from a _____ tends to be viscous; it cools and hardens before spreading far.

a. Mount Baker
b. Mount Overlord
c. Broken Top
d. Stratovolcano

41. The general term '_____' or, more precisely, 'glacial age' denotes a geological period of long-term reduction in the temperature of the Earth's surface and atmosphere, resulting in an expansion of continental ice sheets, polar ice sheets and alpine glaciers. Within a long-term _____, individual pulses of extra cold climate are termed 'glaciations'. Glaciologically, _____ implies the presence of extensive ice sheets in the northern and southern hemispheres; by this definition we are still in an _____.

a. Ice age
b. AL 333
c. AL 129-1
d. AASHTO Soil Classification System

42. _____ describes the large scale motions of Earth's lithosphere. The theory encompasses the older concepts of continental drift, developed during the first decades of the 20th century by Alfred Wegener, and seafloor spreading, understood during the 1960s.

The outermost part of the Earth's interior is made up of two layers: the lithosphere and the asthenosphere.

a. Forearc
b. Thrust fault
c. Plate tectonics
d. Continental crust

43. _____ is a geologic term for a type of topography characterized by a series of separate and parallel mountain ranges with broad valleys interposed, extending over a more or less wide area. It is typified by the topography found in the Great Basin in the western United States, which is part of a larger regional topography known as the _____ Province. _____ topography results from crustal extension.

a. Tidal scour
b. Zechstein
c. Rill
d. Basin and Range

44. The _____ is a large geologic province which includes parts of the southwestern United States and northwestern Mexico, typified by basin and range topography.

The topography of the _____ is a result of crustal extension within this part of the North American Plate. The cause of this extension is as yet not fully understood, although several hypotheses have been offered. The crust here has been stretched up to 100% of its original width. In fact, the crust underneath the _____, especially under the Great Basin, is some of the thinnest in the world.

a. Yilgarn Craton
b. Quaternary
c. Basin and Range Province
d. Canadian Shield

45. The _____ is a mid-ocean ridge, a divergent tectonic plate boundary located along the floor of the Atlantic Ocean, and the longest mountain range in the world. It separates the Eurasian Plate and North American Plate in the North Atlantic, and the African Plate from the South American Plate in the South Atlantic. The MAR extends from a junction with the Gakkel Ridge (Mid-Arctic Ridge) northeast of Greenland southward to the Bouvet Triple Junction in the South Atlantic.

a. 1703 Genroku earthquake
b. 1509 Istanbul earthquake
c. 1700 Cascadia earthquake
d. Mid-Atlantic Ridge

46. The _____ Eon is the current eon in the geologic timescale, and the one during which abundant animal life has existed. It covers roughly 545 million years and goes back to the time when diverse hard-shelled animals first appeared.

a. 1509 Istanbul earthquake
b. 1703 Genroku earthquake
c. 1700 Cascadia earthquake
d. Phanerozoic

47. The _____ is a geological eon representing a period before the first abundant complex life on Earth. The _____ extended from 2500 Ma to 542.0 >± 1.0 Ma (million years ago), and is the most recent part of the old, informally named 'e;Precambrian'e; time.

Chapter 7. The Wrath of Vulcan: Volcanic Eruptions

The Proterozoic consists of 3 geologic eras, from oldest to youngest:

- Paleoproterozoic
- Mesoproterozoic
- Neoproterozoic

The well-identified events were:

- The transition to an oxygenated atmosphere during the Mesoproterozoic.
- Several glaciations, including the hypothesized Snowball Earth during the Cryogenian period in the late Neoproterozoic.
- The Ediacaran Period (635 to 542 Ma) which is characterized by the evolution of abundant soft-bodied multicellular organisms.

The geoloic record of the Proterozoic is much better than that for the preceding Archean. In contrast to the deep-water deposits of the Archean, the Proterozoic features many strata that were laid down in extensive shallow epicontinental seas; furthermore, many of these rocks are less metamorphosed than Archean-age ones, and plenty are unaltered.

a. 1700 Cascadia earthquake
b. 1703 Genroku earthquake
c. 1509 Istanbul earthquake
d. Proterozoic Eon

48. In geology, a _____ is a place where the Earth's crust and lithosphere are being pulled apart and is an example of extensional tectonics.

Typical _____ features are a central linear downdropped fault segment, called a graben, with parallel normal faulting and _____-flank uplifts on either side forming a _____ valley, where the _____ remains above sea level. The axis of the _____ area commonly contains volcanic rocks and active volcanism is a part of many, but not all active _____ systems.

a. 1703 Genroku earthquake
b. 1509 Istanbul earthquake
c. 1700 Cascadia earthquake
d. Rift

49. The _____ is an area where large numbers of earthquakes and volcanic eruptions occur in the basin of the Pacific Ocean. In a 40,000 km horseshoe shape, it is associated with a nearly continuous series of oceanic trenches, volcanic arcs, and volcanic belts and/or plate movements. The _____ has 452 volcanoes and is home to over 75% of the world's active and dormant volcanoes.

a. 1509 Istanbul earthquake
b. 1700 Cascadia earthquake
c. Pacific Ring of Fire
d. 1703 Genroku earthquake

50. A _____ is a chain of volcanic islands or mountains formed by plate tectonics as an oceanic tectonic plate subducts under another tectonic plate and produces magma. There are two types of these: oceanic arcs (commonly called island arcs, a type of archipelago) and continental arcs. In the former, oceanic crust subducts beneath other oceanic crust on an adjacent plate, while in the latter case the oceanic crust subducts beneath continental crust. In some situations, a single subduction zone may show both aspects along its length, as part of a plate subducts beneath a continent and part beneath adjacent oceanic crust.
- a. 1700 Cascadia earthquake
- b. 1703 Genroku earthquake
- c. 1509 Istanbul earthquake
- d. Volcanic arc

51. The _____ was a period of mountain building in western North America, which started in the Late Cretaceous, 70 to 80 million years ago, and ended 35 to 55 million years ago. The exact duration and ages of beginning and end of the orogeny are in dispute, as is the cause. The _____ occurred in a series of pulses, with quiescent phases intervening. The major feature that was created by this orogeny was the Rocky Mountains, but evidence of this orogeny can be found from Alaska to northern Mexico, with the easternmost extent of the mountain-building represented by the Black Hills of South Dakota.
- a. Pan-African orogeny
- b. Kaikoura Orogeny
- c. Sevier orogeny
- d. Laramide orogeny

52. A _____ or trap basalt is the result of a giant volcanic eruption or series of eruptions that coats large stretches of land or the ocean floor with basalt lava. Flood basalts have occurred on continental scales (large igneous provinces) in prehistory, creating great plateaus and mountain ranges. Flood basalts have erupted at random intervals throughout geological history and are clear evidence that the Earth undergoes periods of enhanced activity rather than being in a uniform steady state.
- a. Lopolith
- b. Tuff
- c. Country rock
- d. Flood basalt

53. _____ were originally defined by Coffin and Eldholm (1992) as areas of Earth's surface that contain very large volumes of magmatic rocks (typically basalt but including rhyolites) erupted over extremely short geological time intervals of a few million years or less. These provinces are not associated with normal plate tectonic magmatism, i. e. mid-ocean ridges and island arcs.
- a. Migmatite
- b. Serpentinite
- c. Volcanic rock
- d. Large igneous provinces

54. _____ refers to natural mountain building, and may be studied as a tectonic structural event, (b) as a geographical event, and (c) a chronological event. Orogenic events (a) cause distinctive structural phenomena and related tectonic activity, (b) affect certain regions of rocks and crust, and (c) happen within a specific period of time.
- a. Antler orogeny
- b. Orogenesis
- c. Alice Springs Orogeny
- d. Orogeny

55. _____, (Navajo: >Ts>é Bit'a'>í, 'rock with wings' or 'winged rock') is a rock formation rising nearly 1,800 feet (550 m) above the high-desert plain on the Navajo Nation and in San Juan County, New Mexico.

80 *Chapter 7. The Wrath of Vulcan: Volcanic Eruptions*

_____ is composed of fractured volcanic breccia and black dikes of igneous rock called 'minette'. It is the erosional remnant of the throat of a volcano, and the volcanic breccia formed in a diatreme. The exposed rock probably was originally formed 2,500-3000 feet (750-1,000 meters) below the earth's surface, but it was exposed after millions of years of erosion. Wall-like sheets of minette, known as dikes, radiate away from the central formation. Radiometric age determinations of the minette establish that these volcanic rocks solidified about 27 million years ago.

- a. 1509 Istanbul earthquake
- b. Shiprock
- c. 1700 Cascadia earthquake
- d. 1703 Genroku earthquake

56. _____ is a geological term used to describe particles of rock derived from pre-existing rock through processes of weathering and erosion. Thesel particles can consist of lithic fragments (particles of recognisable rock), or of monomineralic fragments (mineral grains.) These particles are often transported through sedimentary processes into depositional systems such as riverbeds, lakes or the ocean forming sedimentary successions.
- a. Geomechanics
- b. Perched coastline
- c. Medical geology
- d. Detritus

57. The _____ of Thera, also referred to as the Thera eruption or Santorini eruption, was a major catastrophic volcanic eruption (Volcanic Explosivity Index (VEI) = 6 or 7, Dense-rock equivalent (DRE) = 60 km^3) which is estimated to have occurred in the mid second millennium BCE. The eruption was one of the largest volcanic events on Earth in recorded history. The eruption devastated the island of Thera (also called Santorini), including the Minoan settlement at Akrotiri as well as communities and agricultural areas on nearby islands and on the coast of Crete.
- a. Minoan eruption
- b. 1509 Istanbul earthquake
- c. 1703 Genroku earthquake
- d. 1700 Cascadia earthquake

58. An _____ is the result of a sudden release of energy in the Earth's crust that creates seismic waves. They are recorded with a seismometer or the related and mostly obsolete Richter magnitude, with a magnitude 3 or lower _____ being mostly imperceptible and magnitude 7 causing serious damage over large areas.
- a. AL 129-1
- b. AL 333
- c. AASHTO Soil Classification System
- d. Earthquake

59. The _____ is the epoch from 1.8 million to 11550 years BP covering the world's recent period of repeated glaciations. The _____ epoch follows the Pliocene epoch and is followed by the Holocene epoch. The _____ is the third epoch of the Neogene period or 6th epoch of the Cenozoic Era. The end of the _____ corresponds with the retreat of the last continental glacier. It also corresponds with the end of the Paleolithic age used in archaeology.
- a. Tyrrhenian
- b. Pleistocene
- c. Late Pleistocene
- d. Sicilian Stage

60. In geology, a _____ is a location on the Earth's surface that has experienced active volcanism for a long period of time.

J. Tuzo Wilson came up with the idea in 1963 that volcanic chains like the Hawaiian Islands result from the slow movement of a tectonic plate across a 'fixed' _____ deep beneath the surface of the planet.

a. 1700 Cascadia earthquake
b. 1703 Genroku earthquake
c. 1509 Istanbul earthquake
d. Hotspot

Chapter 8. A Violent Pulse: Earthquakes

1. The _____ is a tectonic plate covering most of North America, Greenland and part of Siberia. It extends eastward to the Mid-Atlantic Ridge and westward to the Chersky Range in eastern Siberia. The plate includes both continental and oceanic crust. The interior of the main continental landmass includes an extensive granitic core called a craton. Along most of the edges of this craton are fragments of crustal material called terranes, accreted to the craton by tectonic actions over the long span of geologic time. It is believed that much of North America west of the Rockies is composed of such terranes.
   a. North American Plate
   b. Kermadec Plate
   c. Philippine Sea Plate
   d. Burma Plate

2. The _____ is an oceanic tectonic plate beneath the Pacific Ocean.

   To the north the easterly side is a divergent boundary with the Explorer Plate, the Juan de Fuca Plate and the Gorda Plate forming respectively the Explorer Ridge, the Juan de Fuca Ridge and the Gorda Ridge. In the middle the easterly side is a transform boundary with the North American Plate along the San Andreas Fault and a boundary with the Cocos Plate.

   a. Gorda Plate
   b. Somali Plate
   c. Pacific Plate
   d. Conway Reef Plate

3. An _____ is the result of a sudden release of energy in the Earth's crust that creates seismic waves. They are recorded with a seismometer or the related and mostly obsolete Richter magnitude, with a magnitude 3 or lower _____ being mostly imperceptible and magnitude 7 causing serious damage over large areas.
   a. AL 333
   b. Earthquake
   c. AASHTO Soil Classification System
   d. AL 129-1

4. In geology, a _____ or _____ line is a planar fracture in rock in which the rock on one side of the fracture has moved with respect to the rock on the other side. Large faults within the Earth's crust are the result of differential or shear motion and active _____ zones are the causal locations of most earthquakes. Earthquakes are caused by energy release during rapid slippage along a _____.
   a. Dali
   b. Combe
   c. Stack
   d. Fault

5. The _____ was an ancient oceanic plate, which began subducting under the west coast of the North American Plate-- then located in modern Utah-- as Pangaea broke apart during the Jurassic period. It is named for the Farallon Islands which are located just west of San Francisco, California.

   Over time the central part of the _____ was completely subducted under the southwestern part of the North American Plate. The remains of the _____ are the Juan de Fuca, Explorer and Gorda Plates, subducting under the northern part of the North American Plate, the Cocos Plate subducting under Central America and the Nazca Plate subducting under the South American Plate.

   a. Cocos Plate
   b. Fault trace
   c. Rivera Plate
   d. Farallon Plate

6. _____ are type of elastic wave, also called seismic waves, that can travel through gases, elastic solids and liquids, including the Earth. _____ can be produced by earthquakes and recorded by seismometers.

Chapter 8. A Violent Pulse: Earthquakes 83

a. 1509 Istanbul earthquake
b. 1703 Genroku earthquake
c. P-waves
d. 1700 Cascadia earthquake

7. A type of seismic wave, the _____, secondary wave or shear wave (sometimes called an elastic _____) is one of the two main types of elastic body waves, so named because they move through the body of an object, unlike surface waves.

The _____ move as a shear or transverse wave, so motion is perpendicular to the direction of wave propagation: S-waves, like waves in a rope, as opposed to waves moving through a slinky, the P-wave. The wave moves through elastic media, and the main restoring force comes from shear effects.

a. 1700 Cascadia earthquake
b. 1703 Genroku earthquake
c. 1509 Istanbul earthquake
d. S-wave

8. An _____ is an earthquake that occurs after a previous earthquake (the main shock.) An _____ is in the same region of the main shock but is always of smaller magnitude strength. If an _____ is larger than the main shock, the _____ is redesignated as the main shock and the original main shock is redesignated as a foreshock.

a. Aftershock
b. AL 129-1
c. AL 333
d. AASHTO Soil Classification System

9. Geologically, a _____ is a long, narrow inlet with steep sides, created in a valley carved by glacial activity.

The seeds of a _____ are laid when a glacier cuts a U-shaped valley through abrasion of the surrounding bedrock by the sediment it carries. Many such valleys were formed during the recent ice age.

a. 1703 Genroku earthquake
b. 1700 Cascadia earthquake
c. 1509 Istanbul earthquake
d. Fjord

10. The _____, refers to the site of an earthquake or to that of a nuclear explosion. In the former, it is a synonym of the focus; in the latter, of ground zero.

The location of an earthquake's _____ is the position where the energy stored in the strain in the rock is released, which occurs at the focal depth below the epicentre. The focal depth can be calculated from measurements based on seismic wave phenomena.

a. Receiver function
b. Hypocenter
c. Harmonic tremor
d. Seismic waves

11. A _____ is a geological phenomenon which includes a wide range of ground movement, such as rock falls, deep failure of slopes and shallow debris flows, which can occur in offshore, coastal and onshore environments. Although the action of gravity is the primary driving force for a _____ to occur, there are other contributing factors affecting the original slope stability. Typically, pre-conditional factors build up specific sub-surface conditions that make the area/slope prone to failure, whereas the actual _____ often requires a trigger before being released.

a. Landslide
b. 1509 Istanbul earthquake
c. 1700 Cascadia earthquake
d. Mass wasting

12. _____ is the solid-state recrystallization of pre-existing rocks due to changes in physical and chemical conditions, primarily heat, pressure, and the introduction of chemically active fluids. Both mineralogical, chemical and crystallographic changes can occur during this process.

Three types of _____ exist: dynamic, contact and regional.

a. Compression
b. Detritus
c. Reading Prong
d. Metamorphism

13. The _____ is a geological signature, usually a thin band, dated to (65.5 ± 0.3) Ma (million years ago). The boundary marks the end of the Mesozoic era and the beginning of the Cenozoic era, and is associated with the Cretaceous-Tertiary extinction event, a mass extinction.

a. 1509 Istanbul earthquake
b. K-T boundary
c. 1700 Cascadia earthquake
d. Shiva crater

14. A _____ is the topographic expression of faulting attributed to the displacement of the land surface by movement along the fault. It can be caused by differential erosion along an old inactive geologic fault (a sort of old rupture) with hard and weak rock, or by a movement on an active fault. In many cases, bluffs form from the upthrown block and can be very steep.

a. Bradyseism
b. Fault scarp
c. Rejuvenated
d. Gravitational erosion

15. Since faults do not usually consist of a single, clean fracture, the term fault zone is used when referring to the zone of complex deformation that is associated with the fault plane. The two sides of a non-vertical fault are called the _____ and footwall. By definition, the _____ occurs above the fault and the footwall occurs below the fault.

a. Reverse fault
b. 1700 Cascadia earthquake
c. 1509 Istanbul earthquake
d. Hanging wall

16. _____ describes the large scale motions of Earth's lithosphere. The theory encompasses the older concepts of continental drift, developed during the first decades of the 20th century by Alfred Wegener, and seafloor spreading, understood during the 1960s.

The outermost part of the Earth's interior is made up of two layers: the lithosphere and the asthenosphere.

a. Thrust fault
b. Forearc
c. Continental crust
d. Plate tectonics

17. A _____ is the opposite of a normal fault -- the hanging wall moves up relative to the footwall. They are indicative of shortening of the crust. The dip of a _____ is relatively steep, greater than 45>°.

a. Hanging wall
b. 1700 Cascadia earthquake
c. 1509 Istanbul earthquake
d. Reverse fault

18. The fault surface of _____ is usually near vertical and the footwall moves either left or right or laterally with very little vertical motion. _____ with left-lateral motion are also known as sinistral faults. Those with right-lateral motion are also known as dextral faults.

a. Strike-slip faults
b. Principle of inclusions and components
c. Pahoehoe lava
d. Valley glaciers

19. A _____ column (or _____) is a column of rising air in the lower altitudes of the Earth's atmosphere. They are created by the uneven heating of the Earth's surface from solar radiation, and an example of convection. The Sun warms the ground, which in turn warms the air directly above it.
a. 1703 Genroku earthquake
b. 1509 Istanbul earthquake
c. Thermal
d. 1700 Cascadia earthquake

20. A _____ is a type of fault in which rocks of lower stratigraphic position are pushed up and over higher strata. They are often recognized because they place older rocks above younger. Thrust faults are the result of compressional forces.
a. Juan de Fuca Ridge
b. Subduction
c. Convergent boundary
d. Thrust fault

21. The _____ is a continental transform fault that runs a length of roughly 800 miles (1,300 km) through California in the United States. The fault's motion is right-lateral strike-slip (horizontal motion.) It forms the tectonic boundary between the Pacific Plate and the North American Plate.
a. 1700 Cascadia earthquake
b. 1703 Genroku earthquake
c. San Andreas Fault
d. 1509 Istanbul earthquake

22. An _____ is a fault which has had displacement or seismic activity during the geologically recent period. In the United States, an _____ is generally defined as a fault which displaced earth materials during the Holocene Epoch (during the last 11,000 or so years before present.) Active faults are the most common sources of earthquakes and tectonic movements.
a. AASHTO Soil Classification System
b. AL 129-1
c. AL 333
d. Active fault

23. The _____ was a mountain-building event that affected western North America from Canada to the north to Mexico to the south. This orogeny was the result of convergent boundary tectonism between approximately 140 million years (Ma) ago, and 50 Ma. This orogeny was produced by the collision of the oceanic Farallon Plate and Kula Plate, predecessors of the Pacific Plate, and their subduction underneath the continental North American Plate. The _____ was preceded by several other mountain-building events including the Nevadan orogeny, the Sonoman orogeny, and the Antler orogeny, and partially overlapped in time and space with the Laramide orogeny.
a. Sevier orogeny
b. Trans-Hudson orogeny
c. Pan-African orogeny
d. Kaikoura Orogeny

24. _____ is a common extrusive volcanic rock. It is usually grey to black and fine-grained due to rapid cooling of lava at the surface of a planet. It may be porphyritic containing larger crystals in a fine matrix, or vesicular, or frothy scoria.
a. 1700 Cascadia earthquake
b. 1703 Genroku earthquake
c. 1509 Istanbul earthquake
d. Basalt

25. _____ refers to natural mountain building, and may be studied as a tectonic structural event, (b) as a geographical event, and (c) a chronological event. Orogenic events (a) cause distinctive structural phenomena and related tectonic activity, (b) affect certain regions of rocks and crust, and (c) happen within a specific period of time.

a. Orogenesis
b. Alice Springs Orogeny
c. Antler orogeny
d. Orogeny

26. Study of geological _____ is related to the study of structural geology, rock microstructure or rock texture and fault mechanics.

_____ is the response of a rock to deformation usually by compressive stress and forms particular textures. _____ can be homogeneous or non-homogeneous, and may be pure _____ or simple _____.

a. Sag pond
b. Molasse basin
c. Shear
d. Crenulation

27. In physics, a _____ is a mechanical wave that propagates along the interface between differing media, usually two fluids with different densities. A _____ can also be an electromagnetic wave guided by a refractive index gradient. In radio transmission, a ground wave is a _____ that propagates close to the surface of the Earth.
a. 1509 Istanbul earthquake
b. 1703 Genroku earthquake
c. Surface wave
d. 1700 Cascadia earthquake

28. The lithosphere is broken up into what are called _____. In the case of Earth, there are eight major and many minor plates The lithospheric plates ride on the asthenosphere. These plates move in relation to one another at one of three types of plate boundaries: convergent, or collisional boundaries; divergent boundaries, also called spreading centers; and transform boundaries.
a. Tectonic plates
b. Copperbelt Province
c. Gorda Ridge
d. Thrust fault

29. The _____ is a scale used for measuring the intensity of an earthquake. The scale quantifies the effects of an earthquake on the Earth's surface, humans, objects of nature, and man-made structures on a scale of I through XII, with I denoting not felt, and XII one that causes almost complete destruction. The values will differ based on the distance to the earthquake, with the highest intensities being around the epicentral area.
a. Seismic scale
b. Mercalli intensity scale
c. China Seismic Intensity Scale
d. Richter magnitude scale

30. A _____ is the intersection of a geological fault with the ground surface, leaving a visible mark. The term also applies to a line plotted on a geological map to represent a fault.
a. Sonoma orogeny
b. Cocos Plate
c. Farallon Plate
d. Fault trace

31. A _____ is a body of water, which forms as water collects in the lowest parts of the depression that forms between two strands of an active strike-slip fault . The relative motion of the two fault strands results in a stretching of the land between them, causing the land between them to sink.
a. Graben
b. Michoud fault
c. Sag pond
d. Tectonites

32. The _____ Eon is the current eon in the geologic timescale, and the one during which abundant animal life has existed. It covers roughly 545 million years and goes back to the time when diverse hard-shelled animals first appeared.

a. 1509 Istanbul earthquake
c. 1703 Genroku earthquake
b. 1700 Cascadia earthquake
d. Phanerozoic

33. The _____ is a geological eon representing a period before the first abundant complex life on Earth. The _____ extended from 2500 Ma to 542.0 >± 1.0 Ma (million years ago), and is the most recent part of the old, informally named 'e;Precambrian'e; time.

The Proterozoic consists of 3 geologic eras, from oldest to youngest:

- Paleoproterozoic
- Mesoproterozoic
- Neoproterozoic

The well-identified events were:

- The transition to an oxygenated atmosphere during the Mesoproterozoic.
- Several glaciations, including the hypothesized Snowball Earth during the Cryogenian period in the late Neoproterozoic.
- The Ediacaran Period (635 to 542 Ma) which is characterized by the evolution of abundant soft-bodied multicellular organisms.

The geoloic record of the Proterozoic is much better than that for the preceding Archean. In contrast to the deep-water deposits of the Archean, the Proterozoic features many strata that were laid down in extensive shallow epicontinental seas; furthermore, many of these rocks are less metamorphosed than Archean-age ones, and plenty are unaltered.

a. 1700 Cascadia earthquake
c. Proterozoic Eon
b. 1509 Istanbul earthquake
d. 1703 Genroku earthquake

34. The _____, also known as the local magnitude (M_L) scale, assigns a single number to quantify the amount of seismic energy released by an earthquake. It is a base-10 logarithmic scale obtained by calculating the logarithm of the combined horizontal amplitude of the largest displacement from zero on a Wood-Anderson torsion seismometer output. So, for example, an earthquake that measures 5.0 on the Richter scale has a shaking amplitude 10 times larger than one that measures 4.0.

a. Moment magnitude scale
c. Richter magnitude scale
b. China Seismic Intensity Scale
d. Medvedev-Sponheuer-Karnik scale

35. The _____ is used by seismologists to measure the size of earthquakes in terms of the energy released. The magnitude is based on the moment of the earthquake, which is equal to the rigidity of the Earth multiplied by the average amount of slip on the fault and the size of the area that slipped. The scale was developed in the 1970s to succeed the 1930s-era Richter magnitude scale, M_L.

a. Seismic scale
c. Mercalli intensity scale
b. Medvedev-Sponheuer-Karnik scale
d. Moment magnitude scale

Chapter 8. A Violent Pulse: Earthquakes

36. _____ are waves that travel through the Earth or other elastic body, for example as the result of an earthquake, explosion, or some other process that imparts forces to the body. _____ are also continually excited on Earth by the incessant pounding of ocean waves (referred to as the microseism) and the wind. _____ are studied by seismologists, and measured by a seismograph, which records the output of a seismometer, or geophone.
   a. Seismic waves
   b. Harmonic tremor
   c. Maximum magnitude
   d. Shadow zone

37. The _____ is a mid-ocean ridge, a divergent tectonic plate boundary located along the floor of the Atlantic Ocean, and the longest mountain range in the world. It separates the Eurasian Plate and North American Plate in the North Atlantic, and the African Plate from the South American Plate in the South Atlantic. The MAR extends from a junction with the Gakkel Ridge (Mid-Arctic Ridge) northeast of Greenland southward to the Bouvet Triple Junction in the South Atlantic.
   a. 1509 Istanbul earthquake
   b. 1703 Genroku earthquake
   c. 1700 Cascadia earthquake
   d. Mid-Atlantic Ridge

38. A _____ is a deep active seismic area in a subduction zone. Differential motion along the zone produces deep-seated earthquakes, the foci of which may be as deep as about 700 kilometres (435 miles.) They develop beneath volcanic island arcs and continental margins above active subduction zones.
   a. Pit crater
   b. Lava
   c. Pyroclastic flow
   d. Wadati-Benioff zone

39. _____ is a geologic term for a type of topography characterized by a series of separate and parallel mountain ranges with broad valleys interposed, extending over a more or less wide area. It is typified by the topography found in the Great Basin in the western United States, which is part of a larger regional topography known as the _____ Province. _____ topography results from crustal extension.
   a. Rill
   b. Tidal scour
   c. Zechstein
   d. Basin and Range

40. The _____ is a large geologic province which includes parts of the southwestern United States and northwestern Mexico, typified by basin and range topography.

The topography of the _____ is a result of crustal extension within this part of the North American Plate. The cause of this extension is as yet not fully understood, although several hypotheses have been offered. The crust here has been stretched up to 100% of its original width. In fact, the crust underneath the _____, especially under the Great Basin, is some of the thinnest in the world.

   a. Quaternary
   b. Canadian Shield
   c. Yilgarn Craton
   d. Basin and Range Province

41. In geology, a _____ is a place where the Earth's crust and lithosphere are being pulled apart and is an example of extensional tectonics.

Typical _____ features are a central linear downdropped fault segment, called a graben, with parallel normal faulting and _____-flank uplifts on either side forming a _____ valley, where the _____ remains above sea level. The axis of the _____ area commonly contains volcanic rocks and active volcanism is a part of many, but not all active _____ systems.

a. 1700 Cascadia earthquake
c. 1703 Genroku earthquake
b. 1509 Istanbul earthquake
d. Rift

42. A _____ is an opening in a planet's surface or crust, which allows hot, molten rock, ash, and gases to escape from below the surface. Volcanic activity involving the extrusion of rock tends to form mountains or features like mountains over a period of time.
   a. Volcano
   c. 1703 Genroku earthquake
   b. 1509 Istanbul earthquake
   d. 1700 Cascadia earthquake

43. _____ is any particulate matter that can be transported by fluid flow, and which eventually is deposited.

They are most often transported by water (fluvial processes) transported by wind (aeolian processes) and glaciers. Beach sands and river channel deposits are examples of fluvial transport and deposition, though _____ also often settles out of slow-moving or standing water in lakes and oceans.

   a. Bovey Beds
   c. Quicksand
   b. Brickearth
   d. Sediment

44. The _____ is a tectonic plate located in southeast Asia and commonly considered a part of the Eurasian Plate. The Sunda includes the South China Sea, the Andaman Sea, southern parts of Vietnam and Thailand along with Malaysia and the islands of Borneo, Sumatra, Java, and part of the Celebes in Indonesia, plus the south-western Philippines islands of Palawan and the Sulu Archipelago.

The Sunda is bounded by (clockwise from the east) the Philippine Sea Plate, the Bird's Head Plate (western New Guinea); the Molucca Sea, Banda Sea and Timor microplates; the Australian Plate; the Burma Plate; the Eurasian Plate; and the Yangtze Plate to the north.

   a. Scotia Plate
   c. Kula Plate
   b. Nazca Plate
   d. Sunda plate

45. _____ is a naturally occurring granular material composed of finely divided rock and mineral particles.

As the term is used by geologists, _____ particles range in diameter from 0.0625 (or $>^1\!\!/\!\!>_{16}$ mm, or 62.5 micrometers) to 2 millimeters. An individual particle in this range size is termed a _____ grain.

   a. 1509 Istanbul earthquake
   c. 1703 Genroku earthquake
   b. 1700 Cascadia earthquake
   d. Sand

46. A _____ or sand blow is a cone of sand formed by the ejection of sand onto a surface from a central point. The sand builds up as a cone with slopes at the sand's angle of repose. A crater is commonly seen at the summit. The cone looks like a small volcanic cone and can range in size from millimetres to metres in diameter.
   a. 1509 Istanbul earthquake
   c. 1703 Genroku earthquake
   b. 1700 Cascadia earthquake
   d. Sand volcano

47. _____ are a type of elastic surface wave that travel on solids. They are produced on the Earth by earthquakes, in which case they are also known as 'ground roll', or by other sources of seismic energy such as an explosion or even a sledgehammer impact. They are also produced in materials by acoustic transducers, and are used in non-destructive testing for detecting defects.
- a. Maximum magnitude
- b. Seismic waves
- c. Tornillo event
- d. Rayleigh waves

48. The _____ or epicentre is the point on the Earth's surface that is directly above the hypocenter or focus, the point where an earthquake or underground explosion originates.

The _____ is usually the location of greatest damage. However, in some cases the _____ is above the start of a much larger event.

- a. AL 333
- b. AASHTO Soil Classification System
- c. AL 129-1
- d. Epicenter

49. A _____ is any glacially formed accumulation of unconsolidated glacial debris (soil and rock) which can occur in currently glaciated and formerly glaciated regions, such as those areas acted upon by a past ice age. This debris may have been plucked off the valley floor as a glacier advanced or it may have fallen off the valley walls as a result of frost wedging. Moraines may be composed of silt like glacial flour to large boulders.
- a. 1700 Cascadia earthquake
- b. 1703 Genroku earthquake
- c. 1509 Istanbul earthquake
- d. Moraine

50. A _____ is a segment of an active fault that has not slipped in an unusually long time when compared with other segments along the same structure. _____ hypothesis/theory states that, over long periods of time, the displacement on any segment must be equal to that experienced by all the other parts of the fault. Any large and longstanding gap is therefore considered to be the fault segment most likely to suffer future earthquakes.
- a. Teleseism
- b. Seismic gap
- c. Harmonic tremor
- d. Paleoliquefaction

51. When building a house, regional _____ maps are used to find the best (or the worst) place to locate for earthquake shaking. Although greatly confused with its sister, seismic risk, _____ is the study of expected earthquake ground motions at any point on the earth. Surface motion map for a hypothetical earthquake on the northern portion of the Hayward Fault Zone and its presumed northern extension, the Rodgers Creek Fault Zone

The calculations for _____ can be quite complex.

- a. Seismic risk
- b. Seismic hazard
- c. 1700 Cascadia earthquake
- d. 1509 Istanbul earthquake

52. The _____ is a major active right lateral-moving geologic fault in northern Anatolia which runs along the tectonic boundary between the Eurasian Plate and the Anatolian Plate. The fault extends westward from a junction with the East Anatolian Fault at the Karliova Triple Junction in eastern Turkey, across northern Turkey and into the Aegean Sea. It runs about 20 km south of Istanbul.

a. 1703 Genroku earthquake	b. 1509 Istanbul earthquake
c. 1700 Cascadia earthquake	d. North Anatolian Fault

53. The _____ was a major ice sheet that covered, during glacial periods of the Quaternary, a large area of North America. This included the following areas:

- Western Montana
- The Idaho Panhandle
- Northern Washington state down to about Seattle and Spokane, Washington
- All of British Columbia
- The southwestern third or so of Yukon territory
- All of the Alaska Panhandle
- South Central Alaska
- The Alaska Peninsula
- Almost all of the continental shelf north of the Strait of Juan de Fuca

The ice sheet covered up to two and a half million square kilometres at the Last Glacial Maximum and probably more than that in some previous periods, when it may have extended into the northeast extremity of Oregon and the Salmon River Mountains in Idaho. It is probable, though, that its northern margin also migrated south due to the influence of starvation caused by very low levels of precipitation.

At its eastern end the _____ merged with the Laurentide ice sheet at the Continental Divide, forming an area of ice that contained one and a half times as much water as the Antarctic ice sheet does today.

a. Wolstonian Stage	b. Snowball Earth
c. Cordilleran ice sheet	d. Rock flour

54. The _____ is the layer of igneous, sedimentary, and metamorphic rocks which form the continents and the areas of shallow seabed close to their shores, known as continental shelves. This layer is sometimes called sial due to more felsic, or granitic, bulk composition, which lies in contrast to the oceanic crust, called sima due to its mafic, or basaltic rock. (Based on the change in velocity of seismic waves, it is believed that at a certain depth sial becomes close in its physical properties to sima.

a. Nappe	b. Convergent boundary
c. Tectonic plates	d. Continental crust

55. _____ are the largest glaciers, enormous masses of ice that are not visibly affected by the landscape and that cover the entire surface beneath them, except possibly on the margins where they are thinnest. Antarctica and Greenland are the only places where continental _____ currently exist. These regions contain vast quantities of fresh water.

a. Ice sheets	b. AASHTO Soil Classification System
c. AL 129-1	d. AL 333

56. _____ is the part of Earth's lithosphere that surfaces in the ocean basins. _____ is primarily composed of mafic rocks, or sima. It is thinner than continental crust, or sial, generally less than 10 kilometers thick, however it is denser, having a mean density of about 3.3 grams per cubic centimeter.

a. AASHTO Soil Classification System
c. AL 333
b. AL 129-1
d. Oceanic crust

57. _____ is a sedimentary rock. It is a natural chemical precipitate of carbonate minerals; typically aragonite, but often recrystallized to, or primarily, calcite.

_____ forms as calcium carbonate is deposited from the water of mineral springs or rivulets that are saturated with dissolved calcium bicarbonate. The spring water from which the calcium carbonate precipitates can be hot, warm or cold. The rate of deposition increases with the temperature of the water, or alternatively, when biotic material accelerates the process of precipitation.

a. 1700 Cascadia earthquake
c. 1509 Istanbul earthquake
b. Travertine
d. 1703 Genroku earthquake

58. The _____ Era, is the most recent of the three classic geological eras and covers the period from 65.5 million years ago to the present. It is marked by the Cretaceous-Tertiary extinction event at the end of the Cretaceous that saw the demise of the last non-avian dinosaurs and the end of the Mesozoic Era. The _____ era is ongoing.

a. 1700 Cascadia earthquake
c. 1703 Genroku earthquake
b. 1509 Istanbul earthquake
d. Cenozoic

59. In seismology, _____ are surface seismic waves that cause horizontal shifting of the earth during an earthquake. A.E.H. Love predicted the existence of _____ mathematically in 1911. They form a distinct class, different from other types of seismic waves, such as P-waves and S-waves (both body waves), or Rayleigh waves (another type of surface wave). _____ travel with a slower velocity than P- or S- waves, but faster than Rayleigh waves.

a. Seismic refraction
c. Mazuku
b. Strainmeter
d. Love waves

60. The _____ Era is one of three geologic eras of the Phanerozoic eon. The division of time into eras dates back to Giovanni Arduino, in the 18th century, although his original name for the era now called the '_____' was 'Secondary' (making the modern era the 'Tertiary'.)

The _____ was a time of tectonic, climatic and evolutionary activity. The continents gradually shifted from a state of connectedness into their present configuration; the drifting provided for speciation and other important evolutionary developments.

a. 1509 Istanbul earthquake
c. 1703 Genroku earthquake
b. Mesozoic
d. 1700 Cascadia earthquake

61. The _____ is the earliest of three geologic eras of the Phanerozoic eon. The _____ spanned from roughly 542 to 251 million years ago (ICS, 2004), and is subdivided into six geologic periods; from oldest to youngest they are: the Cambrian, Ordovician, Silurian, Devonian, Carboniferous, and Permian.

The _____ covers the time from the first appearance of abundant, soft-shelled fossils to the time when the continents were beginning to be dominated by large, relatively sophisticated reptiles and modern plants. The lower (oldest) boundary was classically set at the first appearance of creatures known as trilobites and archeocyathids.

a. 1509 Istanbul earthquake
b. 1703 Genroku earthquake
c. 1700 Cascadia earthquake
d. Paleozoic

62. The _____ is the mechanically weak ductily-deforming region of the upper mantle of the Earth. It lies below the lithosphere, at depths between 100 and 200 km (~ 62 and 124 miles) below the surface, but perhaps extending as deep as 400 km (~ 249 miles.)

The _____ is a portion of the upper mantle just below the lithosphere that is involved in plate movements and isostatic adjustments. In spite of its heat, pressures keep it plastic, and it has a relatively low density. Seismic waves pass relatively slowly through the _____, compared to the overlying lithospheric mantle, thus it has been called the low-velocity zone. This was the observation that originally alerted seismologists to its presence and gave some information about its physical properties, as the speed of seismic waves decreases with decreasing rigidity.

a. AL 333
b. AASHTO Soil Classification System
c. AL 129-1
d. Asthenosphere

63. The _____ lies between the Earth's silicate mantle and its liquid iron-nickel outer core. This boundary is located at approximately 2900 km of depth beneath the Earth's surface. The boundary is observed via the discontinuity in seismic wave velocities at that depth. This discontinuity is due to the differences between the acoustic impedances of the solid mantle and the molten outer core. P-wave velocities are much slower in the outer core than in the deep mantle while S-waves do not exist at all in the liquid portion of the core.

a. Brittle-ductile transition zone
b. 1509 Istanbul earthquake
c. Core-mantle boundary
d. Seismogenic layer

64. A _____ is an area in which an S-Wave (secondary seismic wave) is not detected due to it not being able to pass through the outer core of the earth due to it being liquid. When an earthquake occurs, seismographs near the epicenter, out to about 90° distance, are able to record both Primary and Secondary waves, but those at a greater distance no longer detect the S-wave. This is because shear waves cannot pass through liquids.

a. Shadow zone
b. Receiver function
c. Maximum magnitude
d. Tornillo event

65. The _____ is part of the Earth's mantle, and is located between the lower mantle and the upper mantle, between a depth of 410 and 660 km. The Earth's mantle, including the _____, consists primarily of peridotite, a course grained, ultramafic, igneous rock.

The mantle was divided into the upper mantle, _____, and lower mantle as a result of sudden seismic-velocity discontinuities at depths of 410 and 660 km.

a. Transition zone
b. Subfossil
c. Dissolved load
d. Teilzone

66. _____ is an earth science project using geological and geophysical techniques to explore the structure and evolution of the North American continent and to understand the processes controlling earthquakes and volcanoes. Thousands of geophysical instruments will comprise a dense grid covering the continental United States. Scientists from multiple disciplines have joined together to conduct research using the large influx of freely accessible data being produced.

a. AL 129-1
b. AL 333
c. AASHTO Soil Classification System
d. EarthScope

Chapter 9. Crags, Cracks, and Crumples: Crustal Deformation and Mountain Building

1. _____ is soil or sediments deposited by a river or other running water. _____ is typically made up of a variety of materials, including fine particles of silt and clay and larger particles of sand and gravel.

Flowing water associated with glaciers may also deposit _____, but deposits directly from ice are not _____ .

   a. AL 333   b. AL 129-1
   c. AASHTO Soil Classification System   d. Alluvium

2. _____ is the removal of solids (sediment, soil, rock and other particles) in the natural environment. It usually occurs due to transport by wind, water, or ice; by down-slope creep of soil and other material under the force of gravity; or by living organisms, such as burrowing animals, in the case of bioerosion.

_____ is distinguished from weathering, which is the process of chemical or physical breakdown of the minerals in the rocks, although the two processes may occur concurrently.

   a. Erosion   b. AL 333
   c. AASHTO Soil Classification System   d. AL 129-1

3. In geology, a _____ or _____ line is a planar fracture in rock in which the rock on one side of the fracture has moved with respect to the rock on the other side. Large faults within the Earth's crust are the result of differential or shear motion and active _____ zones are the causal locations of most earthquakes. Earthquakes are caused by energy release during rapid slippage along a _____.
   a. Fault   b. Combe
   c. Dali   d. Stack

4. The term _____ is used in geology when one or a stack of originally flat and planar surfaces, such as sedimentary strata, are bent or curved as a result of plastic (i.e. permanent) deformation. Synsedimentary folds are those due to slumping of sedimentary material before it is lithified. Folds in rocks vary in size from microscopic crinkles to mountain-sized folds.
   a. Fold   b. 1700 Cascadia earthquake
   c. 1509 Istanbul earthquake   d. 1703 Genroku earthquake

5. _____ is any penetrative planar fabric present in rocks. _____ is common to rocks affected by regional metamorphic compression typical of orogenic belts. Rocks exhibiting _____ include the typical metamorphic rock sequence of slate, phyllite, schist and gneiss.
   a. Porphyroblast   b. Hornfels
   c. Shock metamorphism   d. Foliation

6. _____ is the solid-state recrystallization of pre-existing rocks due to changes in physical and chemical conditions, primarily heat, pressure, and the introduction of chemically active fluids. Both mineralogical, chemical and crystallographic changes can occur during this process.

Three types of _____ exist: dynamic, contact and regional.

   a. Detritus   b. Reading Prong
   c. Compression   d. Metamorphism

Chapter 9. Crags, Cracks, and Crumples: Crustal Deformation and Mountain Building

7. _____ refers to natural mountain building, and may be studied as a tectonic structural event, (b) as a geographical event, and (c) a chronological event. Orogenic events (a) cause distinctive structural phenomena and related tectonic activity, (b) affect certain regions of rocks and crust, and (c) happen within a specific period of time.
    a. Orogenesis
    b. Antler orogeny
    c. Alice Springs Orogeny
    d. Orogeny

8. A _____ is a natural depression or hole in the surface topography caused by the removal of soil or bedrock, often both, by water. They may vary in size from less than a meter to several hundred meters both in diameter and depth, and vary in form from soil-lined bowls to bedrock-edged chasms. They may be formed gradually or suddenly, and are found worldwide.
    a. Sinkhole
    b. 1509 Istanbul earthquake
    c. 1700 Cascadia earthquake
    d. 1703 Genroku earthquake

9. Geologically, a _____ is a long, narrow inlet with steep sides, created in a valley carved by glacial activity.

The seeds of a _____ are laid when a glacier cuts a U-shaped valley through abrasion of the surrounding bedrock by the sediment it carries. Many such valleys were formed during the recent ice age.

    a. 1703 Genroku earthquake
    b. 1700 Cascadia earthquake
    c. Fjord
    d. 1509 Istanbul earthquake

10. _____ is a geological term referring to the appearance of bedrock or superficial deposits exposed at the surface of the Earth. In most places the bedrock or superficial deposits are covered by a mantle of soil and vegetation and cannot be seen or examined closely. However in places where the overlying cover is removed through erosion, the rock may be exposed, or crop out.
    a. AL 333
    b. AASHTO Soil Classification System
    c. Outcrop
    d. AL 129-1

11. Study of geological _____ is related to the study of structural geology, rock microstructure or rock texture and fault mechanics.

_____ is the response of a rock to deformation usually by compressive stress and forms particular textures. _____ can be homogeneous or non-homogeneous, and may be pure _____ or simple _____.

    a. Shear
    b. Sag pond
    c. Molasse basin
    d. Crenulation

12. The _____ is a geological signature, usually a thin band, dated to (65.5 ± 0.3) Ma (million years ago). The boundary marks the end of the Mesozoic era and the beginning of the Cenozoic era, and is associated with the Cretaceous-Tertiary extinction event, a mass extinction.
    a. K-T boundary
    b. 1700 Cascadia earthquake
    c. Shiva crater
    d. 1509 Istanbul earthquake

Chapter 9. Crags, Cracks, and Crumples: Crustal Deformation and Mountain Building   97

13. The _____ was a mountain-building event that affected western North America from Canada to the north to Mexico to the south. This orogeny was the result of convergent boundary tectonism between approximately 140 million years (Ma) ago, and 50 Ma. This orogeny was produced by the collision of the oceanic Farallon Plate and Kula Plate, predecessors of the Pacific Plate, and their subduction underneath the continental North American Plate. The _____ was preceded by several other mountain-building events including the Nevadan orogeny, the Sonoman orogeny, and the Antler orogeny, and partially overlapped in time and space with the Laramide orogeny.

   a. Trans-Hudson orogeny
   b. Sevier orogeny
   c. Pan-African orogeny
   d. Kaikoura Orogeny

14. _____ is a common extrusive volcanic rock. It is usually grey to black and fine-grained due to rapid cooling of lava at the surface of a planet. It may be porphyritic containing larger crystals in a fine matrix, or vesicular, or frothy scoria.

   a. 1509 Istanbul earthquake
   b. 1703 Genroku earthquake
   c. 1700 Cascadia earthquake
   d. Basalt

15. In geology the term _____ refers to the system of forces that tend to decrease the volume of or shorten rocks. Compressive strength refers to the maximum compressive stress that can be applied to a material before failure occurs. In tectonics, plates are always subjected to compressive stress.

   a. Seismic to simulation
   b. Compression
   c. Metamorphic reaction
   d. Seismic inversion

16. A _____, denoted τ (tau), is defined as a stress which is applied parallel or tangential to a face of a material, as opposed to a normal stress which is applied perpendicularly. In other words, considering that weight is a force, hanging something from a wall creates a _____ on the wall, since the weight of the object is acting parallel to the wall, as opposed to hanging something from the ceiling which creates a normal stress on the ceiling, since the weight is acting perpendicular to the ceiling.

The formula to calculate average _____ is:

$$\tau = \frac{F}{A}$$

where

   τ = the _____
   F = the force applied
   A = the cross sectional area

Beam shear is defined as the internal _____ of a beam caused by the shear force applied to the beam.

   a. Tensile stress
   b. Viscosity
   c. Thixotropy
   d. Shear stress

98   Chapter 9. Crags, Cracks, and Crumples: Crustal Deformation and Mountain Building

17. The _____ is the epoch from 1.8 million to 11550 years BP covering the world's recent period of repeated glaciations. The _____ epoch follows the Pliocene epoch and is followed by the Holocene epoch. The _____ is the third epoch of the Neogene period or 6th epoch of the Cenozoic Era. The end of the _____ corresponds with the retreat of the last continental glacier. It also corresponds with the end of the Paleolithic age used in archaeology.
   a. Late Pleistocene
   b. Sicilian Stage
   c. Pleistocene
   d. Tyrrhenian

18. The general term '_____' or, more precisely, 'glacial age' denotes a geological period of long-term reduction in the temperature of the Earth's surface and atmosphere, resulting in an expansion of continental ice sheets, polar ice sheets and alpine glaciers. Within a long-term _____, individual pulses of extra cold climate are termed 'glaciations'. Glaciologically, _____ implies the presence of extensive ice sheets in the northern and southern hemispheres; by this definition we are still in an _____.
   a. Ice age
   b. AL 333
   c. AASHTO Soil Classification System
   d. AL 129-1

19. The _____ was an ancient oceanic plate, which began subducting under the west coast of the North American Plate-- then located in modern Utah-- as Pangaea broke apart during the Jurassic period. It is named for the Farallon Islands which are located just west of San Francisco, California.

Over time the central part of the _____ was completely subducted under the southwestern part of the North American Plate. The remains of the _____ are the Juan de Fuca, Explorer and Gorda Plates, subducting under the northern part of the North American Plate, the Cocos Plate subducting under Central America and the Nazca Plate subducting under the South American Plate.

   a. Rivera Plate
   b. Cocos Plate
   c. Fault trace
   d. Farallon Plate

20. The _____ is a continental transform fault that runs a length of roughly 800 miles (1,300 km) through California in the United States. The fault's motion is right-lateral strike-slip (horizontal motion.) It forms the tectonic boundary between the Pacific Plate and the North American Plate.
   a. 1700 Cascadia earthquake
   b. San Andreas Fault
   c. 1509 Istanbul earthquake
   d. 1703 Genroku earthquake

21. An _____ is the result of a sudden release of energy in the Earth's crust that creates seismic waves. They are recorded with a seismometer or the related and mostly obsolete Richter magnitude, with a magnitude 3 or lower _____ being mostly imperceptible and magnitude 7 causing serious damage over large areas.
   a. AL 129-1
   b. AASHTO Soil Classification System
   c. Earthquake
   d. AL 333

22. An _____ is a fault which has had displacement or seismic activity during the geologically recent period. In the United States, an _____ is generally defined as a fault which displaced earth materials during the Holocene Epoch (during the last 11,000 or so years before present.) Active faults are the most common sources of earthquakes and tectonic movements.
   a. AL 129-1
   b. Active fault
   c. AASHTO Soil Classification System
   d. AL 333

Chapter 9. Crags, Cracks, and Crumples: Crustal Deformation and Mountain Building

23. _____ can be again classified into the types 'reverse' and 'normal'. A normal fault occurs when the crust is extended. Alternatively such a fault can be called an extensional fault.
    a. 1509 Istanbul earthquake
    b. 1700 Cascadia earthquake
    c. Hanging wall
    d. Dip-slip faults

24. _____ describes the large scale motions of Earth's lithosphere. The theory encompasses the older concepts of continental drift, developed during the first decades of the 20th century by Alfred Wegener, and seafloor spreading, understood during the 1960s.

    The outermost part of the Earth's interior is made up of two layers: the lithosphere and the asthenosphere.

    a. Thrust fault
    b. Forearc
    c. Plate tectonics
    d. Continental crust

25. A _____ is the opposite of a normal fault -- the hanging wall moves up relative to the footwall. They are indicative of shortening of the crust. The dip of a _____ is relatively steep, greater than 45>°.
    a. Reverse fault
    b. 1509 Istanbul earthquake
    c. 1700 Cascadia earthquake
    d. Hanging wall

26. The fault surface of _____ is usually near vertical and the footwall moves either left or right or laterally with very little vertical motion. _____ with left-lateral motion are also known as sinistral faults. Those with right-lateral motion are also known as dextral faults.
    a. Strike-slip faults
    b. Pahoehoe lava
    c. Valley glaciers
    d. Principle of inclusions and components

27. A _____ column (or _____) is a column of rising air in the lower altitudes of the Earth's atmosphere. They are created by the uneven heating of the Earth's surface from solar radiation, and an example of convection. The Sun warms the ground, which in turn warms the air directly above it.
    a. 1700 Cascadia earthquake
    b. 1703 Genroku earthquake
    c. 1509 Istanbul earthquake
    d. Thermal

28. A _____ is a type of fault in which rocks of lower stratigraphic position are pushed up and over higher strata. They are often recognized because they place older rocks above younger. Thrust faults are the result of compressional forces.
    a. Convergent boundary
    b. Subduction
    c. Juan de Fuca Ridge
    d. Thrust fault

29. _____ is a rock composed of angular fragments of minerals or rocks in a matrix (cementing material), that may be similar or different in composition to the fragments. A _____ may have a variety of different origins, as indicated by the named types including sedimentary _____, tectonic _____, igneous _____, impact _____ and hydrothermal _____.

Sedimentary breccias are a type of clastic sedimentary rock which are composed of angular to subangular, randomly oriented clasts of other sedimentary rocks.

Chapter 9. Crags, Cracks, and Crumples: Crustal Deformation and Mountain Building

    a. Fault breccia
    b. 1509 Istanbul earthquake
    c. Breccia
    d. Ventifacts

30. _____, or tectonic breccia is a breccia (a rock type consisting of angular clasts) that was formed by tectonic forces. _____ has no cohesion, it is normally an unconsolidated rock type, unless cementation took place at a later stage. Sometimes a distinction is made between fault gouge and _____, the first has a smaller grain size.
    a. Ventifacts
    b. Fault breccia
    c. 1509 Istanbul earthquake
    d. Coprolite

31. A _____ is the topographic expression of faulting attributed to the displacement of the land surface by movement along the fault. It can be caused by differential erosion along an old inactive geologic fault (a sort of old rupture) with hard and weak rock, or by a movement on an active fault. In many cases, bluffs form from the upthrown block and can be very steep.
    a. Bradyseism
    b. Rejuvenated
    c. Gravitational erosion
    d. Fault scarp

32. _____ is a geologic term for a type of topography characterized by a series of separate and parallel mountain ranges with broad valleys interposed, extending over a more or less wide area. It is typified by the topography found in the Great Basin in the western United States, which is part of a larger regional topography known as the _____ Province. _____ topography results from crustal extension.
    a. Rill
    b. Zechstein
    c. Tidal scour
    d. Basin and Range

33. The _____ is a large geologic province which includes parts of the southwestern United States and northwestern Mexico, typified by basin and range topography.

The topography of the _____ is a result of crustal extension within this part of the North American Plate. The cause of this extension is as yet not fully understood, although several hypotheses have been offered. The crust here has been stretched up to 100% of its original width. In fact, the crust underneath the _____, especially under the Great Basin, is some of the thinnest in the world.

    a. Basin and Range Province
    b. Canadian Shield
    c. Yilgarn Craton
    d. Quaternary

34. A type of seismic wave, the _____, secondary wave or shear wave (sometimes called an elastic _____) is one of the two main types of elastic body waves, so named because they move through the body of an object, unlike surface waves.

The _____ move as a shear or transverse wave, so motion is perpendicular to the direction of wave propagation: S-waves, like waves in a rope, as opposed to waves moving through a slinky, the P-wave. The wave moves through elastic media, and the main restoring force comes from shear effects.

    a. 1700 Cascadia earthquake
    b. S-wave
    c. 1703 Genroku earthquake
    d. 1509 Istanbul earthquake

Chapter 9. Crags, Cracks, and Crumples: Crustal Deformation and Mountain Building

35. In structural geology, an _____ is a fold that is convex up and has its oldest beds at its core. The term is not to be confused with antiform, which is a purely descriptive term for any fold that is convex up. Therefore if age relationships (i.e. younging direction) between various strata are unknown, the term antiform must be used.
   a. AL 129-1
   b. AASHTO Soil Classification System
   c. AL 333
   d. Anticline

36. A _____ is a geological phenomenon which includes a wide range of ground movement, such as rock falls, deep failure of slopes and shallow debris flows, which can occur in offshore, coastal and onshore environments. Although the action of gravity is the primary driving force for a _____ to occur, there are other contributing factors affecting the original slope stability. Typically, pre-conditional factors build up specific sub-surface conditions that make the area/slope prone to failure, whereas the actual _____ often requires a trigger before being released.
   a. 1509 Istanbul earthquake
   b. Mass wasting
   c. 1700 Cascadia earthquake
   d. Landslide

37. A _____ is an area in which an S-Wave (secondary seismic wave) is not detected due to it not being able to pass through the outer core of the earth due to it being liquid. When an earthquake occurs, seismographs near the epicenter, out to about 90° distance, are able to record both Primary and Secondary waves, but those at a greater distance no longer detect the S-wave. This is because shear waves cannot pass through liquids.
   a. Tornillo event
   b. Receiver function
   c. Maximum magnitude
   d. Shadow zone

38. In structural geology, a _____ is a downward-curving fold, with layers that dip toward the center of the structure. A synclinorium is a large _____ with superimposed smaller folds.

On a geologic map, they are recognized by a sequence of rock layers that grow progressively younger, followed by the youngest layer at the fold's center or hinge, and by a reverse sequence of the same rock layers on the opposite side of the hinge.

   a. Michoud fault
   b. Syncline
   c. Petermann Orogeny
   d. Shear

39. The _____ is a geological eon representing a period before the first abundant complex life on Earth. The _____ extended from 2500 Ma to 542.0 >± 1.0 Ma (million years ago), and is the most recent part of the old, informally named 'e;Precambrian'e; time.

The Proterozoic consists of 3 geologic eras, from oldest to youngest:

- Paleoproterozoic
- Mesoproterozoic
- Neoproterozoic

Chapter 9. Crags, Cracks, and Crumples: Crustal Deformation and Mountain Building

The well-identified events were:

- The transition to an oxygenated atmosphere during the Mesoproterozoic.
- Several glaciations, including the hypothesized Snowball Earth during the Cryogenian period in the late Neoproterozoic.
- The Ediacaran Period (635 to 542 Ma) which is characterized by the evolution of abundant soft-bodied multicellular organisms.

The geoloic record of the Proterozoic is much better than that for the preceding Archean. In contrast to the deep-water deposits of the Archean, the Proterozoic features many strata that were laid down in extensive shallow epicontinental seas; furthermore, many of these rocks are less metamorphosed than Archean-age ones, and plenty are unaltered.

a. 1509 Istanbul earthquake
b. Proterozoic Eon
c. 1703 Genroku earthquake
d. 1700 Cascadia earthquake

40. _____ is a phenomenon of the plate tectonics of Earth that occurs at convergent boundaries. _____ is a variation on the fundamental process of subduction, whereby the subduction zone is destroyed, mountains produced, and two continents sutured together. _____ is known only from this planet and is an interesting example of how our different crusts, oceanic and continental, behave during subduction.

a. Continental collision
b. Forearc
c. Divergent boundary
d. Motagua Fault

41. A _____ is a large, slow-moving mass of ice, formed from compacted layers of snow, that slowly deforms and flows in response to gravity and high pressure.

_____ ice is the largest reservoir of fresh water on Earth, and second only to oceans as the largest reservoir of total water.

a. Glacier
b. Little Ice Age
c. Keeling Curve
d. Pacific Decadal Oscillation

42. _____ is a term used in geology to refer to the state of gravitational equilibrium between the earth's lithosphere and asthenosphere such that the tectonic plates 'float' at an elevation which depends on their thickness and density. This concept is invoked to explain how different topographic heights can exist at the Earth's surface. When a certain area of lithosphere reaches the state of _____, it is said to be in isostatic equilibrium.

a. Orientation Tensor
b. Isograd
c. Isostasy
d. Economic geology

43. The _____ is the level at which the ground water pressure is equal to atmospheric pressure. It may be conveniently visualized as the 'surface' of the ground water in a given vicinity. It usually coincides with the phreatic surface, but can be many feet above it. As water infiltrates through pore spaces in the soil, it first passes through the zone of aeration, where the soil is unsaturated. At increasing depths water fills in more spaces, until the zone of saturation is reached. The relatively horizontal plane atop this zone constitutes the _____.

Chapter 9. Crags, Cracks, and Crumples: Crustal Deformation and Mountain Building

a. Water table
b. Rock bolt
c. Crosshole sonic logging
d. Shaft construction

44. The _____ is the earliest of three geologic eras of the Phanerozoic eon. The _____ spanned from roughly 542 to 251 million years ago (ICS, 2004), and is subdivided into six geologic periods; from oldest to youngest they are: the Cambrian, Ordovician, Silurian, Devonian, Carboniferous, and Permian.

The _____ covers the time from the first appearance of abundant, soft-shelled fossils to the time when the continents were beginning to be dominated by large, relatively sophisticated reptiles and modern plants. The lower (oldest) boundary was classically set at the first appearance of creatures known as trilobites and archeocyathids.

a. 1509 Istanbul earthquake
b. Paleozoic
c. 1703 Genroku earthquake
d. 1700 Cascadia earthquake

45. A _____ is an opening in a planet's surface or crust, which allows hot, molten rock, ash, and gases to escape from below the surface. Volcanic activity involving the extrusion of rock tends to form mountains or features like mountains over a period of time.

a. 1703 Genroku earthquake
b. 1509 Istanbul earthquake
c. 1700 Cascadia earthquake
d. Volcano

46. A _____ is a series of mountainous foothills, adjacent to an orogenic belt, that form due to compression. They commonly form in the forelands adjacent to major orogens as deformation propagates outwards. They usually comprise both folds and thrust faults, commonly interrelated.

a. Nevadan orogeny
b. Pan-African orogeny
c. Trans-Hudson orogeny
d. Fold and thrust belt

47. A _____ is a mountain rising from the ocean seafloor that does not reach to the water's surface (sea level), and thus is not an island. These are typically formed from extinct volcanoes, that rise abruptly and are usually found rising from a seafloor of 1,000-4,000 meters depth. They are defined by oceanographers as independent features that rise to at least 1,000 meters above the seafloor.

a. Seamount
b. 1509 Istanbul earthquake
c. 1703 Genroku earthquake
d. 1700 Cascadia earthquake

48. In geology, a _____ is a place where the Earth's crust and lithosphere are being pulled apart and is an example of extensional tectonics.

Typical _____ features are a central linear downdropped fault segment, called a graben, with parallel normal faulting and _____-flank uplifts on either side forming a _____ valley, where the _____ remains above sea level. The axis of the _____ area commonly contains volcanic rocks and active volcanism is a part of many, but not all active _____ systems.

a. 1509 Istanbul earthquake
b. 1700 Cascadia earthquake
c. 1703 Genroku earthquake
d. Rift

Chapter 9. Crags, Cracks, and Crumples: Crustal Deformation and Mountain Building

49. A _____ is a chain of volcanic islands or mountains formed by plate tectonics as an oceanic tectonic plate subducts under another tectonic plate and produces magma. There are two types of these: oceanic arcs (commonly called island arcs, a type of archipelago) and continental arcs. In the former, oceanic crust subducts beneath other oceanic crust on an adjacent plate, while in the latter case the oceanic crust subducts beneath continental crust. In some situations, a single subduction zone may show both aspects along its length, as part of a plate subducts beneath a continent and part beneath adjacent oceanic crust.
   a. 1509 Istanbul earthquake
   b. Volcanic arc
   c. 1703 Genroku earthquake
   d. 1700 Cascadia earthquake

50. A _____ is an old and stable part of the continental crust that has survived the merging and splitting of continents and supercontinents for at least 500 million years. Some are over two billion years old. They are generally found in the interiors of continents and are characteristically composed of ancient crystalline basement crust of lightweight felsic igneous rock such as granite.
   a. Superior craton
   b. Craton
   c. Sebakwe proto-craton
   d. Kalahari craton

51. _____ landforms (mountains, hills, ridges, etc.) are created when large areas of bedrock are widely broken up by faults creating large vertical displacements of continental crust.

Vertical motion of the resulting blocks, sometimes accompanied by tilting, can then lead to high escarpments. These mountains are formed by the earth's crust being stretched and extended by tensional forces. Fault block mountains commonly accompany rifting, another indicator of tensional tectonic forces.

   a. Shutter ridge
   b. Fault scarp
   c. Gravitational erosion
   d. Fault-block

52. In geology, a _____ is a continental area covered by relatively flat or gently tilted, mainly sedimentary strata, which overlie a basement of consolidated igneous or metamorphic rocks of an earlier deformation. They as well as, shields and the basement rocks together constitute cratons.

It is also common practice to use the term _____ as a very general term for a sequence of shallow water carbonate _____.

   a. Streak
   b. Platform
   c. Cleavage
   d. Fault

53. A _____ is generally a large area of exposed Precambrian crystalline igneous and high-grade metamorphic rocks that form tectonically stable areas. In all cases, the age of these rocks is greater than 570 million years and sometimes dates back 2 to 3.5 billion years. They have been little affected by tectonic events following the end of the Precambrian Era, and are relatively flat regions where mountain building, faulting, and other tectonic processes are greatly diminished compared with the activity that occurs at the margins of the shields and the boundaries between tectonic plates.
   a. 1509 Istanbul earthquake
   b. 1700 Cascadia earthquake
   c. 1703 Genroku earthquake
   d. Shield

Chapter 9. Crags, Cracks, and Crumples: Crustal Deformation and Mountain Building

54. In geology, _____ is the process that takes place at convergent boundaries by which one tectonic plate moves under another tectonic plate, sinking into the Earth's mantle, as the plates converge. A _____ zone is an area on Earth where two tectonic plates move towards one another and _____ occurs. Rates of _____ are typically measured in centimeters per year, with the average rate of convergence being approximately 2 to 8 centimeters per year (about the rate a fingernail grows.)
   a. Subduction
   b. Motagua Fault
   c. Forearc
   d. Divergent boundary

55. The _____ is an oceanic tectonic plate beneath the Pacific Ocean.

   To the north the easterly side is a divergent boundary with the Explorer Plate, the Juan de Fuca Plate and the Gorda Plate forming respectively the Explorer Ridge, the Juan de Fuca Ridge and the Gorda Ridge. In the middle the easterly side is a transform boundary with the North American Plate along the San Andreas Fault and a boundary with the Cocos Plate.

   a. Somali Plate
   b. Conway Reef Plate
   c. Gorda Plate
   d. Pacific Plate

56. _____ are the preserved remains or traces of animals, plants, and other organisms from the remote past. The totality of _____, both discovered and undiscovered, and their placement in fossiliferous rock formations and sedimentary layers (strata) is known as the fossil record. The study of _____ across geological time, how they were formed, and the evolutionary relationships between taxa (phylogeny) are some of the most important functions of the science of paleontology.
   a. 1703 Genroku earthquake
   b. 1700 Cascadia earthquake
   c. 1509 Istanbul earthquake
   d. Fossils

57. _____ is the result of the transformation of an existing rock type, the protolith, in a process called metamorphism, which means 'change in form'. The protolith is subjected to heat and pressure (temperatures greater than 150 to 200 >°C and pressures of 1500 bars) causing profound physical and/or chemical change. The protolith may be sedimentary rock, igneous rock or another older _____.
   a. Sedimentary rock
   b. Migmatite
   c. Metamorphic rock
   d. Metavolcanic rock

58. _____ is one of the three main rock types (the others being igneous and metamorphic rock.) _____ is formed by deposition and consolidation of mineral and organic material and from precipitation of minerals from solution. The processes that form _____ occur at the surface of the Earth and within bodies of water.
   a. Sedimentary rock
   b. Petrology
   c. Serpentinite
   d. Rock cycle

59. _____ is a process of fossilization in which mineral deposits form internal casts of organism. Carried by water, these minerals fill the spaces within organic tissue. Because of the nature of the casts, _____ is particularly useful in studies of the internal structures of organisms, usually of plants.
   a. Hydrothermal circulation
   b. Permineralization
   c. Hydraulic action
   d. Deposition

Chapter 9. Crags, Cracks, and Crumples: Crustal Deformation and Mountain Building

60. _____ is a type of fossil: it consists of fossil wood where all the organic materials have been replaced with minerals, while retaining the original structure of the wood. The petrifaction process occurs underground, when wood becomes buried under sediment and is initially preserved due to a lack of oxygen. Mineral-rich water flowing through the sediment deposits minerals in the plant's cells and as the plant's lignin and cellulose decay away, a stone mould forms in its place.
   a. Pteridospermatophyta
   b. Petrified wood
   c. 1509 Istanbul earthquake
   d. Glossopteris

61. _____ is a sedimentary rock composed largely of the mineral calcite (calcium carbonate: $CaCO_3$.) The deposition of _____ strata is often a by-product and indicator of biological activity in the geologic record. Calcium (along with nitrogen, phosphorus, and potassium) is a key mineral to plant nutrition: soils overlying _____ bedrock tend to be pre-fertilized with calcium.
   a. 1703 Genroku earthquake
   b. 1509 Istanbul earthquake
   c. Limestone
   d. 1700 Cascadia earthquake

62. _____ are geological records of biological activity. _____ may be impressions made on the substrate by an organism: for example, burrows, borings, footprints and feeding marks, and root cavities. The term in its broadest sense also includes the remains of other organic material produced by an organism - for example coprolites or chemical markers - or sedimentological structures produced by biological means - for example, stromatolites.
   a. 1700 Cascadia earthquake
   b. 1703 Genroku earthquake
   c. 1509 Istanbul earthquake
   d. Trace fossils

63. The _____ Formation is one of the world's most celebrated fossil localities, and is famous for the exceptional preservation of the fossils found within it, in which the soft parts are preserved. It is 505 million years (Middle Cambrian) in age, making it one of the earliest fossil beds to preserve the soft parts of animals. The pre-Cambrian fossil record of animals is sparse and ambiguous.
   a. 1700 Cascadia earthquake
   b. 1703 Genroku earthquake
   c. 1509 Istanbul earthquake
   d. Burgess Shale

64. _____ is a fine-grained sedimentary rock whose original constituents were clay minerals or muds. It is characterized by thin laminae breaking with an irregular curving fracture, often splintery and usually parallel to the often-indistinguishable bedding plane. This property is called fissility.
   a. Pelagic sediments
   b. Metasediment
   c. Mudstone
   d. Shale

65. _____ are an extinct group of marine animals of the subclass Ammonoidea in the class Cephalopoda, phylum Mollusca. They are excellent index fossils, and it is often possible to link the rock layer in which they are found to specific geological time periods.

   _____' closest living relative is probably not the modern Nautilus (which they outwardly resemble), but rather the subclass Coleoidea (octopus, squid, and cuttlefish.)

   a. AASHTO Soil Classification System
   b. AL 129-1
   c. AL 333
   d. Ammonites

Chapter 9. Crags, Cracks, and Crumples: Crustal Deformation and Mountain Building

66. In mineralogy and crystallography, a _____ is a unique arrangement of atoms in a crystal. A _____ is composed of a motif, a set of atoms arranged in a particular way, and a lattice. Motifs are located upon the points of a lattice, which is an array of points repeating periodically in three dimensions.
   a. 1509 Istanbul earthquake
   b. Crystal structure
   c. 1703 Genroku earthquake
   d. 1700 Cascadia earthquake

67. A _____ is a piece of rock that differs from the size and type of rock native to the area in which it rests. They are carried by glacial ice, often over distances of hundreds of kilometres and can range in size from pebbles to large boulders such as Big Rock (16,500 tons) in Alberta.
   a. 1509 Istanbul earthquake
   b. Glacial erratic
   c. 1703 Genroku earthquake
   d. 1700 Cascadia earthquake

68. _____, originally Gondwanaland, is the name given to a southern precursor-supercontinent and then as a remnant separated from Laurasia 180-200 million years ago during the breakup of the Pangaea supercontinent that existed about 500 to 200 Ma ago into two large segments. While the corresponding northern hemisphere continent Laurasia moved further north, the nearly equal in area _____ included most of the landmasses in today's southern hemisphere, including Antarctica, South America, Africa, Madagascar, Australia-New Guinea, and New Zealand, as well as Arabia and the Indian subcontinent, which have now moved into the Northern Hemisphere.
   a. 1509 Istanbul earthquake
   b. Laurasia
   c. 1700 Cascadia earthquake
   d. Gondwana

69. A _____ is a natural formation (or landform) where a rock arch forms, with a natural passageway through underneath. Most natural arches form as a narrow ridge, walled by cliffs, become narrower from erosion, with a softer rock stratum under the cliff-forming stratum gradually eroding out until the rock shelters thus formed meet underneath the ridge, thus forming the arch. They commonly form where cliffs are subject to erosion from the sea, rivers or weathering (sub-aerial processes); the processes 'find' weaknesses in rocks and work on them, making them bigger until they break through.
   a. 1703 Genroku earthquake
   b. 1700 Cascadia earthquake
   c. 1509 Istanbul earthquake
   d. Natural arch

70. In the natural sciences, _____ is a theory which holds that profound change is the cumulative product of slow but continuous processes, often contrasted with catastrophism. The theory was proposed in 1795 by James Hutton, a Scottish geologist, and was later incorporated into Charles Lyell's theory of uniformitarianism.
   a. Detritus
   b. Gradualism
   c. Type locality
   d. Medical geology

71. A _____ is an underwater mountain range, typically having a valley known as a rift running along its spine, formed by plate tectonics. This type of oceanic ridge is characteristic of what is known as an oceanic spreading center, which is responsible for seafloor spreading. The uplifted sea floor results from convection currents which rise in the mantle as magma at a linear weakness in the oceanic crust, and emerge as lava, creating new crust upon cooling.
   a. Permineralization
   b. Mid-ocean ridge
   c. Transgression
   d. Seafloor spreading

72. _____ is a naturally occurring granular material composed of finely divided rock and mineral particles.

As the term is used by geologists, _____ particles range in diameter from 0.0625 (or $>^1\!\!/_{16}$ mm, or 62.5 micrometers) to 2 millimeters. An individual particle in this range size is termed a _____ grain.

a. 1509 Istanbul earthquake
c. Sand

b. 1700 Cascadia earthquake
d. 1703 Genroku earthquake

Chapter 10. Deep Time: How Old Is Old?

1. The _____ is a chronologic schema (or idealized model) relating stratigraphy to time that is used by geologists, paleontologists and other earth scientists to describe the timing and relationships between events that have occurred during the history of the Earth. The table of geologic time spans presented here agrees with the dates and nomenclature proposed by the International Commission on Stratigraphy, and uses the standard color codes of the United States Geological Survey.

Evidence from radiometric dating indicates that the Earth is about 4.570 billion years old.

   a. 1700 Cascadia earthquake
   b. Geologic time scale
   c. 1509 Istanbul earthquake
   d. 1703 Genroku earthquake

2. A _____ is a mountain rising from the ocean seafloor that does not reach to the water's surface (sea level), and thus is not an island. These are typically formed from extinct volcanoes, that rise abruptly and are usually found rising from a seafloor of 1,000-4,000 meters depth. They are defined by oceanographers as independent features that rise to at least 1,000 meters above the seafloor.
   a. 1700 Cascadia earthquake
   b. 1509 Istanbul earthquake
   c. 1703 Genroku earthquake
   d. Seamount

3. A _____ is an opening in a planet's surface or crust, which allows hot, molten rock, ash, and gases to escape from below the surface. Volcanic activity involving the extrusion of rock tends to form mountains or features like mountains over a period of time.
   a. 1700 Cascadia earthquake
   b. 1703 Genroku earthquake
   c. 1509 Istanbul earthquake
   d. Volcano

4. _____ is the concept of geologic time first recognized in the 11th century by the Persian geologist and polymath, Avicenna , and the Chinese naturalist and polymath Shen Kuo (1031-1095.) In the Western world, the modern scientific concept was developed in the 1700s by Scottish geologist James Hutton.

Science in succeeding centuries has established the age of the Earth as between four and five billion years, with an exceedingly long history of change and development.

   a. Deep time
   b. 1703 Genroku earthquake
   c. 1700 Cascadia earthquake
   d. 1509 Istanbul earthquake

5. Geologically, a _____ is a long, narrow inlet with steep sides, created in a valley carved by glacial activity.

The seeds of a _____ are laid when a glacier cuts a U-shaped valley through abrasion of the surrounding bedrock by the sediment it carries. Many such valleys were formed during the recent ice age.

   a. 1700 Cascadia earthquake
   b. 1703 Genroku earthquake
   c. 1509 Istanbul earthquake
   d. Fjord

6. _____ is the principle that the same scientific laws and processes are constant throughout space and time. It applies specifically to sciences that require a long timescale such as geology, astronomy, and paleontology. It was first defined by Charles Lyell (1797 - 1875), who incorporated James Hutton's gradualism into the idea of _____.
   a. AASHTO Soil Classification System
   b. AL 129-1
   c. AL 333
   d. Uniformitarianism

7. The _____ is a geological signature, usually a thin band, dated to (65.5 ± 0.3) Ma (million years ago). The boundary marks the end of the Mesozoic era and the beginning of the Cenozoic era, and is associated with the Cretaceous-Tertiary extinction event, a mass extinction.
   a. 1509 Istanbul earthquake
   b. 1700 Cascadia earthquake
   c. K-T boundary
   d. Shiva crater

8. The _____ is a geological eon representing a period before the first abundant complex life on Earth. The _____ extended from 2500 Ma to 542.0 >± 1.0 Ma (million years ago), and is the most recent part of the old, informally named 'e;Precambrian'e; time.

The Proterozoic consists of 3 geologic eras, from oldest to youngest:

- Paleoproterozoic
- Mesoproterozoic
- Neoproterozoic

The well-identified events were:

- The transition to an oxygenated atmosphere during the Mesoproterozoic.
- Several glaciations, including the hypothesized Snowball Earth during the Cryogenian period in the late Neoproterozoic.
- The Ediacaran Period (635 to 542 Ma) which is characterized by the evolution of abundant soft-bodied multicellular organisms.

The geoloic record of the Proterozoic is much better than that for the preceding Archean. In contrast to the deep-water deposits of the Archean, the Proterozoic features many strata that were laid down in extensive shallow epicontinental seas; furthermore, many of these rocks are less metamorphosed than Archean-age ones, and plenty are unaltered.

   a. 1700 Cascadia earthquake
   b. 1509 Istanbul earthquake
   c. Proterozoic Eon
   d. 1703 Genroku earthquake

9. _____ are the preserved remains or traces of animals, plants, and other organisms from the remote past. The totality of _____, both discovered and undiscovered, and their placement in fossiliferous rock formations and sedimentary layers (strata) is known as the fossil record. The study of _____ across geological time, how they were formed, and the evolutionary relationships between taxa (phylogeny) are some of the most important functions of the science of paleontology.
   a. 1509 Istanbul earthquake
   b. 1700 Cascadia earthquake
   c. 1703 Genroku earthquake
   d. Fossils

10. _____ are fossils used to define and identify geologic periods They work on the premise that, although different sediments may look different depending on the conditions under which they were laid down, they may include the remains of the same species of fossil. If the species concerned were short-lived, then it is certain that the sediments in question were deposited within that narrow time period.

Chapter 10. Deep Time: How Old Is Old?

a. Allotrioceras
b. Invertebrate paleontology
c. Index fossils
d. Indian bead

11. The lithosphere is broken up into what are called _____. In the case of Earth, there are eight major and many minor plates The lithospheric plates ride on the asthenosphere. These plates move in relation to one another at one of three types of plate boundaries: convergent, or collisional boundaries; divergent boundaries, also called spreading centers; and transform boundaries.

a. Gorda Ridge
b. Copperbelt Province
c. Thrust fault
d. Tectonic plates

12. _____ is a paramount and base concept in archaeology, especially in the course of excavation. It is largely based on the Law of Superposition. When archaeological finds are below the surface of the ground (as is most commonly the case), the identification of the context of each find is vital in enabling the archaeologist to draw conclusions about the site and about the nature and date of its occupation.

a. Geothermal
b. Cleavage
c. Stack
d. Stratification

13. A marine _____ is a geologic event during which sea level rises relative to the land and the shoreline moves toward higher ground, resulting in flooding. They can be caused either by the land sinking or the ocean basins filling with water (or decreasing in capacity.) Transgresssions and regressions may be caused by tectonic events such as orogenies, severe climate change such as ice ages or isostatic adjustments following removal of ice or sediment load.

a. Stoping
b. Spheroidal weathering
c. Wave pounding
d. Transgression

14. An _____ is the result of a sudden release of energy in the Earth's crust that creates seismic waves. They are recorded with a seismometer or the related and mostly obsolete Richter magnitude, with a magnitude 3 or lower _____ being mostly imperceptible and magnitude 7 causing serious damage over large areas.

a. AL 333
b. Earthquake
c. AASHTO Soil Classification System
d. AL 129-1

15. The _____ zone is the area that is exposed to the air at low tide and submerged at high tide, for example, the area between tide marks. This area can include many different types of habitats, including steep rocky cliffs, sandy beaches, or wetlands The area can be a narrow strip, as in Pacific islands that have only a narrow tidal range, or can include many meters of shoreline where shallow beach slope interacts with high tidal excursion.

a. Eutrophication
b. AASHTO Soil Classification System
c. Overland flow
d. Intertidal

16. A _____ is a special-purpose map made to show geological features.

The stratigraphic contour lines are drawn on the surface of a selected deep stratum, so that they can show the topographic trends of the strata under the ground. It is not always possible to properly show this when the strata are extremely fractured, mixed, in some discontinuities, or where they are otherwise disturbed.

a. 1703 Genroku earthquake
b. 1509 Istanbul earthquake
c. Geologic map
d. 1700 Cascadia earthquake

17. The _____ is the first geological period of the Phanerozoic eon, lasting from 542 ± 0.3 million years ago to 488.3 ± 1.7 million years ago (ICS, 2004); it is succeeded by the Ordovician. Its subdivisions, and indeed its base, are somewhat in flux. The period was established by Adam Sedgwick, who named it after Cambria, the classical name for Wales, where Britain's _____ rocks are best exposed.

- a. 1700 Cascadia earthquake
- b. 1509 Istanbul earthquake
- c. 1703 Genroku earthquake
- d. Cambrian

18. The _____ or Cambrian radiation was the seemingly rapid appearance of most major groups of complex animals around 530 million years ago, as evidenced by the fossil record. This was accompanied by a major diversification of other organisms, including animals, phytoplankton, and calcimicrobes. Before about 580 million years ago, most organisms were simple, composed of individual cells occasionally organized into colonies.

- a. Conodont Alteration Index
- b. Romer's Gap
- c. Labyrinthodont
- d. Cambrian explosion

19. An _____ is an animal lacking a vertebral column. The group includes 98% of all animal species -- all animals except those in the Chordate subphylum Vertebrata (fish, reptiles, amphibians, birds, and mammals.)

Carolus Linnaeus' Systema Naturae divided these animals into only two groups, the Insecta and the now-obsolete vermes (worms.)

- a. AASHTO Soil Classification System
- b. AL 129-1
- c. AL 333
- d. Invertebrate

20. A _____ is a geological phenomenon which includes a wide range of ground movement, such as rock falls, deep failure of slopes and shallow debris flows, which can occur in offshore, coastal and onshore environments. Although the action of gravity is the primary driving force for a _____ to occur, there are other contributing factors affecting the original slope stability. Typically, pre-conditional factors build up specific sub-surface conditions that make the area/slope prone to failure, whereas the actual _____ often requires a trigger before being released.

- a. Landslide
- b. 1509 Istanbul earthquake
- c. Mass wasting
- d. 1700 Cascadia earthquake

21. The _____ is the level at which the ground water pressure is equal to atmospheric pressure. It may be conveniently visualized as the 'surface' of the ground water in a given vicinity. It usually coincides with the phreatic surface, but can be many feet above it. As water infiltrates through pore spaces in the soil, it first passes through the zone of aeration, where the soil is unsaturated. At increasing depths water fills in more spaces, until the zone of saturation is reached. The relatively horizontal plane atop this zone constitutes the _____.

- a. Rock bolt
- b. Shaft construction
- c. Water table
- d. Crosshole sonic logging

22. The _____ is a geologic period and system, the second of six of the Paleozoic era, and covers the time between 488.3>±1.7 to 443.7>±1.5 million years ago (ICS, 2004.) It follows the Cambrian period and is followed by the Silurian period. The _____ was defined by Charles Lapworth in 1879, to resolve a dispute between followers of Adam Sedgwick and Roderick Murchison, who were placing the same rock beds in northern Wales into the Cambrian and Silurian periods respectively.

Chapter 10. Deep Time: How Old Is Old?

a. AL 129-1
b. AL 333
c. AASHTO Soil Classification System
d. Ordovician

23. The _____ is an active transform fault, located between the North American Plate and the Pacific Plate, Canada's equivalent of the San Andreas Fault. The _____ forms a triple junction on its south with the Cascadia subduction zone and the Explorer Ridge (the Queen Charlotte Triple Junction.) The fault is named for Queen Charlotte Island which lies just north of the triple junction.
   a. 1703 Genroku earthquake
   b. Queen Charlotte fault
   c. 1509 Istanbul earthquake
   d. 1700 Cascadia earthquake

24. The _____ is a geologic period and system that extends from about 251 to 199 Mya (million years ago.) As the first period of the Mesozoic Era, the _____ follows the Permian and is followed by the Jurassic. Both the start and end of the _____ are marked by major extinction events.
   a. 1509 Istanbul earthquake
   b. Rhaetian
   c. 1700 Cascadia earthquake
   d. Triassic

25. In geology, a _____ or _____ line is a planar fracture in rock in which the rock on one side of the fracture has moved with respect to the rock on the other side. Large faults within the Earth's crust are the result of differential or shear motion and active _____ zones are the causal locations of most earthquakes. Earthquakes are caused by energy release during rapid slippage along a _____.
   a. Stack
   b. Combe
   c. Fault
   d. Dali

26. The _____ of a quantity whose value decreases with time is the interval required for the quantity to decay to half of its initial value. The concept originated in describing how long it takes atoms to undergo radioactive decay but also applies in a wide variety of other situations.
   a. 1703 Genroku earthquake
   b. 1509 Istanbul earthquake
   c. 1700 Cascadia earthquake
   d. Half-life

27. A _____ is an atom with an unstable nucleus, which is a nucleus characterized by excess energy which is available to be imparted either to a newly-created radiation particle within the nucleus, or else to an atomic electron. The _____, in this process, undergoes radioactive decay, and emits a gamma ray(s) and/or subatomic particles. These particles constitute ionizing radiation.
   a. 1703 Genroku earthquake
   b. 1700 Cascadia earthquake
   c. 1509 Istanbul earthquake
   d. Radionuclide

28. _____ is a technique used to date materials, usually based on a comparison between the observed abundance of a naturally occurring radioactive isotope and its decay products, using known decay rates. It is the principal source of information about the absolute age of rocks and other geological features, including the age of the Earth itself, and can be used to date a wide range of natural and man-made materials. Together with stratigraphic principles, _____ methods are used in geochronology to establish the geological time scale.
   a. Global Standard Stratigraphic Age
   b. Chronozone
   c. Paleomagnetism
   d. Radiometric dating

29. _____ are a type of elastic surface wave that travel on solids. They are produced on the Earth by earthquakes, in which case they are also known as 'ground roll', or by other sources of seismic energy such as an explosion or even a sledgehammer impact. They are also produced in materials by acoustic transducers, and are used in non-destructive testing for detecting defects.
   a. Maximum magnitude
   b. Tornillo event
   c. Seismic waves
   d. Rayleigh waves

30. A _____ is any glacially formed accumulation of unconsolidated glacial debris (soil and rock) which can occur in currently glaciated and formerly glaciated regions, such as those areas acted upon by a past ice age. This debris may have been plucked off the valley floor as a glacier advanced or it may have fallen off the valley walls as a result of frost wedging. Moraines may be composed of silt like glacial flour to large boulders.
   a. 1700 Cascadia earthquake
   b. 1509 Istanbul earthquake
   c. 1703 Genroku earthquake
   d. Moraine

31. A _____ is a large, slow-moving mass of ice, formed from compacted layers of snow, that slowly deforms and flows in response to gravity and high pressure.

_____ ice is the largest reservoir of fresh water on Earth, and second only to oceans as the largest reservoir of total water.

   a. Little Ice Age
   b. Keeling Curve
   c. Glacier
   d. Pacific Decadal Oscillation

32. _____ is one of the three main rock types (the others being igneous and metamorphic rock.) _____ is formed by deposition and consolidation of mineral and organic material and from precipitation of minerals from solution. The processes that form _____ occur at the surface of the Earth and within bodies of water.
   a. Rock cycle
   b. Petrology
   c. Serpentinite
   d. Sedimentary rock

Chapter 11. A Biography of Earth

1. _____ is a soft, white, porous sedimentary rock, a form of limestone composed of the mineral calcite. It forms under relatively deep marine conditions from the gradual accumulation of minute calcite plates shed from micro-organisms called coccolithophores. It is common to find flint and chert nodules embedded in _____.
   - a. 1703 Genroku earthquake
   - b. 1509 Istanbul earthquake
   - c. 1700 Cascadia earthquake
   - d. Chalk

2. A _____ is a mountain rising from the ocean seafloor that does not reach to the water's surface (sea level), and thus is not an island. These are typically formed from extinct volcanoes, that rise abruptly and are usually found rising from a seafloor of 1,000-4,000 meters depth. They are defined by oceanographers as independent features that rise to at least 1,000 meters above the seafloor.
   - a. 1700 Cascadia earthquake
   - b. 1703 Genroku earthquake
   - c. Seamount
   - d. 1509 Istanbul earthquake

3. The _____ is a chronologic schema (or idealized model) relating stratigraphy to time that is used by geologists, paleontologists and other earth scientists to describe the timing and relationships between events that have occurred during the history of the Earth. The table of geologic time spans presented here agrees with the dates and nomenclature proposed by the International Commission on Stratigraphy, and uses the standard color codes of the United States Geological Survey.

   Evidence from radiometric dating indicates that the Earth is about 4.570 billion years old.

   - a. 1700 Cascadia earthquake
   - b. 1703 Genroku earthquake
   - c. 1509 Istanbul earthquake
   - d. Geologic time scale

4. A _____ is a piece of rock that differs from the size and type of rock native to the area in which it rests. They are carried by glacial ice, often over distances of hundreds of kilometres and can range in size from pebbles to large boulders such as Big Rock (16,500 tons) in Alberta.
   - a. 1703 Genroku earthquake
   - b. Glacial erratic
   - c. 1700 Cascadia earthquake
   - d. 1509 Istanbul earthquake

5. The _____ was a major ice sheet that covered, during glacial periods of the Quaternary, a large area of North America. This included the following areas:

   - Western Montana
   - The Idaho Panhandle
   - Northern Washington state down to about Seattle and Spokane, Washington
   - All of British Columbia
   - The southwestern third or so of Yukon territory
   - All of the Alaska Panhandle
   - South Central Alaska
   - The Alaska Peninsula
   - Almost all of the continental shelf north of the Strait of Juan de Fuca

The ice sheet covered up to two and a half million square kilometres at the Last Glacial Maximum and probably more than that in some previous periods, when it may have extended into the northeast extremity of Oregon and the Salmon River Mountains in Idaho. It is probable, though, that its northern margin also migrated south due to the influence of starvation caused by very low levels of precipitation.

At its eastern end the _____ merged with the Laurentide ice sheet at the Continental Divide, forming an area of ice that contained one and a half times as much water as the Antarctic ice sheet does today.

a. Wolstonian Stage
b. Snowball Earth
c. Rock flour
d. Cordilleran ice sheet

6. The _____ is the geologic eon before the Archean. It started at Earth's formation about 4.6 billion years ago (4,600 Ma), and ended roughly 3.8 billion years ago, though the latter date varies according to different sources.

a. 1703 Genroku earthquake
b. 1700 Cascadia earthquake
c. 1509 Istanbul earthquake
d. Hadean

7. Geologically, a _____ is a long, narrow inlet with steep sides, created in a valley carved by glacial activity.

The seeds of a _____ are laid when a glacier cuts a U-shaped valley through abrasion of the surrounding bedrock by the sediment it carries. Many such valleys were formed during the recent ice age.

a. 1509 Istanbul earthquake
b. Fjord
c. 1703 Genroku earthquake
d. 1700 Cascadia earthquake

8. _____ are the largest glaciers, enormous masses of ice that are not visibly affected by the landscape and that cover the entire surface beneath them, except possibly on the margins where they are thinnest. Antarctica and Greenland are the only places where continental _____ currently exist. These regions contain vast quantities of fresh water.

a. Ice sheets
b. AL 129-1
c. AL 333
d. AASHTO Soil Classification System

9.

A widely accepted theory of planet formation, the so-called _____ hypothesis of Viktor Safronov, states that planets form out of dust grains that collide and stick to form larger and larger bodies. When the bodies reach sizes of approximately one kilometer, then they can attract each other directly through their mutual gravity, aiding further growth into moon-sized protoplanets enormously.

a. 1700 Cascadia earthquake
b. 1509 Istanbul earthquake
c. 1703 Genroku earthquake
d. Planetesimal

10. _____ is a sedimentary rock. It is a natural chemical precipitate of carbonate minerals; typically aragonite, but often recrystallized to, or primarily, calcite.

_____ forms as calcium carbonate is deposited from the water of mineral springs or rivulets that are saturated with dissolved calcium bicarbonate. The spring water from which the calcium carbonate precipitates can be hot, warm or cold. The rate of deposition increases with the temperature of the water, or alternatively, when biotic material accelerates the process of precipitation.

a. Travertine
b. 1700 Cascadia earthquake
c. 1703 Genroku earthquake
d. 1509 Istanbul earthquake

11. A _____ is an old and stable part of the continental crust that has survived the merging and splitting of continents and supercontinents for at least 500 million years. Some are over two billion years old. They are generally found in the interiors of continents and are characteristically composed of ancient crystalline basement crust of lightweight felsic igneous rock such as granite.
a. Superior craton
b. Kalahari craton
c. Sebakwe proto-craton
d. Craton

12. _____ is the solid-state recrystallization of pre-existing rocks due to changes in physical and chemical conditions, primarily heat, pressure, and the introduction of chemically active fluids. Both mineralogical, chemical and crystallographic changes can occur during this process.

Three types of _____ exist: dynamic, contact and regional.

a. Detritus
b. Metamorphism
c. Compression
d. Reading Prong

13. A _____ in geology is an intrusive igneous rock body that crystallized from a magma slowly cooling below the surface of the Earth. Plutons include batholiths, dikes, sills, laccoliths, lopoliths, and other igneous bodies. In practice, '_____' usually refers to a distinctive mass of igneous rock, typically kilometers in dimension, without a tabular shape like those of dikes and sills.
a. Migmatite
b. Vesicular texture
c. Metamorphic zone
d. Pluton

14. The _____ is a geological signature, usually a thin band, dated to (65.5 ± 0.3) Ma (million years ago). The boundary marks the end of the Mesozoic era and the beginning of the Cenozoic era, and is associated with the Cretaceous-Tertiary extinction event, a mass extinction.
a. K-T boundary
b. Shiva crater
c. 1700 Cascadia earthquake
d. 1509 Istanbul earthquake

15. _____, is a phylum of bacteria that obtain their energy through photosynthesis. The name '_____' comes from the color of the bacteria . They are a significant component of the marine nitrogen cycle and an important primary producer in many areas of the ocean, but are also found in habitats other than the marine environment; in particular _____ are known to occur in both freshwater, hypersaline inland lakes and in arid areas where they are a major component of biological soil crusts.

Stromatolites of fossilized oxygen-producing _____ have been found from 2.8 billion years ago. The ability of _____ to perform oxygenic photosynthesis is thought to have converted the early reducing atmosphere into an oxidizing one, which dramatically changed the composition of life forms on Earth by provoking an explosion of biodiversity and leading to the near-extinction of oxygen-intolerant organisms.

a. 1700 Cascadia earthquake
b. Cyanobacteria
c. 1509 Istanbul earthquake
d. 1703 Genroku earthquake

Chapter 11. A Biography of Earth

16. _____ are the preserved remains or traces of animals, plants, and other organisms from the remote past. The totality of _____, both discovered and undiscovered, and their placement in fossiliferous rock formations and sedimentary layers (strata) is known as the fossil record. The study of _____ across geological time, how they were formed, and the evolutionary relationships between taxa (phylogeny) are some of the most important functions of the science of paleontology.
   a. 1700 Cascadia earthquake
   b. 1703 Genroku earthquake
   c. 1509 Istanbul earthquake
   d. Fossils

17. A _____ is a geological phenomenon which includes a wide range of ground movement, such as rock falls, deep failure of slopes and shallow debris flows, which can occur in offshore, coastal and onshore environments. Although the action of gravity is the primary driving force for a _____ to occur, there are other contributing factors affecting the original slope stability. Typically, pre-conditional factors build up specific sub-surface conditions that make the area/slope prone to failure, whereas the actual _____ often requires a trigger before being released.
   a. 1700 Cascadia earthquake
   b. Landslide
   c. Mass wasting
   d. 1509 Istanbul earthquake

18. _____ are layered accretionary structures formed in shallow water by the trapping, binding and cementation of sedimentary grains by biofilms of microorganisms, especially cyanobacteria (commonly known as blue-green algae.)

A variety of stromatolite morphologies exist including conical, stratiform, branching, domal, and columnar types. _____ occur widely in the fossil record of the Precambrian, but are rare today.

   a. 1700 Cascadia earthquake
   b. 1509 Istanbul earthquake
   c. 1703 Genroku earthquake
   d. Stromatolites

19. The _____, is a geologic eon before the Proterozoic and Paleoproterozoic, before 2.5 Ga (billion years ago, or 2,500 Ma.) Instead of being based on stratigraphy, this date is defined chronometrically. The lower boundary (starting point) has not been officially recognized by the International Commission on Stratigraphy, but it is usually set to 3.8 Ga, at the end of the Hadean eon.
   a. AL 129-1
   b. AL 333
   c. Archean
   d. AASHTO Soil Classification System

20. The _____ is a geological eon representing a period before the first abundant complex life on Earth. The _____ extended from 2500 Ma to 542.0 >± 1.0 Ma (million years ago), and is the most recent part of the old, informally named 'e;Precambrian'e; time.

The Proterozoic consists of 3 geologic eras, from oldest to youngest:

- Paleoproterozoic
- Mesoproterozoic
- Neoproterozoic

The well-identified events were:

- The transition to an oxygenated atmosphere during the Mesoproterozoic.
- Several glaciations, including the hypothesized Snowball Earth during the Cryogenian period in the late Neoproterozoic.
- The Ediacaran Period (635 to 542 Ma) which is characterized by the evolution of abundant soft-bodied multicellular organisms.

The geoloic record of the Proterozoic is much better than that for the preceding Archean. In contrast to the deep-water deposits of the Archean, the Proterozoic features many strata that were laid down in extensive shallow epicontinental seas; furthermore, many of these rocks are less metamorphosed than Archean-age ones, and plenty are unaltered.

a. 1700 Cascadia earthquake
b. 1703 Genroku earthquake
c. 1509 Istanbul earthquake
d. Proterozoic Eon

21. A _____ or sea vent, is a type of hydrothermal vent found on the ocean floor. They are formed in fields hundreds of meters wide when superheated water from below Earth's crust comes through the ocean floor. This water is rich in dissolved minerals from the crust, most notably sulfides.

a. 1700 Cascadia earthquake
b. 1703 Genroku earthquake
c. 1509 Istanbul earthquake
d. Black smoker

22. _____, like all craton land, was created as continents moved about the surface of the Earth, bumping into other continents and drifting away.

Many times in its past, _____ has been a separate continent as it is now in the form of North America. During other times in its past, _____ has been part of a supercontinent.

a. North China craton
b. Congo craton
c. Laurentia
d. South China

23. The _____ Eon is the current eon in the geologic timescale, and the one during which abundant animal life has existed. It covers roughly 545 million years and goes back to the time when diverse hard-shelled animals first appeared.

a. 1703 Genroku earthquake
b. Phanerozoic
c. 1700 Cascadia earthquake
d. 1509 Istanbul earthquake

24. In geology, _____ is the name of a supercontinent, a continent which contained most or all of Earth's landmass. According to plate tectonic reconstructions, _____ existed between 1100 and 750 million years ago, in the Neoproterozoic era.

In contrast with Pangaea, the last supercontinent about 300 million years ago, little is known yet about the exact configuration and geodynamic history of _____.

a. Laurasia
b. Rodinia
c. 1700 Cascadia earthquake
d. 1509 Istanbul earthquake

25. In geology, a _____ is a continental area covered by relatively flat or gently tilted, mainly sedimentary strata, which overlie a basement of consolidated igneous or metamorphic rocks of an earlier deformation. They as well as, shields and the basement rocks together constitute cratons.

It is also common practice to use the term _____ as a very general term for a sequence of shallow water carbonate _____.

a. Fault
b. Platform
c. Cleavage
d. Streak

26. A _____ is generally a large area of exposed Precambrian crystalline igneous and high-grade metamorphic rocks that form tectonically stable areas. In all cases, the age of these rocks is greater than 570 million years and sometimes dates back 2 to 3.5 billion years. They have been little affected by tectonic events following the end of the Precambrian Era, and are relatively flat regions where mountain building, faulting, and other tectonic processes are greatly diminished compared with the activity that occurs at the margins of the shields and the boundaries between tectonic plates.

a. 1703 Genroku earthquake
b. 1509 Istanbul earthquake
c. 1700 Cascadia earthquake
d. Shield

27. The _____ Period is the last geological period of the Neoproterozoic Era and of the Proterozoic Eon, immediately preceding the Cambrian Period, the first period of the Paleozoic Era and of the Phanerozoic Eon. Its status as an official geological period was ratified in 2004 by the International Union of Geological Sciences (IUGS), making it the first new geological period declared in 120 years. The type section is in the Flinders Ranges in South Australia.

a. AASHTO Soil Classification System
b. AL 129-1
c. AL 333
d. Ediacaran

28. A _____ is a large, slow-moving mass of ice, formed from compacted layers of snow, that slowly deforms and flows in response to gravity and high pressure.

_____ ice is the largest reservoir of fresh water on Earth, and second only to oceans as the largest reservoir of total water.

a. Little Ice Age
b. Pacific Decadal Oscillation
c. Keeling Curve
d. Glacier

29. _____, originally Gondwanaland, is the name given to a southern precursor-supercontinent and then as a remnant separated from Laurasia 180-200 million years ago during the breakup of the Pangaea supercontinent that existed about 500 to 200 Ma ago into two large segments. While the corresponding northern hemisphere continent Laurasia moved further north, the nearly equal in area _____ included most of the landmasses in today's southern hemisphere, including Antarctica, South America, Africa, Madagascar, Australia-New Guinea, and New Zealand, as well as Arabia and the Indian subcontinent, which have now moved into the Northern Hemisphere.

a. Laurasia
b. 1700 Cascadia earthquake
c. 1509 Istanbul earthquake
d. Gondwana

Chapter 11. A Biography of Earth

30. The _____ is an oceanic tectonic plate beneath the Pacific Ocean.

To the north the easterly side is a divergent boundary with the Explorer Plate, the Juan de Fuca Plate and the Gorda Plate forming respectively the Explorer Ridge, the Juan de Fuca Ridge and the Gorda Ridge. In the middle the easterly side is a transform boundary with the North American Plate along the San Andreas Fault and a boundary with the Cocos Plate.

   a. Somali Plate
   b. Gorda Plate
   c. Conway Reef Plate
   d. Pacific Plate

31. The _____ is the earliest of three geologic eras of the Phanerozoic eon. The _____ spanned from roughly 542 to 251 million years ago (ICS, 2004), and is subdivided into six geologic periods; from oldest to youngest they are: the Cambrian, Ordovician, Silurian, Devonian, Carboniferous, and Permian.

The _____ covers the time from the first appearance of abundant, soft-shelled fossils to the time when the continents were beginning to be dominated by large, relatively sophisticated reptiles and modern plants. The lower (oldest) boundary was classically set at the first appearance of creatures known as trilobites and archeocyathids.

   a. 1703 Genroku earthquake
   b. 1700 Cascadia earthquake
   c. 1509 Istanbul earthquake
   d. Paleozoic

32. An _____ is a large shallow sea that either extends far into a continent, such as the Persian Gulf, or overlies a large part of a continent.

They are usually associated with the marine transgressions of the early Cenozoic era and may be semi-cyclic--during eras of glacial recession given a period of low mountains coupled with a warming under the influence of plate tectonics. They can be warm or cold; indeed, several were present at the end of the last Ice Age, when sea levels rose more rapidly than some areas could isostatically adjust.

   a. AASHTO Soil Classification System
   b. AL 129-1
   c. AL 333
   d. Epeiric sea

33. _____ refers to hypotheses regarding paleoclimatic global-scale glaciation, claiming that the Earth's surface was nearly or entirely frozen at some points in its past. The occurrence of _____ remains controversial. Proponents claim it best explains sedimentary deposits generally regarded as of glacial origin at tropical latitudes and other enigmatic features of the geological record.
   a. Pre-Pastonian Stage
   b. Snowball Earth
   c. Pastonian Stage
   d. Cirque glacier

34. The _____ is the first geological period of the Phanerozoic eon, lasting from 542 ± 0.3 million years ago to 488.3 ± 1.7 million years ago (ICS, 2004); it is succeeded by the Ordovician. Its subdivisions, and indeed its base, are somewhat in flux. The period was established by Adam Sedgwick, who named it after Cambria, the classical name for Wales, where Britain's _____ rocks are best exposed.

a. 1703 Genroku earthquake
c. 1700 Cascadia earthquake
b. 1509 Istanbul earthquake
d. Cambrian

35. The _____ or Cambrian radiation was the seemingly rapid appearance of most major groups of complex animals around 530 million years ago, as evidenced by the fossil record. This was accompanied by a major diversification of other organisms, including animals, phytoplankton, and calcimicrobes. Before about 580 million years ago, most organisms were simple, composed of individual cells occasionally organized into colonies.
   a. Conodont Alteration Index
   b. Labyrinthodont
   c. Romer's Gap
   d. Cambrian explosion

36. A _____ is a natural formation (or landform) where a rock arch forms, with a natural passageway through underneath. Most natural arches form as a narrow ridge, walled by cliffs, become narrower from erosion, with a softer rock stratum under the cliff-forming stratum gradually eroding out until the rock shelters thus formed meet underneath the ridge, thus forming the arch. They commonly form where cliffs are subject to erosion from the sea, rivers or weathering (sub-aerial processes); the processes 'find' weaknesses in rocks and work on them, making them bigger until they break through.
   a. 1700 Cascadia earthquake
   b. 1703 Genroku earthquake
   c. 1509 Istanbul earthquake
   d. Natural arch

37. In mineralogy and crystallography, a _____ is a unique arrangement of atoms in a crystal. A _____ is composed of a motif, a set of atoms arranged in a particular way, and a lattice. Motifs are located upon the points of a lattice, which is an array of points repeating periodically in three dimensions.
   a. 1703 Genroku earthquake
   b. 1700 Cascadia earthquake
   c. 1509 Istanbul earthquake
   d. Crystal structure

38. _____ is molten rock expelled by a volcano during eruption. When first expelled from a volcanic vent, it is a liquid at temperatures from 700 >°C to 1,200 >°C (1,300 >°F to 2,200 >°F.) Although _____ is quite viscous, with about 100,000 times the viscosity of water, it can flow great distances before cooling and solidifying, because of both its thixotropic and shear thinning properties.
   a. Volcanic ash
   b. Pit crater
   c. Supervolcano
   d. Lava

39. _____ refers to natural mountain building, and may be studied as a tectonic structural event, (b) as a geographical event, and (c) a chronological event. Orogenic events (a) cause distinctive structural phenomena and related tectonic activity, (b) affect certain regions of rocks and crust, and (c) happen within a specific period of time.
   a. Orogenesis
   b. Alice Springs Orogeny
   c. Antler orogeny
   d. Orogeny

40. A _____ is a natural depression or hole in the surface topography caused by the removal of soil or bedrock, often both, by water. They may vary in size from less than a meter to several hundred meters both in diameter and depth, and vary in form from soil-lined bowls to bedrock-edged chasms. They may be formed gradually or suddenly, and are found worldwide.
   a. 1703 Genroku earthquake
   b. 1700 Cascadia earthquake
   c. 1509 Istanbul earthquake
   d. Sinkhole

41. The _____ is the level at which the ground water pressure is equal to atmospheric pressure. It may be conveniently visualized as the 'surface' of the ground water in a given vicinity. It usually coincides with the phreatic surface, but can be many feet above it. As water infiltrates through pore spaces in the soil, it first passes through the zone of aeration, where the soil is unsaturated. At increasing depths water fills in more spaces, until the zone of saturation is reached. The relatively horizontal plane atop this zone constitutes the _____.
   a. Crosshole sonic logging
   b. Shaft construction
   c. Rock bolt
   d. Water table

42. A _____ refers to a very large-scale lithostratigraphic sequence that covers a complete marine transgressive-regressive cycle across a craton. They are also known as 'megasequences', 'stratigraphic sequences', or simply 'sequences.'

They were first proposed by Lawrence Sloss in 1963; each one represents a time when epeiric seas deposited sediments across the craton, while the upper and lower edges of the sequence are bounded by craton-wide unconformities eroded when the seas receded.

These sequences may in part represent eustatic or global change in sea level; however, when the proper names are used they usually refer to the North American continent.

   a. Cornbrash
   b. Tyrrell Sea
   c. Paleoseismology
   d. Cratonic sequence

43. The _____ or Appalachian orogeny is one of the geological mountain-forming events (orogeny) that formed the Appalachian Mountains and Allegheny Mountains. The term and spelling 'Alleghany Orogeny' (sic) originally proposed by H.P. Woodward (1957, 1958) is preferred usage. Approximately 350 million to 300 million years ago, in the Carboniferous period, the combined continents of Europe and Africa (Gondwana) collided with North America to form the supercontinent of Pangaea.
   a. Alleghenian orogeny
   b. Antler orogeny
   c. Alice Springs Orogeny
   d. Alpine orogeny

44. The _____ is a mountain-building episode that extensively deformed Paleozoic rocks of the Great Basin in Nevada and western Utah during Late Devonian and Early Mississippian time. In the late Devonian, the Antler volcanic island arc terrane collided with was then the west coast of North America in the vicinity of today's border between Utah and Nevada.
   a. Alleghenian orogeny
   b. Orogenesis
   c. Orogeny
   d. Antler orogeny

45. The _____ was an ocean that existed in the Neoproterozoic and Paleozoic eras of the geologic timescale (between 600 and 400 million years ago.) The _____ was situated in the southern hemisphere, between the paleocontinents of Laurentia, Baltica and Avalonia. The ocean disappeared with the Caledonian, Taconic and Acadian orogenies, when these three continents joined to form one big landmass called Laurussia.
   a. Iapetus Ocean
   b. AL 129-1
   c. AL 333
   d. AASHTO Soil Classification System

46. _____ was the supercontinent that is theorized to have existed during the Paleozoic and Mesozoic eras about 250 million years ago, before the component continents were separated into their current configuration.

124 Chapter 11. A Biography of Earth

The name was first used by the German originator of the continental drift theory, Alfred Wegener, in the 1920 edition of his book The Origin of Continents and Oceans , in which a postulated supercontinent _____ played a key role.

The single enormous ocean which surrounded Pangaea is known as Panthalassa.

- a. 1703 Genroku earthquake
- b. 1509 Istanbul earthquake
- c. 1700 Cascadia earthquake
- d. Pangea

47. The _____ is the epoch from 1.8 million to 11550 years BP covering the world's recent period of repeated glaciations. The _____ epoch follows the Pliocene epoch and is followed by the Holocene epoch. The _____ is the third epoch of the Neogene period or 6th epoch of the Cenozoic Era. The end of the _____ corresponds with the retreat of the last continental glacier. It also corresponds with the end of the Paleolithic age used in archaeology.
- a. Pleistocene
- b. Tyrrhenian
- c. Sicilian Stage
- d. Late Pleistocene

48. A _____ is an opening in a planet's surface or crust, which allows hot, molten rock, ash, and gases to escape from below the surface. Volcanic activity involving the extrusion of rock tends to form mountains or features like mountains over a period of time.
- a. 1700 Cascadia earthquake
- b. 1703 Genroku earthquake
- c. Volcano
- d. 1509 Istanbul earthquake

49. _____ is a phenomenon of the plate tectonics of Earth that occurs at convergent boundaries. _____ is a variation on the fundamental process of subduction, whereby the subduction zone is destroyed, mountains produced, and two continents sutured together. _____ is known only from this planet and is an interesting example of how our different crusts, oceanic and continental, behave during subduction.
- a. Continental collision
- b. Divergent boundary
- c. Forearc
- d. Motagua Fault

50. The terms _____ and icehouse Earth refer to the prevailing global climate on a timescale of millions of years.

During a _____ Earth period, the planet's atmosphere contains sufficient _____ gases such as carbon dioxide and methane for ice to be entirely absent from the planet's surface.

During icehouse periods, glaciers are present in fluctuating amounts; variations in the Earth's orbit may result in many ice ages, glacials, and interglacials.

- a. 1703 Genroku earthquake
- b. Greenhouse
- c. 1509 Istanbul earthquake
- d. 1700 Cascadia earthquake

51. The general term '_____' or, more precisely, 'glacial age' denotes a geological period of long-term reduction in the temperature of the Earth's surface and atmosphere, resulting in an expansion of continental ice sheets, polar ice sheets and alpine glaciers. Within a long-term _____, individual pulses of extra cold climate are termed 'glaciations'. Glaciologically, _____ implies the presence of extensive ice sheets in the northern and southern hemispheres; by this definition we are still in an _____.

Chapter 11. A Biography of Earth

    a. AL 333
    b. AL 129-1
    c. AASHTO Soil Classification System
    d. Ice age

52. The _____ Era is one of three geologic eras of the Phanerozoic eon. The division of time into eras dates back to Giovanni Arduino, in the 18th century, although his original name for the era now called the '_____' was 'Secondary' (making the modern era the 'Tertiary'.)

The _____ was a time of tectonic, climatic and evolutionary activity. The continents gradually shifted from a state of connectedness into their present configuration; the drifting provided for speciation and other important evolutionary developments.

    a. 1509 Istanbul earthquake
    b. 1700 Cascadia earthquake
    c. Mesozoic
    d. 1703 Genroku earthquake

53. The _____ is a mid-ocean ridge, a divergent tectonic plate boundary located along the floor of the Atlantic Ocean, and the longest mountain range in the world. It separates the Eurasian Plate and North American Plate in the North Atlantic, and the African Plate from the South American Plate in the South Atlantic. The MAR extends from a junction with the Gakkel Ridge (Mid-Arctic Ridge) northeast of Greenland southward to the Bouvet Triple Junction in the South Atlantic.

    a. Mid-Atlantic Ridge
    b. 1700 Cascadia earthquake
    c. 1703 Genroku earthquake
    d. 1509 Istanbul earthquake

54. The _____ was a period of mountain building in western North America, which started in the Late Cretaceous, 70 to 80 million years ago, and ended 35 to 55 million years ago. The exact duration and ages of beginning and end of the orogeny are in dispute, as is the cause. The _____ occurred in a series of pulses, with quiescent phases intervening. The major feature that was created by this orogeny was the Rocky Mountains, but evidence of this orogeny can be found from Alaska to northern Mexico, with the easternmost extent of the mountain-building represented by the Black Hills of South Dakota.

    a. Kaikoura Orogeny
    b. Laramide orogeny
    c. Sevier orogeny
    d. Pan-African orogeny

55. The _____ was a mountain-building event that affected western North America from Canada to the north to Mexico to the south. This orogeny was the result of convergent boundary tectonism between approximately 140 million years (Ma) ago, and 50 Ma. This orogeny was produced by the collision of the oceanic Farallon Plate and Kula Plate, predecessors of the Pacific Plate, and their subduction underneath the continental North American Plate. The _____ was preceded by several other mountain-building events including the Nevadan orogeny, the Sonoman orogeny, and the Antler orogeny, and partially overlapped in time and space with the Laramide orogeny.

    a. Trans-Hudson orogeny
    b. Sevier orogeny
    c. Pan-African orogeny
    d. Kaikoura Orogeny

56. A _____ is an underwater mountain range, typically having a valley known as a rift running along its spine, formed by plate tectonics. This type of oceanic ridge is characteristic of what is known as an oceanic spreading center, which is responsible for seafloor spreading. The uplifted sea floor results from convection currents which rise in the mantle as magma at a linear weakness in the oceanic crust, and emerge as lava, creating new crust upon cooling.

    a. Transgression
    b. Mid-ocean ridge
    c. Permineralization
    d. Seafloor spreading

Chapter 11. A Biography of Earth

57. _____ occurs at mid-ocean ridges, where new oceanic crust is formed through volcanic activity and then gradually moves away from the ridge. _____ helps explain continental drift in the theory of plate tectonics.

Earlier theories (e.g., by Alfred Wegener) of continental drift were that continents 'plowed' through the sea. The idea that the seafloor itself moves (and carries the continents with it) as it expands from a central axis was proposed by Harry Hess from Princeton University in the 1960s. The theory is well-accepted now, and the phenomenon is known to be caused by convection currents in the plastic, very weak upper mantle, or asthenosphere.

a. Saltation
b. Deposition
c. Diagenesis
d. Seafloor spreading

58. _____ is a geologic term for a type of topography characterized by a series of separate and parallel mountain ranges with broad valleys interposed, extending over a more or less wide area. It is typified by the topography found in the Great Basin in the western United States, which is part of a larger regional topography known as the _____ Province. _____ topography results from crustal extension.

a. Rill
b. Zechstein
c. Tidal scour
d. Basin and Range

59. The _____ is a large geologic province which includes parts of the southwestern United States and northwestern Mexico, typified by basin and range topography.

The topography of the _____ is a result of crustal extension within this part of the North American Plate. The cause of this extension is as yet not fully understood, although several hypotheses have been offered. The crust here has been stretched up to 100% of its original width. In fact, the crust underneath the _____, especially under the Great Basin, is some of the thinnest in the world.

a. Yilgarn Craton
b. Basin and Range Province
c. Quaternary
d. Canadian Shield

60. In geology, a _____ or _____ line is a planar fracture in rock in which the rock on one side of the fracture has moved with respect to the rock on the other side. Large faults within the Earth's crust are the result of differential or shear motion and active _____ zones are the causal locations of most earthquakes. Earthquakes are caused by energy release during rapid slippage along a _____.

a. Stack
b. Fault
c. Dali
d. Combe

61. The _____ is an active transform fault, located between the North American Plate and the Pacific Plate, Canada's equivalent of the San Andreas Fault. The _____ forms a triple junction on its south with the Cascadia subduction zone and the Explorer Ridge (the Queen Charlotte Triple Junction.) The fault is named for Queen Charlotte Island which lies just north of the triple junction.

a. 1509 Istanbul earthquake
b. 1700 Cascadia earthquake
c. 1703 Genroku earthquake
d. Queen Charlotte fault

Chapter 11. A Biography of Earth

62. The _____ is a continental transform fault that runs a length of roughly 800 miles (1,300 km) through California in the United States. The fault's motion is right-lateral strike-slip (horizontal motion.) It forms the tectonic boundary between the Pacific Plate and the North American Plate.
   a. 1703 Genroku earthquake
   b. 1700 Cascadia earthquake
   c. 1509 Istanbul earthquake
   d. San Andreas Fault

63. The _____ was an ocean that existed between the continents of Gondwana and Laurasia during the Mesozoic era before the opening of the Indian Ocean.

About 250 million years ago, during the Triassic, a new ocean began forming in the southern end of the Paleo-_____. A rift formed along the northern continental shelf of Southern Pangaea (Gondwana.) Over the next 60 million years, that piece of shelf, known as Cimmeria, traveled north, pushing the floor of the Paleo-_____ under the eastern end of Northern Pangaea (Laurasia). The _____ formed between Cimmeria and Gondwana, directly over where the Paleo-Tethys used to be.

   a. Tethys Ocean
   b. 1703 Genroku earthquake
   c. 1700 Cascadia earthquake
   d. 1509 Istanbul earthquake

64. The _____ was an ancient oceanic plate, which began subducting under the west coast of the North American Plate-- then located in modern Utah-- as Pangaea broke apart during the Jurassic period. It is named for the Farallon Islands which are located just west of San Francisco, California.

Over time the central part of the _____ was completely subducted under the southwestern part of the North American Plate. The remains of the _____ are the Juan de Fuca, Explorer and Gorda Plates, subducting under the northern part of the North American Plate, the Cocos Plate subducting under Central America and the Nazca Plate subducting under the South American Plate.

   a. Fault trace
   b. Rivera Plate
   c. Cocos Plate
   d. Farallon Plate

65. The _____ Era, is the most recent of the three classic geological eras and covers the period from 65.5 million years ago to the present. It is marked by the Cretaceous-Tertiary extinction event at the end of the Cretaceous that saw the demise of the last non-avian dinosaurs and the end of the Mesozoic Era. The _____ era is ongoing.
   a. 1703 Genroku earthquake
   b. 1509 Istanbul earthquake
   c. Cenozoic
   d. 1700 Cascadia earthquake

66. The _____ is a physiographic region of the Intermontane Plateaus, roughly centered on the Four Corners region of the southwestern United States. The province covers an area of 337,000 km^2 within western Colorado, northwestern New Mexico, southern and eastern Utah, and northern Arizona. About 90% of the area is drained by the Colorado River and its main tributaries; the Green, San Juan and Little Colorado.

Development of the province has in large part been influenced by structural features in its oldest rocks. Part of the Wasatch Line and its various faults form the western edge of the province. Faults that run parallel to the Wasatch Fault that lies along the Wasatch Range form the boundaries between the plateaus in the High Plateaus Section. The Uinta Basin, Uncompahgre Uplift, and the Paradox Basin were also created by movement along structural weaknesses in the region's oldest rock.

Chapter 11. A Biography of Earth

a. Colorado Plateau
b. 1703 Genroku earthquake
c. 1509 Istanbul earthquake
d. 1700 Cascadia earthquake

67. In geology, a _____ is a place where the Earth's crust and lithosphere are being pulled apart and is an example of extensional tectonics.

Typical _____ features are a central linear downdropped fault segment, called a graben, with parallel normal faulting and _____-flank uplifts on either side forming a _____ valley, where the _____ remains above sea level. The axis of the _____ area commonly contains volcanic rocks and active volcanism is a part of many, but not all active _____ systems.

a. 1703 Genroku earthquake
b. 1700 Cascadia earthquake
c. 1509 Istanbul earthquake
d. Rift

68. A _____, in biogeography, is an isthmus or wider land connection between otherwise separate areas, which allows terrestrial animals and plants to cross over and colonise new lands. They can be created by marine regression, in which sea levels fall, exposing shallow, previously submerged sections of continental shelf; or when new land is created by plate tectonics; or occasionally when the sea floor rises due to post-glacial rebound after an ice age.

a. 1700 Cascadia earthquake
b. Land bridge
c. 1703 Genroku earthquake
d. 1509 Istanbul earthquake

69. _____ is an extinct species of the genus Homo, believed to have been the first hominin to leave Africa.

_____ originally migrated from Africa during the Early Pleistocene, possibly as a result of the operation of the Saharan pump, around 2.0 million years ago, and dispersed throughout most of the Old World.

a. 1509 Istanbul earthquake
b. 1700 Cascadia earthquake
c. 1703 Genroku earthquake
d. Homo erectus

70. The _____ is an extinct member of the Homo genus that is known from Pleistocene specimens found in Europe and parts of western and central Asia. Neanderthals are either classified as a subspecies of humans (Homo sapiens neanderthalensis) or as a separate species (Homo neanderthalensis.) The first proto-_____ traits appeared in Europe as early as 600,000-350,000 years ago.

a. Neanderthal
b. 1703 Genroku earthquake
c. 1700 Cascadia earthquake
d. 1509 Istanbul earthquake

Chapter 12. Riches in Rock: Energy and Mineral Resources

1. In geology, _____ refers to heat sources within the planet. _____ is technically an adjective (e.g., _____ energy) but in U.S. English the word has attained frequent use as a noun .

The planet's internal heat was originally generated during its accretion, due to gravitational binding energy, and since then additional heat has continued to be generated by decay heat from the radioactive decay of elements.

 a. Dali
 b. Diamond Head
 c. Stratification
 d. Geothermal

2. _____ is power extracted from heat stored in the earth. This geothermal energy originates from the original formation of the planet, from radioactive decay of minerals, and from solar energy absorbed at the surface. It has been used for space heating and bathing since ancient roman times, but is now better known for generating electricity.
 a. Geothermal gradient
 b. Geothermal power
 c. Geothermal desalination
 d. Hot Dry Rock Geothermal Energy

3. _____ is a mixture of organic chemical compounds that make up a portion of the organic matter in sedimentary rocks. It is insoluble in normal organic solvents because of the huge molecular weight (upwards of 1,000 Daltons) of its component compounds. The soluble portion is known as bitumen.
 a. Kerogen
 b. 1703 Genroku earthquake
 c. 1509 Istanbul earthquake
 d. 1700 Cascadia earthquake

4. _____ is an organic-rich fine-grained sedimentary rock. It contains significant amounts of kerogen, a solid mixture of organic chemical compounds from which liquid hydrocarbons can be extracted. Deposits of _____ occur around the world, including major deposits in the United States of America. Estimates of global deposits range from 2.8 trillion to 3.3 trillion barrels >(450 >× 10^9 to 520 >× 10^9 m^3) of recoverable oil.
 a. AASHTO Soil Classification System
 b. AL 129-1
 c. AL 333
 d. Oil shale

5. _____ is a fine-grained sedimentary rock whose original constituents were clay minerals or muds. It is characterized by thin laminae breaking with an irregular curving fracture, often splintery and usually parallel to the often-indistinguishable bedding plane. This property is called fissility.
 a. Mudstone
 b. Pelagic sediments
 c. Shale
 d. Metasediment

6. _____ or kerogen oil is a non-conventional oil produced by the destructive distillation of oil shale. This process, a controlled form of pyrolysis, converts the organic matter within the rock (kerogen) into synthetic oil and gas. The resulting oil can be used immediately as a fuel or upgraded to meet refinery feedstock specifications by adding hydrogen and removing impurities such as sulfur and nitrogen.
 a. 1703 Genroku earthquake
 b. 1700 Cascadia earthquake
 c. 1509 Istanbul earthquake
 d. Shale Oil

7. _____ in the earth sciences (commonly symbolized as κ a rock or k) is a measure of the ability of a material (typically unconsolidated material) to transmit fluids. It is of great importance in determining the flow characteristics of hydrocarbons in oil and gas reservoirs, and of groundwater in aquifers. It is typically measured in the lab by application of Darcy's law under steady state conditions or, more generally, by application of various solutions to the diffusion equation for unsteady flow conditions.

a. Porosity
b. Phreatic zone
c. Permeability
d. Saltwater intrusion

8. _____ is a measure of the void spaces in a material, and is measured as a fraction, between 0-1, or as a percentage between 0-100%. The term is used in multiple fields including ceramics, metallurgy, materials, manufacturing, earth sciences and construction.

Used in geology, hydrogeology, soil science, and building science, the _____ of a porous medium (such as rock or sediment) describes the fraction of void space in the material, where the void may contain, for example, air or water.

a. Saltwater intrusion
b. Phreatic zone
c. Permeability
d. Porosity

9. A _____, is a device attached to the end of the drill string that breaks apart, cuts or crushes the rock formations when drilling a wellbore (water, gas or oil.)

The _____ is hollow and has jets to allow for the expulsion of the drilling fluid at high velocity and high pressure to help clean the bit and help to break apart the rock (for softer formations.)

a. Conductor pipe
b. Drill line
c. Casing head
d. Drill bit

10.

A _____ is a device which converts ground movement into voltage, which may be recorded at a recording station. The deviation of this measured voltage from the base line is called the seismic response and is analyzed for structure of the earth.

a. Gutenberg-Richter law
b. Coulomb stress transfer
c. Depth conversion
d. Geophone

11. The lithosphere is broken up into what are called _____. In the case of Earth, there are eight major and many minor plates The lithospheric plates ride on the asthenosphere. These plates move in relation to one another at one of three types of plate boundaries: convergent, or collisional boundaries; divergent boundaries, also called spreading centers; and transform boundaries.
a. Gorda Ridge
b. Tectonic plates
c. Copperbelt Province
d. Thrust fault

12. In structural geology, an _____ is a fold that is convex up and has its oldest beds at its core. The term is not to be confused with antiform, which is a purely descriptive term for any fold that is convex up. Therefore if age relationships (i.e. younging direction) between various strata are unknown, the term antiform must be used.
a. AL 129-1
b. AASHTO Soil Classification System
c. AL 333
d. Anticline

Chapter 12. Riches in Rock: Energy and Mineral Resources 131

13. In geology, a _____ or _____ line is a planar fracture in rock in which the rock on one side of the fracture has moved with respect to the rock on the other side. Large faults within the Earth's crust are the result of differential or shear motion and active _____ zones are the causal locations of most earthquakes. Earthquakes are caused by energy release during rapid slippage along a _____.
   a. Combe
   b. Stack
   c. Fault
   d. Dali

14. An _____ is the result of a sudden release of energy in the Earth's crust that creates seismic waves. They are recorded with a seismometer or the related and mostly obsolete Richter magnitude, with a magnitude 3 or lower _____ being mostly imperceptible and magnitude 7 causing serious damage over large areas.
   a. Earthquake
   b. AL 129-1
   c. AL 333
   d. AASHTO Soil Classification System

15. _____ or extra heavy oil, is a type of bitumen deposit. The sands are naturally occurring mixtures of sand or clay, water and an extremely dense and viscous form of petroleum called bitumen. They are found in large amounts in many countries throughout the world, but are found in extremely large quantities in Canada and Venezuela.
   a. AASHTO Soil Classification System
   b. AL 333
   c. AL 129-1
   d. Oil sands

16. _____ is a naturally occurring granular material composed of finely divided rock and mineral particles.

As the term is used by geologists, _____ particles range in diameter from 0.0625 (or $>^1\!/_{16}$ mm, or 62.5 micrometers) to 2 millimeters. An individual particle in this range size is termed a _____ grain.

   a. 1703 Genroku earthquake
   b. 1700 Cascadia earthquake
   c. Sand
   d. 1509 Istanbul earthquake

17. A _____ is a natural formation (or landform) where a rock arch forms, with a natural passageway through underneath. Most natural arches form as a narrow ridge, walled by cliffs, become narrower from erosion, with a softer rock stratum under the cliff-forming stratum gradually eroding out until the rock shelters thus formed meet underneath the ridge, thus forming the arch. They commonly form where cliffs are subject to erosion from the sea, rivers or weathering (sub-aerial processes); the processes 'find' weaknesses in rocks and work on them, making them bigger until they break through.
   a. 1509 Istanbul earthquake
   b. 1700 Cascadia earthquake
   c. 1703 Genroku earthquake
   d. Natural arch

18. _____ is the solid-state recrystallization of pre-existing rocks due to changes in physical and chemical conditions, primarily heat, pressure, and the introduction of chemically active fluids. Both mineralogical, chemical and crystallographic changes can occur during this process.

Three types of _____ exist: dynamic, contact and regional.

   a. Detritus
   b. Metamorphism
   c. Reading Prong
   d. Compression

19. The _____ is a geological signature, usually a thin band, dated to (65.5 ± 0.3) Ma (million years ago). The boundary marks the end of the Mesozoic era and the beginning of the Cenozoic era, and is associated with the Cretaceous-Tertiary extinction event, a mass extinction.
   a. 1700 Cascadia earthquake
   b. Shiva crater
   c. K-T boundary
   d. 1509 Istanbul earthquake

20. _____ are the preserved remains or traces of animals, plants, and other organisms from the remote past. The totality of _____, both discovered and undiscovered, and their placement in fossiliferous rock formations and sedimentary layers (strata) is known as the fossil record. The study of _____ across geological time, how they were formed, and the evolutionary relationships between taxa (phylogeny) are some of the most important functions of the science of paleontology.
   a. Fossils
   b. 1509 Istanbul earthquake
   c. 1700 Cascadia earthquake
   d. 1703 Genroku earthquake

21. _____ is an accumulation of partially decayed vegetation matter. _____ forms in wetlands or peatlands, variously called bogs, moors, muskegs, pocosins, mires, and _____ swamp forests. By volume there are about 4 trillion mÂ³ of _____ in the world covering a total of around 2% of global land mass (about 3 million km²), containing about 8 billion terajoules of energy.
   a. 1703 Genroku earthquake
   b. Peat
   c. 1509 Istanbul earthquake
   d. 1700 Cascadia earthquake

22. _____ is a hard, compact variety of mineral coal that has a high lustre. It has the highest carbon count and contains the fewest impurities of all coals, despite its lower calorific content.

_____ is the highest of the metamorphic rank, in which the carbon content is between 92% and 98%.

   a. AASHTO Soil Classification System
   b. Anthracite
   c. AL 333
   d. AL 129-1

23. _____ is a relatively soft coal containing a tarlike substance called bitumen. It is of higher quality than lignite coal but of poorer quality than anthracite coal.

_____ is a sedimorphic rock formed by diagenetic and submetamorphic compression of peat bog material.

   a. 1700 Cascadia earthquake
   b. 1509 Istanbul earthquake
   c. 1703 Genroku earthquake
   d. Bituminous coal

24. A marine _____ is a geologic event during which sea level rises relative to the land and the shoreline moves toward higher ground, resulting in flooding. They can be caused either by the land sinking or the ocean basins filling with water (or decreasing in capacity.) Transgresssions and regressions may be caused by tectonic events such as orogenies, severe climate change such as ice ages or isostatic adjustments following removal of ice or sediment load.
   a. Wave pounding
   b. Transgression
   c. Spheroidal weathering
   d. Stoping

Chapter 12. Riches in Rock: Energy and Mineral Resources   133

25. _____ is a soft, white, porous sedimentary rock, a form of limestone composed of the mineral calcite. It forms under relatively deep marine conditions from the gradual accumulation of minute calcite plates shed from micro-organisms called coccolithophores. It is common to find flint and chert nodules embedded in _____.
   a. 1509 Istanbul earthquake
   b. 1700 Cascadia earthquake
   c. 1703 Genroku earthquake
   d. Chalk

26. Geologically, a _____ is a long, narrow inlet with steep sides, created in a valley carved by glacial activity.

The seeds of a _____ are laid when a glacier cuts a U-shaped valley through abrasion of the surrounding bedrock by the sediment it carries. Many such valleys were formed during the recent ice age.

   a. 1703 Genroku earthquake
   b. Fjord
   c. 1509 Istanbul earthquake
   d. 1700 Cascadia earthquake

27. A _____ is a piece of rock that differs from the size and type of rock native to the area in which it rests. They are carried by glacial ice, often over distances of hundreds of kilometres and can range in size from pebbles to large boulders such as Big Rock (16,500 tons) in Alberta.
   a. Glacial erratic
   b. 1703 Genroku earthquake
   c. 1509 Istanbul earthquake
   d. 1700 Cascadia earthquake

28. A _____ is a large, slow-moving mass of ice, formed from compacted layers of snow, that slowly deforms and flows in response to gravity and high pressure.

_____ ice is the largest reservoir of fresh water on Earth, and second only to oceans as the largest reservoir of total water.

   a. Keeling Curve
   b. Pacific Decadal Oscillation
   c. Glacier
   d. Little Ice Age

29. The terms _____ and icehouse Earth refer to the prevailing global climate on a timescale of millions of years.

During a _____ Earth period, the planet's atmosphere contains sufficient _____ gases such as carbon dioxide and methane for ice to be entirely absent from the planet's surface.

During icehouse periods, glaciers are present in fluctuating amounts; variations in the Earth's orbit may result in many ice ages, glacials, and interglacials.

   a. 1703 Genroku earthquake
   b. 1509 Istanbul earthquake
   c. 1700 Cascadia earthquake
   d. Greenhouse

30. In mineralogy and crystallography, a _____ is a unique arrangement of atoms in a crystal. A _____ is composed of a motif, a set of atoms arranged in a particular way, and a lattice. Motifs are located upon the points of a lattice, which is an array of points repeating periodically in three dimensions.
   a. 1509 Istanbul earthquake
   b. 1703 Genroku earthquake
   c. Crystal structure
   d. 1700 Cascadia earthquake

Chapter 12. Riches in Rock: Energy and Mineral Resources

31. The _____ is a geologic period and system, the second of six of the Paleozoic era, and covers the time between 488.3>±1.7 to 443.7>±1.5 million years ago (ICS, 2004.) It follows the Cambrian period and is followed by the Silurian period. The _____ was defined by Charles Lapworth in 1879, to resolve a dispute between followers of Adam Sedgwick and Roderick Murchison, who were placing the same rock beds in northern Wales into the Cambrian and Silurian periods respectively.
   a. AL 129-1
   b. Ordovician
   c. AASHTO Soil Classification System
   d. AL 333

32. _____ is a silvery white and ductile member of the boron group of chemical elements. It has the symbol Al; its atomic number is 13. It is not soluble in water under normal circumstances. _____ is the most abundant metal in the Earth's crust, and the third most abundant element therein, after oxygen and silicon. It makes up about 8% by weight of the Earth'e;s solid surface.
   a. AL 333
   b. Aluminum
   c. AL 129-1
   d. AASHTO Soil Classification System

33. _____ is a fine-grained silica-rich microcrystalline, cryptocrystalline or microfibrous sedimentary rock that may contain small fossils. It varies greatly in color (from white to black), but most often manifests as gray, brown, grayish brown and light green to rusty red; its color is an expression of trace elements present in the rock, and both red and green are most often related to traces of iron (in its oxidized and reduced forms respectively.)

    _____ occurs as oval to irregular nodules in greensand, limestone, chalk, and dolostone formations as a replacement mineral, where it is formed as a result of some type of diagenesis.

   a. 1703 Genroku earthquake
   b. 1700 Cascadia earthquake
   c. Chert
   d. 1509 Istanbul earthquake

34. A _____ is a geological phenomenon which includes a wide range of ground movement, such as rock falls, deep failure of slopes and shallow debris flows, which can occur in offshore, coastal and onshore environments. Although the action of gravity is the primary driving force for a _____ to occur, there are other contributing factors affecting the original slope stability. Typically, pre-conditional factors build up specific sub-surface conditions that make the area/slope prone to failure, whereas the actual _____ often requires a trigger before being released.
   a. Mass wasting
   b. 1509 Istanbul earthquake
   c. 1700 Cascadia earthquake
   d. Landslide

35. An _____ is a type of rock that contains minerals such as gemstones and metals that can be extracted through mining and refined for use. Samples of _____ in the form of exceptionally beautiful crystals, exotic layering visible when sectioned or polished or metallic presentations such as large nuggets or crystalline formations of metals such as gold or copper may command a value far beyond their value as mere _____ or raw metal for subsequent reduction to utilitarian purposes.

    The grade or concentration of an _____ mineral, or metal, as well as its form of occurrence, will directly affect the costs associated with mining the _____.

   a. Ore genesis
   b. Ore
   c. AL 129-1
   d. AASHTO Soil Classification System

Chapter 12. Riches in Rock: Energy and Mineral Resources   135

36. A _____ is a mountain rising from the ocean seafloor that does not reach to the water's surface (sea level), and thus is not an island. These are typically formed from extinct volcanoes, that rise abruptly and are usually found rising from a seafloor of 1,000-4,000 meters depth. They are defined by oceanographers as independent features that rise to at least 1,000 meters above the seafloor.
   a. Seamount
   b. 1700 Cascadia earthquake
   c. 1703 Genroku earthquake
   d. 1509 Istanbul earthquake

37. _____ is molten rock expelled by a volcano during eruption. When first expelled from a volcanic vent, it is a liquid at temperatures from 700 >°C to 1,200 >°C (1,300 >°F to 2,200 >°F.) Although _____ is quite viscous, with about 100,000 times the viscosity of water, it can flow great distances before cooling and solidifying, because of both its thixotropic and shear thinning properties.
   a. Lava
   b. Pit crater
   c. Volcanic ash
   d. Supervolcano

38. _____ are natural conduits through which lava travels beneath the surface of a lava flow, expelled by a volcano during an eruption. They can be actively draining lava from a source, or can be extinct, meaning the lava flow has ceased and the rock has cooled and left a long, cave-like channel.

_____ are formed when an active low-viscosity lava flow develops a continuous and hard crust, which thickens and forms a roof above the still-flowing lava stream.

   a. 1700 Cascadia earthquake
   b. 1703 Genroku earthquake
   c. 1509 Istanbul earthquake
   d. Lava tubes

39. A _____ or sea vent, is a type of hydrothermal vent found on the ocean floor. They are formed in fields hundreds of meters wide when superheated water from below Earth's crust comes through the ocean floor. This water is rich in dissolved minerals from the crust, most notably sulfides.
   a. 1700 Cascadia earthquake
   b. Black smoker
   c. 1703 Genroku earthquake
   d. 1509 Istanbul earthquake

40. _____ are rock concretions on the sea bottom formed of concentric layers of iron and manganese hydroxides around a core. The core may be microscopically small and is sometimes completely transformed into manganese minerals by crystallization. When visible to the naked eye, it can be a small test of a microfossil, a phosphatized shark tooth, basalt debris or even fragments of earlier nodules.
   a. 1700 Cascadia earthquake
   b. Polymetallic nodules
   c. 1509 Istanbul earthquake
   d. 1703 Genroku earthquake

41. A _____ in petrology or mineralogy is a secondary structure, generally spherical or irregularly rounded in shape. They are typically solid replacement bodies of chert or iron oxides formed during diagenesis of a sedimentary rock. They may be hollow as geodes or vugs or filled with crystals and intricate geometric shrinkage patterns as in septarian nodules.
   a. Streak
   b. Diamond Head
   c. Combe
   d. Nodule

42. _____ is a sedimentary rock. It is a natural chemical precipitate of carbonate minerals; typically aragonite, but often recrystallized to, or primarily, calcite.

Chapter 12. Riches in Rock: Energy and Mineral Resources

_____ forms as calcium carbonate is deposited from the water of mineral springs or rivulets that are saturated with dissolved calcium bicarbonate. The spring water from which the calcium carbonate precipitates can be hot, warm or cold. The rate of deposition increases with the temperature of the water, or alternatively, when biotic material accelerates the process of precipitation.

- a. 1509 Istanbul earthquake
- b. 1703 Genroku earthquake
- c. 1700 Cascadia earthquake
- d. Travertine

43. In geology, a _____ deposit or _____ is an accumulation of valuable minerals formed by deposition of dense mineral phases in a trap site. Types of _____ deposits include alluvium, eluvium, beach placers, and paleoplacers.

Typical locations for alluvial _____ deposits are on the inside bends of rivers and creeks, in natural hollows, at the break of slope on a stream, the base of an escarpment, waterfall or other barrier, within sand dunes, beach profiles or in gravel beds.

- a. 1700 Cascadia earthquake
- b. 1509 Istanbul earthquake
- c. 1703 Genroku earthquake
- d. Placer

44. _____ are type of elastic wave, also called seismic waves, that can travel through gases, elastic solids and liquids, including the Earth. _____ can be produced by earthquakes and recorded by seismometers.
- a. P-waves
- b. 1509 Istanbul earthquake
- c. 1703 Genroku earthquake
- d. 1700 Cascadia earthquake

45. The _____ is a geological eon representing a period before the first abundant complex life on Earth. The _____ extended from 2500 Ma to 542.0 >± 1.0 Ma (million years ago), and is the most recent part of the old, informally named 'e;Precambrian'e; time.

The Proterozoic consists of 3 geologic eras, from oldest to youngest:

- Paleoproterozoic
- Mesoproterozoic
- Neoproterozoic

The well-identified events were:

- The transition to an oxygenated atmosphere during the Mesoproterozoic.
- Several glaciations, including the hypothesized Snowball Earth during the Cryogenian period in the late Neoproterozoic.
- The Ediacaran Period (635 to 542 Ma) which is characterized by the evolution of abundant soft-bodied multicellular organisms.

Chapter 12. Riches in Rock: Energy and Mineral Resources 137

The geoloic record of the Proterozoic is much better than that for the preceding Archean. In contrast to the deep-water deposits of the Archean, the Proterozoic features many strata that were laid down in extensive shallow epicontinental seas; furthermore, many of these rocks are less metamorphosed than Archean-age ones, and plenty are unaltered.

- a. 1703 Genroku earthquake
- b. 1509 Istanbul earthquake
- c. 1700 Cascadia earthquake
- d. Proterozoic Eon

46. A _____ is a deep active seismic area in a subduction zone. Differential motion along the zone produces deep-seated earthquakes, the foci of which may be as deep as about 700 kilometres (435 miles.) They develop beneath volcanic island arcs and continental margins above active subduction zones.
- a. Wadati-Benioff zone
- b. Lava
- c. Pit crater
- d. Pyroclastic flow

47. _____ is a common extrusive volcanic rock. It is usually grey to black and fine-grained due to rapid cooling of lava at the surface of a planet. It may be porphyritic containing larger crystals in a fine matrix, or vesicular, or frothy scoria.
- a. Basalt
- b. 1700 Cascadia earthquake
- c. 1509 Istanbul earthquake
- d. 1703 Genroku earthquake

48. _____ refers to natural mountain building, and may be studied as a tectonic structural event, (b) as a geographical event, and (c) a chronological event. Orogenic events (a) cause distinctive structural phenomena and related tectonic activity, (b) affect certain regions of rocks and crust, and (c) happen within a specific period of time.
- a. Antler orogeny
- b. Alice Springs Orogeny
- c. Orogenesis
- d. Orogeny

49. _____ describes the large scale motions of Earth's lithosphere. The theory encompasses the older concepts of continental drift, developed during the first decades of the 20th century by Alfred Wegener, and seafloor spreading, understood during the 1960s.

The outermost part of the Earth's interior is made up of two layers: the lithosphere and the asthenosphere.

- a. Plate tectonics
- b. Continental crust
- c. Forearc
- d. Thrust fault

50. A _____ is an area in which an S-Wave (secondary seismic wave) is not detected due to it not being able to pass through the outer core of the earth due to it being liquid. When an earthquake occurs, seismographs near the epicenter, out to about 90° distance, are able to record both Primary and Secondary waves, but those at a greater distance no longer detect the S-wave. This is because shear waves cannot pass through liquids.
- a. Receiver function
- b. Tornillo event
- c. Shadow zone
- d. Maximum magnitude

51. A _____ is a natural depression or hole in the surface topography caused by the removal of soil or bedrock, often both, by water. They may vary in size from less than a meter to several hundred meters both in diameter and depth, and vary in form from soil-lined bowls to bedrock-edged chasms. They may be formed gradually or suddenly, and are found worldwide.

a. 1703 Genroku earthquake
b. 1700 Cascadia earthquake
c. Sinkhole
d. 1509 Istanbul earthquake

52. _____ are the materials left over after the process of separating the valuable fraction from the worthless fraction of an ore.

_____ represent external costs of mining. As mining techniques and the price of minerals improve, it is not unusual for _____ to be reprocessed using new methods, or more thoroughly with old methods, to recover additional minerals.

a. 1509 Istanbul earthquake
b. 1700 Cascadia earthquake
c. 1703 Genroku earthquake
d. Tailings

53. A _____ column (or _____) is a column of rising air in the lower altitudes of the Earth's atmosphere. They are created by the uneven heating of the Earth's surface from solar radiation, and an example of convection. The Sun warms the ground, which in turn warms the air directly above it.

a. Thermal
b. 1509 Istanbul earthquake
c. 1703 Genroku earthquake
d. 1700 Cascadia earthquake

54. _____ is the geological process by which material is added to a landform or land mass. Fluids such as wind and water, as well as sediment gravity flows, transport previously eroded sediment, which, at the loss of enough kinetic energy in the fluid, is deposited, building up layers of sediment.

_____ occurs when the forces responsible for sediment transportation are no longer sufficient to overcome the forces of particle weight and friction, which resist motion.

a. Downcutting
b. Diagenesis
c. Headward erosion
d. Deposition

55. _____ is the removal of solids (sediment, soil, rock and other particles) in the natural environment. It usually occurs due to transport by wind, water, or ice; by down-slope creep of soil and other material under the force of gravity; or by living organisms, such as burrowing animals, in the case of bioerosion.

_____ is distinguished from weathering, which is the process of chemical or physical breakdown of the minerals in the rocks, although the two processes may occur concurrently.

a. AASHTO Soil Classification System
b. AL 333
c. AL 129-1
d. Erosion

56. _____ are those structures formed during sediment deposition.

_____ such as cross bedding, graded bedding and ripple marks are utilized in stratigraphic studies to indicate original position of strata in geologically complex terranes.

There are two kinds of flow regimes, which at varying speeds and velocities produce different structures.

Chapter 12. Riches in Rock: Energy and Mineral Resources

a. 1703 Genroku earthquake
b. 1700 Cascadia earthquake
c. Sedimentary structures
d. 1509 Istanbul earthquake

57. In geology, engineering, and surveying, _____ is the motion of a surface (usually, the Earth's surface) as it shifts downward relative to a datum such as sea-level. The opposite of _____ is uplift, which results in an increase in elevation. There are several types of _____.
a. 1509 Istanbul earthquake
b. 1700 Cascadia earthquake
c. Pothole
d. Subsidence

58. A _____ is an opening in a planet's surface or crust, which allows hot, molten rock, ash, and gases to escape from below the surface. Volcanic activity involving the extrusion of rock tends to form mountains or features like mountains over a period of time.
a. Volcano
b. 1509 Istanbul earthquake
c. 1703 Genroku earthquake
d. 1700 Cascadia earthquake

59. The _____ describes the continuous movement of water on, above, and below the surface of the Earth. Since the _____ is truly a 'cycle,' there is no beginning or end. Water can change states among liquid, vapor, and ice at various places in the _____.
a. Cone of depression
b. Vadose zone
c. Hydraulic conductivity
d. Water cycle

60. _____ is water located beneath the ground surface in soil pore spaces and in the fractures of lithologic formations. A unit of rock or an unconsolidated deposit is called an aquifer when it can yield a usable quantity of water. The depth at which soil pore spaces or fractures and voids in rock become completely saturated with water is called the water table.
a. Groundwater
b. 1509 Istanbul earthquake
c. 1700 Cascadia earthquake
d. Depression focused recharge

61. The _____ is the level at which the ground water pressure is equal to atmospheric pressure. It may be conveniently visualized as the 'surface' of the ground water in a given vicinity. It usually coincides with the phreatic surface, but can be many feet above it. As water infiltrates through pore spaces in the soil, it first passes through the zone of aeration, where the soil is unsaturated. At increasing depths water fills in more spaces, until the zone of saturation is reached. The relatively horizontal plane atop this zone constitutes the _____.
a. Crosshole sonic logging
b. Water table
c. Rock bolt
d. Shaft construction

62. The _____ is the epoch from 1.8 million to 11550 years BP covering the world's recent period of repeated glaciations. The _____ epoch follows the Pliocene epoch and is followed by the Holocene epoch. The _____ is the third epoch of the Neogene period or 6th epoch of the Cenozoic Era. The end of the _____ corresponds with the retreat of the last continental glacier. It also corresponds with the end of the Paleolithic age used in archaeology.
a. Pleistocene
b. Sicilian Stage
c. Tyrrhenian
d. Late Pleistocene

Chapter 12. Riches in Rock: Energy and Mineral Resources

63. _____ is the geomorphic process by which soil, regolith, and rock move downslope under the force of gravity. Types of _____ include creep, slides, flows, topples, and falls, each with its own characteristic features, and taking place over timescales from seconds to years. _____ occurs on both terrestrial and submarine slopes, and has been observed on Earth, Mars, and Venus.
   a. Soil liquefaction
   b. 1509 Istanbul earthquake
   c. 1700 Cascadia earthquake
   d. Mass wasting

64. _____ is a broadly useful concept that expresses how fast something moves through a system in equilibrium. It is the average time a substance spends within a specified region of space, such as a reservoir. For example, the _____ of water stored in deep groundwater, as part of the water cycle, is about 10,000 years.
   a. 1703 Genroku earthquake
   b. 1700 Cascadia earthquake
   c. 1509 Istanbul earthquake
   d. Residence time

Chapter 13. Unsafe Ground: Landslides and Other Mass Movements

1. _____ is a layer of loose, heterogeneous material covering solid rock. It includes dust, soil, broken rock, and other related materials and is present on Earth, the Moon, some asteroids, and other planets. The term was first defined by George P. Merrill in 1897 who stated, 'In places this covering is made up of material originating through rock-weathering or plant growth in situ. In other instances it is of fragmental and more or less decomposed matter drifted by wind, water or ice from other sources. This entire mantle of unconsolidated material, whatever its nature or origin, it is proposed to call the _____.'
   a. 1700 Cascadia earthquake
   b. Regolith
   c. 1703 Genroku earthquake
   d. 1509 Istanbul earthquake

2. A _____ is a mountain rising from the ocean seafloor that does not reach to the water's surface (sea level), and thus is not an island. These are typically formed from extinct volcanoes, that rise abruptly and are usually found rising from a seafloor of 1,000-4,000 meters depth. They are defined by oceanographers as independent features that rise to at least 1,000 meters above the seafloor.
   a. 1703 Genroku earthquake
   b. Seamount
   c. 1700 Cascadia earthquake
   d. 1509 Istanbul earthquake

3. _____ is a sedimentary rock composed largely of the mineral calcite (calcium carbonate: $CaCO_3$.) The deposition of _____ strata is often a by-product and indicator of biological activity in the geologic record. Calcium (along with nitrogen, phosphorus, and potassium) is a key mineral to plant nutrition: soils overlying _____ bedrock tend to be pre-fertilized with calcium.
   a. 1509 Istanbul earthquake
   b. 1700 Cascadia earthquake
   c. 1703 Genroku earthquake
   d. Limestone

4. The _____ is a geological eon representing a period before the first abundant complex life on Earth. The _____ extended from 2500 Ma to 542.0 >± 1.0 Ma (million years ago), and is the most recent part of the old, informally named 'e;Precambrian'e; time.

The Proterozoic consists of 3 geologic eras, from oldest to youngest:

- Paleoproterozoic
- Mesoproterozoic
- Neoproterozoic

The well-identified events were:

- The transition to an oxygenated atmosphere during the Mesoproterozoic.
- Several glaciations, including the hypothesized Snowball Earth during the Cryogenian period in the late Neoproterozoic.
- The Ediacaran Period (635 to 542 Ma) which is characterized by the evolution of abundant soft-bodied multicellular organisms.

The geoloic record of the Proterozoic is much better than that for the preceding Archean. In contrast to the deep-water deposits of the Archean, the Proterozoic features many strata that were laid down in extensive shallow epicontinental seas; furthermore, many of these rocks are less metamorphosed than Archean-age ones, and plenty are unaltered.

Chapter 13. Unsafe Ground: Landslides and Other Mass Movements

a. 1700 Cascadia earthquake
b. 1703 Genroku earthquake
c. Proterozoic Eon
d. 1509 Istanbul earthquake

5. _____ are the preserved remains or traces of animals, plants, and other organisms from the remote past. The totality of _____, both discovered and undiscovered, and their placement in fossiliferous rock formations and sedimentary layers (strata) is known as the fossil record. The study of _____ across geological time, how they were formed, and the evolutionary relationships between taxa (phylogeny) are some of the most important functions of the science of paleontology.
  a. 1700 Cascadia earthquake
  b. Fossils
  c. 1703 Genroku earthquake
  d. 1509 Istanbul earthquake

6. A _____ is the topographic expression of faulting attributed to the displacement of the land surface by movement along the fault. It can be caused by differential erosion along an old inactive geologic fault (a sort of old rupture) with hard and weak rock, or by a movement on an active fault. In many cases, bluffs form from the upthrown block and can be very steep.
  a. Rejuvenated
  b. Bradyseism
  c. Fault scarp
  d. Gravitational erosion

7. _____ is a form of mass wasting event that occurs when loosely consolidated materials or rock layers move a short distance down a slope. The landmass and the surface it slumps upon is called a failure surface. When the movement occurs in soil, there is often a distinctive rotational movement to the mass, that cuts vertically through bedding planes (landslides take place along a bedding plane or fault). This rotational movement moves along a curved slip surface of regolith (the failure surface) which overlies bedrock. This results in internal deformation of the moving mass consisting chiefly of overturned folds called 'sheath folds.'
  a. Topsoil
  b. Soil
  c. 1509 Istanbul earthquake
  d. Slump

8. In geology, _____ is a type of mass wasting where waterlogged sediment slowly moves downslope over impermeable material. It can occur in any climate where the ground is saturated by water, though it is most often found in periglacial environments where the ground is permanently frozen, under which conditions the process is often called gelifluction. During warm seasonal periods the surface layer melts and slides over the frozen underlayer, slowly moving downslope due to frost heave that occurs normal to the slope.
  a. Solifluction
  b. Cryoseism
  c. Rockfall
  d. Sturzstrom

9. A _____ is a fast moving mass of unconsolidated, saturated debris that looks like flowing concrete. They differentiate from a mudflow by terms of the viscosity of the flow. Flows can carry clasts ranging in size from clay particles to boulders, and also often contains a large amount of woody debris.
  a. Geohazard
  b. Cryoseism
  c. Debris flow
  d. Predator trap

10. A _____ is a type of mudflow or landslide composed of pyroclastic material and water that flows down from a volcano, typically along a river valley. The term '_____' originated in the Javanese language of Indonesia. They can be best described as volcanic mudflows. They may not necessarily be caused by volcanic activity, but at the very least do originate from some type of volcanism.

Chapter 13. Unsafe Ground: Landslides and Other Mass Movements

a. 1703 Genroku earthquake
b. 1509 Istanbul earthquake
c. Lahar
d. 1700 Cascadia earthquake

11. A _____ is a geological phenomenon which includes a wide range of ground movement, such as rock falls, deep failure of slopes and shallow debris flows, which can occur in offshore, coastal and onshore environments. Although the action of gravity is the primary driving force for a _____ to occur, there are other contributing factors affecting the original slope stability. Typically, pre-conditional factors build up specific sub-surface conditions that make the area/slope prone to failure, whereas the actual _____ often requires a trigger before being released.
 a. Mass wasting
 b. 1700 Cascadia earthquake
 c. 1509 Istanbul earthquake
 d. Landslide

12. A _____ or mudslide is the most rapid (up to 80 km/h, or 50 mph) and fluid type of downhill mass wasting. It is a rapid movement of a large mass of mud formed from loose earth and water. Similar terms are mudslide (not very liquid), mud stream, debris flow (e.g. in high mountains), j>ökulhlaup, and lahar
 a. Mudflow
 b. 1703 Genroku earthquake
 c. 1509 Istanbul earthquake
 d. 1700 Cascadia earthquake

13. _____ is the result of the transformation of an existing rock type, the protolith, in a process called metamorphism, which means 'change in form'. The protolith is subjected to heat and pressure (temperatures greater than 150 to 200 >°C and pressures of 1500 bars) causing profound physical and/or chemical change. The protolith may be sedimentary rock, igneous rock or another older _____.
 a. Migmatite
 b. Metavolcanic rock
 c. Sedimentary rock
 d. Metamorphic rock

14. An _____ is a fan-shaped deposit formed where a fast flowing stream flattens, slows, and spreads typically at the exit of a canyon onto a flatter plain. A convergence of neighboring fans into a single apron of deposits against a slope is called a bajada, or compound _____.
 a. Alluvial fan
 b. AL 129-1
 c. AL 333
 d. AASHTO Soil Classification System

15. An _____ is a rapid flow of snow down a slope, from either natural triggers or human activity. Typically occurring in mountainous terrain, an _____ can mix air and water with the descending snow. Powerful avalanches have the capability to entrain ice, rocks, trees, and other material on the slope; however avalanches are always initiated in snow, are primarily composed of flowing snow, and are distinct from mudslides, rock slides, rock avalanches, and serac collapses from an icefall.
 a. Avalanche
 b. AL 333
 c. AASHTO Soil Classification System
 d. AL 129-1

16. A _____ is an elongated whale-shaped hill formed by glacial action. Its long axis is parallel with the movement of the ice, with the blunter end facing into the glacial movement. They may be more than 45 m (150 ft) high and more than 0.8 km (1/2 mile) long, and are often in _____ fields of similarly shaped, sized and oriented hills. They usually have layers indicating that the material was repeatedly added to a core, which may be of rock or glacial till.
 a. Drumlin
 b. Monadnock
 c. Sandur
 d. 1509 Istanbul earthquake

Chapter 13. Unsafe Ground: Landslides and Other Mass Movements

17. _____ is a term given to an accumulation of broken rock fragments at the base of crags, mountain cliffs, or valley shoulders. Landforms associated with these materials are sometimes called _____ slopes or talus piles. These deposits typically have a concave upwards form, while the maximum inclination of such deposits corresponds to the angle of repose of the mean debris size.
   a. 1700 Cascadia earthquake
   b. 1703 Genroku earthquake
   c. 1509 Istanbul earthquake
   d. Scree

18. The _____ was an ancient oceanic plate, which began subducting under the west coast of the North American Plate-- then located in modern Utah-- as Pangaea broke apart during the Jurassic period. It is named for the Farallon Islands which are located just west of San Francisco, California.

   Over time the central part of the _____ was completely subducted under the southwestern part of the North American Plate. The remains of the _____ are the Juan de Fuca, Explorer and Gorda Plates, subducting under the northern part of the North American Plate, the Cocos Plate subducting under Central America and the Nazca Plate subducting under the South American Plate.

   a. Rivera Plate
   b. Farallon Plate
   c. Fault trace
   d. Cocos Plate

19. The _____ is a geological signature, usually a thin band, dated to (65.5 ± 0.3) Ma (million years ago). The boundary marks the end of the Mesozoic era and the beginning of the Cenozoic era, and is associated with the Cretaceous-Tertiary extinction event, a mass extinction.
   a. 1700 Cascadia earthquake
   b. Shiva crater
   c. 1509 Istanbul earthquake
   d. K-T boundary

20. A _____ is an opening in a planet's surface or crust, which allows hot, molten rock, ash, and gases to escape from below the surface. Volcanic activity involving the extrusion of rock tends to form mountains or features like mountains over a period of time.
   a. 1703 Genroku earthquake
   b. 1509 Istanbul earthquake
   c. 1700 Cascadia earthquake
   d. Volcano

21. _____ is a soft, white, porous sedimentary rock, a form of limestone composed of the mineral calcite. It forms under relatively deep marine conditions from the gradual accumulation of minute calcite plates shed from micro-organisms called coccolithophores. It is common to find flint and chert nodules embedded in _____.
   a. 1509 Istanbul earthquake
   b. 1700 Cascadia earthquake
   c. 1703 Genroku earthquake
   d. Chalk

22. _____ is the geomorphic process by which soil, regolith, and rock move downslope under the force of gravity. Types of _____ include creep, slides, flows, topples, and falls, each with its own characteristic features, and taking place over timescales from seconds to years. _____ occurs on both terrestrial and submarine slopes, and has been observed on Earth, Mars, and Venus.
   a. 1509 Istanbul earthquake
   b. Soil liquefaction
   c. 1700 Cascadia earthquake
   d. Mass wasting

23. The field of _____ encompasses the analysis of static and dynamic stability of slopes of earth and rock-fill dams, slopes of other types of embankments, excavated slopes, and natural slopes in soil and soft rock.

Chapter 13. Unsafe Ground: Landslides and Other Mass Movements

Earthen slopes can develop a cut-spherical weakness zone. The probability of this happening can be calculated in advance using a simple 2-D circular analysis package. A primary difficulty with analysis is locating the most-probable slip plane for any given situation. Many landslides have only been analyzed after the fact.

a. Pore water pressure
b. Groundwater-related subsidence
c. Vibro replacement stone columns
d. Slope stability

24. The _____ is an engineering property of granular materials. The _____ is the maximum angle of a stable slope determined by friction, cohesion and the shapes of the particles.

When bulk granular materials are poured onto a horizontal surface, a conical pile will form. The internal angle between the surface of the pile and the horizontal surface is known as the _____ and is related to the density, surface area, and coefficient of friction of the material.

a. AL 129-1
b. AASHTO Soil Classification System
c. AL 333
d. Angle of repose

25. An _____ is the result of a sudden release of energy in the Earth's crust that creates seismic waves. They are recorded with a seismometer or the related and mostly obsolete Richter magnitude, with a magnitude 3 or lower _____ being mostly imperceptible and magnitude 7 causing serious damage over large areas.

a. Earthquake
b. AL 333
c. AASHTO Soil Classification System
d. AL 129-1

26. In geology a _____ is the smallest division of a geologic formation or stratigraphic rock series marked by well-defined divisional planes (bedding planes) separating it from layers above and below. A _____ is the smallest lithostratigraphic unit, usually ranging in thickness from a centimeter to several meters and distinguishable from beds above and below it. Beds can be differentiated in various ways, including rock or mineral type and particle size.

a. Biozones
b. Bed
c. Cyclostratigraphy
d. Sequence stratigraphy

27. _____ is any penetrative planar fabric present in rocks. _____ is common to rocks affected by regional metamorphic compression typical of orogenic belts. Rocks exhibiting _____ include the typical metamorphic rock sequence of slate, phyllite, schist and gneiss.

a. Porphyroblast
b. Hornfels
c. Shock metamorphism
d. Foliation

28. _____ is any particulate matter that can be transported by fluid flow, and which eventually is deposited.

They are most often transported by water (fluvial processes) transported by wind (aeolian processes) and glaciers. Beach sands and river channel deposits are examples of fluvial transport and deposition, though _____ also often settles out of slow-moving or standing water in lakes and oceans.

a. Bovey Beds
b. Sediment
c. Brickearth
d. Quicksand

Chapter 13. Unsafe Ground: Landslides and Other Mass Movements

29. A _____ is a natural depression or hole in the surface topography caused by the removal of soil or bedrock, often both, by water. They may vary in size from less than a meter to several hundred meters both in diameter and depth, and vary in form from soil-lined bowls to bedrock-edged chasms. They may be formed gradually or suddenly, and are found worldwide.
   a. Sinkhole
   b. 1703 Genroku earthquake
   c. 1509 Istanbul earthquake
   d. 1700 Cascadia earthquake

30. _____ is a fine-grained sedimentary rock whose original constituents were clay minerals or muds. It is characterized by thin laminae breaking with an irregular curving fracture, often splintery and usually parallel to the often-indistinguishable bedding plane. This property is called fissility.
   a. Metasediment
   b. Shale
   c. Pelagic sediments
   d. Mudstone

31. Two important classifications of weathering processes exist -- physical and _____. Mechanical or physical weathering involves the breakdown of rocks and soils through direct contact with atmospheric conditions, such as heat, water, ice and pressure. The second classification, _____, involves the direct effect of atmospheric chemicals or biologically produced chemicals (also known as biological weathering) in the breakdown of rocks, soils and minerals.
   a. Chemical weathering
   b. 1509 Istanbul earthquake
   c. Physical weathering
   d. Weathering

32. Two important classifications of weathering processes exist -- _____ and chemical weathering. Mechanical or _____ involves the breakdown of rocks and soils through direct contact with atmospheric conditions, such as heat, water, ice and pressure. The second classification, chemical weathering, involves the direct effect of atmospheric chemicals or biologically produced chemicals (also known as biological weathering) in the breakdown of rocks, soils and minerals.
   a. Weathering
   b. 1509 Istanbul earthquake
   c. Physical weathering
   d. Frost disintegration

33. _____ is the decomposition of Earth rocks, soils and their minerals through direct contact with the planet's atmosphere. _____ occurs in situ, or 'with no movement', and thus should not be confused with erosion, which involves the movement of rocks and minerals by agents such as water, ice, wind and gravity.

   Two important classifications of _____ processes exist -- physical and chemical _____.

   a. 1509 Istanbul earthquake
   b. Weathering
   c. Physical weathering
   d. Frost disintegration

1. A _____ is a deep active seismic area in a subduction zone. Differential motion along the zone produces deep-seated earthquakes, the foci of which may be as deep as about 700 kilometres (435 miles.) They develop beneath volcanic island arcs and continental margins above active subduction zones.
   a. Pit crater
   b. Wadati-Benioff zone
   c. Pyroclastic flow
   d. Lava

2. A _____ is a mountain rising from the ocean seafloor that does not reach to the water's surface (sea level), and thus is not an island. These are typically formed from extinct volcanoes, that rise abruptly and are usually found rising from a seafloor of 1,000-4,000 meters depth. They are defined by oceanographers as independent features that rise to at least 1,000 meters above the seafloor.
   a. 1700 Cascadia earthquake
   b. 1509 Istanbul earthquake
   c. Seamount
   d. 1703 Genroku earthquake

3. _____ is a soft, white, porous sedimentary rock, a form of limestone composed of the mineral calcite. It forms under relatively deep marine conditions from the gradual accumulation of minute calcite plates shed from micro-organisms called coccolithophores. It is common to find flint and chert nodules embedded in _____.
   a. 1703 Genroku earthquake
   b. Chalk
   c. 1509 Istanbul earthquake
   d. 1700 Cascadia earthquake

4. _____, also called erosional _____ or downward erosion or vertical erosion is a geological process that deepens the channel of a stream or valley by removing material from the stream's bed or the valley's floor. How fast _____ occurs depends on the stream's base level, which is the lowest point to which the stream can erode. Sea level is the ultimate base level, but many streams have a higher 'temporary' base level because they empty into another body of water that is above sea level or encounter bedrock that resists erosion.
   a. Seafloor spreading
   b. Downcutting
   c. Transgression
   d. Deposition

5. _____ is the removal of solids (sediment, soil, rock and other particles) in the natural environment. It usually occurs due to transport by wind, water, or ice; by down-slope creep of soil and other material under the force of gravity; or by living organisms, such as burrowing animals, in the case of bioerosion.

   _____ is distinguished from weathering, which is the process of chemical or physical breakdown of the minerals in the rocks, although the two processes may occur concurrently.

   a. AL 129-1
   b. AASHTO Soil Classification System
   c. Erosion
   d. AL 333

6. _____ is water located beneath the ground surface in soil pore spaces and in the fractures of lithologic formations. A unit of rock or an unconsolidated deposit is called an aquifer when it can yield a usable quantity of water. The depth at which soil pore spaces or fractures and voids in rock become completely saturated with water is called the water table.
   a. 1509 Istanbul earthquake
   b. Depression focused recharge
   c. 1700 Cascadia earthquake
   d. Groundwater

Chapter 14. Streams and Associated Flooding: The Geology of Running Water

7. _____ is a fluvial process of erosion that lengthens a stream, a valley or a gully at its head and also enlarges its drainage basin. The stream erodes away at the rock and soil at its headwaters in the opposite direction that it flows. Once a stream has begun to cut back, the erosion is sped up by the steep gradient the water is flowing down. As water erodes a path from its headwaters to its mouth at a standing body of water, it tries to cut an ever-shallower path. This leads to increased erosion at the steepest parts, which is _____.
   a. Transgression
   b. Saltation
   c. Headward erosion
   d. Mid-ocean ridge

8. The _____ describes the continuous movement of water on, above, and below the surface of the Earth. Since the _____ is truly a 'cycle,' there is no beginning or end. Water can change states among liquid, vapor, and ice at various places in the _____.
   a. Water cycle
   b. Vadose zone
   c. Cone of depression
   d. Hydraulic conductivity

9. The _____ is an active transform fault, located between the North American Plate and the Pacific Plate, Canada's equivalent of the San Andreas Fault. The _____ forms a triple junction on its south with the Cascadia subduction zone and the Explorer Ridge (the Queen Charlotte Triple Junction.) The fault is named for Queen Charlotte Island which lies just north of the triple junction.
   a. 1703 Genroku earthquake
   b. 1509 Istanbul earthquake
   c. 1700 Cascadia earthquake
   d. Queen Charlotte fault

10. _____ are a type of elastic surface wave that travel on solids. They are produced on the Earth by earthquakes, in which case they are also known as 'ground roll', or by other sources of seismic energy such as an explosion or even a sledgehammer impact. They are also produced in materials by acoustic transducers, and are used in non-destructive testing for detecting defects.
    a. Tornillo event
    b. Seismic waves
    c. Maximum magnitude
    d. Rayleigh waves

11. _____ is the natural or artificial removal of surface and sub-surface water from an area. Many agricultural soils need _____ to improve production or to manage water supplies.

The earliest archaeological record of an advanced system of _____ comes from the Indus Valley Civilization from around 3100 BC in what is now Pakistan and North India.

   a. 1700 Cascadia earthquake
   b. 1703 Genroku earthquake
   c. 1509 Istanbul earthquake
   d. Drainage

12. A _____ is an extent of land where water from rain or snow melt drains downhill into a body of water, such as a river, lake, reservoir, estuary, wetland, sea or ocean. The _____ includes both the streams and rivers that convey the water as well as the land surfaces from which water drains into those channels, and is separated from adjacent basins by a drainage divide.

The _____ acts like a funnel, collecting all the water within the area covered by the basin and channelling it into a waterway.

Chapter 14. Streams and Associated Flooding: The Geology of Running Water 149

   a. 1703 Genroku earthquake   b. 1700 Cascadia earthquake
   c. 1509 Istanbul earthquake   d. Drainage basin

13. A _____, is the line separating neighbouring drainage basins (catchments.) In hilly country, the divide lies along topographical peaks and ridges, but in flat country (especially where the ground is marshy) the divide may be invisible - just a more or less notional line on the ground on either side of which falling raindrops will start a journey to different rivers, and even to different sides of a region or continent.
   a. Drainage divide   b. 1703 Genroku earthquake
   c. 1509 Istanbul earthquake   d. 1700 Cascadia earthquake

14. In geology, a _____ or _____ line is a planar fracture in rock in which the rock on one side of the fracture has moved with respect to the rock on the other side. Large faults within the Earth's crust are the result of differential or shear motion and active _____ zones are the causal locations of most earthquakes. Earthquakes are caused by energy release during rapid slippage along a _____.
   a. Dali   b. Stack
   c. Fault   d. Combe

15. A _____ is any glacially formed accumulation of unconsolidated glacial debris (soil and rock) which can occur in currently glaciated and formerly glaciated regions, such as those areas acted upon by a past ice age. This debris may have been plucked off the valley floor as a glacier advanced or it may have fallen off the valley walls as a result of frost wedging. Moraines may be composed of silt like glacial flour to large boulders.
   a. 1700 Cascadia earthquake   b. 1509 Istanbul earthquake
   c. 1703 Genroku earthquake   d. Moraine

16. The lithosphere is broken up into what are called _____. In the case of Earth, there are eight major and many minor plates The lithospheric plates ride on the asthenosphere. These plates move in relation to one another at one of three types of plate boundaries: convergent, or collisional boundaries; divergent boundaries, also called spreading centers; and transform boundaries.
   a. Copperbelt Province   b. Thrust fault
   c. Gorda Ridge   d. Tectonic plates

17. _____ is mechanical scraping of a rock surface by friction between rocks and moving particles during their transport in wind, glacier, waves, gravity or running water, after friction, the moving particles dislodge loose and weak debris from the side of the rock, these particles can be dissolved in the water source.

The intensity of _____ depends on the hardness, concentration, velocity and mass of moving particles.

A virtually smooth marine platform cut by the ocean waves at a coastline.

   a. AASHTO Soil Classification System   b. AL 129-1
   c. Abrasion   d. AL 333

18. In mineralogy and crystallography, a _____ is a unique arrangement of atoms in a crystal. A _____ is composed of a motif, a set of atoms arranged in a particular way, and a lattice. Motifs are located upon the points of a lattice, which is an array of points repeating periodically in three dimensions.

Chapter 14. Streams and Associated Flooding: The Geology of Running Water

    a. 1700 Cascadia earthquake
    b. Crystal structure
    c. 1703 Genroku earthquake
    d. 1509 Istanbul earthquake

19. _____ is any particulate matter that can be transported by fluid flow, and which eventually is deposited.

They are most often transported by water (fluvial processes) transported by wind (aeolian processes) and glaciers. Beach sands and river channel deposits are examples of fluvial transport and deposition, though _____ also often settles out of slow-moving or standing water in lakes and oceans.

    a. Brickearth
    b. Bovey Beds
    c. Quicksand
    d. Sediment

20. _____ is a common extrusive volcanic rock. It is usually grey to black and fine-grained due to rapid cooling of lava at the surface of a planet. It may be porphyritic containing larger crystals in a fine matrix, or vesicular, or frothy scoria.

    a. 1509 Istanbul earthquake
    b. 1703 Genroku earthquake
    c. 1700 Cascadia earthquake
    d. Basalt

21. In geology a _____ is the smallest division of a geologic formation or stratigraphic rock series marked by well-defined divisional planes (bedding planes) separating it from layers above and below. A _____ is the smallest lithostratigraphic unit, usually ranging in thickness from a centimeter to several meters and distinguishable from beds above and below it. Beds can be differentiated in various ways, including rock or mineral type and particle size.

    a. Biozones
    b. Bed
    c. Sequence stratigraphy
    d. Cyclostratigraphy

22. The term _____ describes particles in a flowing fluid (usually a river) that are transported along the bed. This is in opposition to suspended load and wash load which are carried entirely in suspension.

_____ moves by a variety of methods, including rolling, sliding, traction, and saltation.

    a. Coastal erosion
    b. Gravitational erosion
    c. Bed load
    d. Fault-block

23. _____ is the term for material, especially ions from chemical weathering, that are carried in solution by a stream.

    a. Marine clay
    b. Cap carbonates
    c. Palynomorph
    d. Dissolved load

24. In geology, _____ is a specific type of particle transport by fluids such as wind, or the denser fluid water. It occurs when loose material is removed from a bed and carried by the fluid, before being transported back to the surface. Examples include pebble transport by rivers, sand drift over desert surfaces, soil blowing over fields, or even snow drift over smooth surfaces such as those in the Arctic or Canadian Prairies.

    a. Transgression
    b. Permineralization
    c. Hydrothermal circulation
    d. Saltation

Chapter 14. Streams and Associated Flooding: The Geology of Running Water 151

25. The _____ or Appalachian orogeny is one of the geological mountain-forming events (orogeny) that formed the Appalachian Mountains and Allegheny Mountains. The term and spelling 'Alleghany Orogeny' (sic) originally proposed by H.P. Woodward (1957, 1958) is preferred usage. Approximately 350 million to 300 million years ago, in the Carboniferous period, the combined continents of Europe and Africa (Gondwana) collided with North America to form the supercontinent of Pangaea.
    a. Alpine orogeny
    b. Alice Springs Orogeny
    c. Alleghenian orogeny
    d. Antler orogeny

26. _____ is the largest volcano on earth in terms of area covered and one of five volcanoes that form the Island of Hawaii in the U.S. state of Hawai>Ê»i in the Pacific Ocean. It is an active shield volcano, with a volume estimated at approximately 18,000 cubic miles (75,000 kmÂ³), although its peak is about 120 feet (37 m) lower than that of its neighbor, Mauna Kea. The Hawaiian name '_____' means 'Long Mountain'.
    a. 1700 Cascadia earthquake
    b. 1703 Genroku earthquake
    c. 1509 Istanbul earthquake
    d. Mauna Loa

27. A _____ is an opening in a planet's surface or crust, which allows hot, molten rock, ash, and gases to escape from below the surface. Volcanic activity involving the extrusion of rock tends to form mountains or features like mountains over a period of time.
    a. 1700 Cascadia earthquake
    b. 1509 Istanbul earthquake
    c. 1703 Genroku earthquake
    d. Volcano

28. _____ is soil or sediments deposited by a river or other running water. _____ is typically made up of a variety of materials, including fine particles of silt and clay and larger particles of sand and gravel.

Flowing water associated with glaciers may also deposit _____, but deposits directly from ice are not _____ .

    a. AL 129-1
    b. AL 333
    c. AASHTO Soil Classification System
    d. Alluvium

29. A _____ is flat or nearly flat land adjacent to a stream or river that experiences occasional or periodic flooding. It includes the floodway, which consists of the stream channel and adjacent areas that carry flood flows, and the flood fringe, which are areas covered by the flood, but which do not experience a strong current.

They generally contain unconsolidated sediments, often extending below the bed of the stream.

    a. 1703 Genroku earthquake
    b. 1509 Istanbul earthquake
    c. 1700 Cascadia earthquake
    d. Floodplain

30. A _____ in general is a bend in a sinuous watercourse. A _____ is formed when the moving water in a river erodes the outer banks and widens its valley. A stream of any volume may assume a meandering course, alternatively eroding sediments from the outside of a bend and depositing them on the inside.
    a. Meander
    b. 1703 Genroku earthquake
    c. 1509 Istanbul earthquake
    d. 1700 Cascadia earthquake

Chapter 14. Streams and Associated Flooding: The Geology of Running Water

31. _____ refers to natural mountain building, and may be studied as a tectonic structural event, (b) as a geographical event, and (c) a chronological event. Orogenic events (a) cause distinctive structural phenomena and related tectonic activity, (b) affect certain regions of rocks and crust, and (c) happen within a specific period of time.
- a. Orogeny
- b. Orogenesis
- c. Antler orogeny
- d. Alice Springs Orogeny

32. The _____ is a physiographic region of the Intermontane Plateaus, roughly centered on the Four Corners region of the southwestern United States. The province covers an area of 337,000 km^2 within western Colorado, northwestern New Mexico, southern and eastern Utah, and northern Arizona. About 90% of the area is drained by the Colorado River and its main tributaries; the Green, San Juan and Little Colorado.

Development of the province has in large part been influenced by structural features in its oldest rocks. Part of the Wasatch Line and its various faults form the western edge of the province. Faults that run parallel to the Wasatch Fault that lies along the Wasatch Range form the boundaries between the plateaus in the High Plateaus Section. The Uinta Basin, Uncompahgre Uplift, and the Paradox Basin were also created by movement along structural weaknesses in the region's oldest rock.

- a. Colorado Plateau
- b. 1703 Genroku earthquake
- c. 1509 Istanbul earthquake
- d. 1700 Cascadia earthquake

33. The _____ is the epoch from 1.8 million to 11550 years BP covering the world's recent period of repeated glaciations. The _____ epoch follows the Pliocene epoch and is followed by the Holocene epoch. The _____ is the third epoch of the Neogene period or 6th epoch of the Cenozoic Era. The end of the _____ corresponds with the retreat of the last continental glacier. It also corresponds with the end of the Paleolithic age used in archaeology.
- a. Sicilian Stage
- b. Tyrrhenian
- c. Pleistocene
- d. Late Pleistocene

34. The general term '_____' or, more precisely, 'glacial age' denotes a geological period of long-term reduction in the temperature of the Earth's surface and atmosphere, resulting in an expansion of continental ice sheets, polar ice sheets and alpine glaciers. Within a long-term _____, individual pulses of extra cold climate are termed 'glaciations'. Glaciologically, _____ implies the presence of extensive ice sheets in the northern and southern hemispheres; by this definition we are still in an _____.
- a. AASHTO Soil Classification System
- b. AL 333
- c. Ice age
- d. AL 129-1

35. _____ or dolomite rock is a sedimentary carbonate rock that contains a high percentage of the mineral dolomite. In old U.S.G.S. publications it was referred to as magnesian limestone. Most _____ formed as a magnesium replacement of limestone or lime mud prior to lithification.
- a. Jasperoid
- b. Lithification
- c. Pelagic sediments
- d. Dolostone

36. An _____ is a fan-shaped deposit formed where a fast flowing stream flattens, slows, and spreads typically at the exit of a canyon onto a flatter plain. A convergence of neighboring fans into a single apron of deposits against a slope is called a bajada, or compound _____.

Chapter 14. Streams and Associated Flooding: The Geology of Running Water

a. AASHTO Soil Classification System
b. AL 333
c. AL 129-1
d. Alluvial fan

37. A _____ is a natural formation (or landform) where a rock arch forms, with a natural passageway through underneath. Most natural arches form as a narrow ridge, walled by cliffs, become narrower from erosion, with a softer rock stratum under the cliff-forming stratum gradually eroding out until the rock shelters thus formed meet underneath the ridge, thus forming the arch. They commonly form where cliffs are subject to erosion from the sea, rivers or weathering (sub-aerial processes); the processes 'find' weaknesses in rocks and work on them, making them bigger until they break through.
   a. 1703 Genroku earthquake
   b. 1509 Istanbul earthquake
   c. 1700 Cascadia earthquake
   d. Natural arch

38. A _____ is a stream that branches off and flows away from a main stream channel. They are a common feature of river deltas. The phenomenon is known as river bifurcation.
   a. Distributary
   b. 1509 Istanbul earthquake
   c. 1703 Genroku earthquake
   d. 1700 Cascadia earthquake

39. A _____ is a geological phenomenon which includes a wide range of ground movement, such as rock falls, deep failure of slopes and shallow debris flows, which can occur in offshore, coastal and onshore environments. Although the action of gravity is the primary driving force for a _____ to occur, there are other contributing factors affecting the original slope stability. Typically, pre-conditional factors build up specific sub-surface conditions that make the area/slope prone to failure, whereas the actual _____ often requires a trigger before being released.
   a. Mass wasting
   b. 1700 Cascadia earthquake
   c. 1509 Istanbul earthquake
   d. Landslide

40. _____ is the geological process by which material is added to a landform or land mass. Fluids such as wind and water, as well as sediment gravity flows, transport previously eroded sediment, which, at the loss of enough kinetic energy in the fluid, is deposited, building up layers of sediment.

_____ occurs when the forces responsible for sediment transportation are no longer sufficient to overcome the forces of particle weight and friction, which resist motion.

   a. Headward erosion
   b. Diagenesis
   c. Downcutting
   d. Deposition

41. The _____ is a continental transform fault that runs a length of roughly 800 miles (1,300 km) through California in the United States. The fault's motion is right-lateral strike-slip (horizontal motion.) It forms the tectonic boundary between the Pacific Plate and the North American Plate.
   a. 1700 Cascadia earthquake
   b. San Andreas Fault
   c. 1509 Istanbul earthquake
   d. 1703 Genroku earthquake

42. _____ is a naturally occurring granular material composed of finely divided rock and mineral particles.

As the term is used by geologists, _____ particles range in diameter from 0.0625 (or $>^1\!\!/_{16}$ mm, or 62.5 micrometers) to 2 millimeters. An individual particle in this range size is termed a _____ grain.

a. Sand
b. 1700 Cascadia earthquake
c. 1509 Istanbul earthquake
d. 1703 Genroku earthquake

43. A _____ or sand blow is a cone of sand formed by the ejection of sand onto a surface from a central point. The sand builds up as a cone with slopes at the sand's angle of repose. A crater is commonly seen at the summit. The cone looks like a small volcanic cone and can range in size from millimetres to metres in diameter.
   a. 1700 Cascadia earthquake
   b. 1509 Istanbul earthquake
   c. Sand volcano
   d. 1703 Genroku earthquake

Chapter 15. Restless Realm: Oceans and Coasts

1. The _____ is the zone of the ocean floor that separates the thin oceanic crust from thick continental crust. Continental margins constitute about 28% of the oceanic area.

The transition from continental to oceanic crust commonly occurs within the outer part of the margin, called continental rise.

a. Cuspate forelands
b. Continental margin
c. Longshore drift
d. 1509 Istanbul earthquake

2. The _____ is the extended perimeter of each continent and associated coastal plain, and was part of the continent during the glacial periods, but is undersea during interglacial periods such as the current epoch by relatively shallow seas (known as shelf seas) and gulfs.

The continental rise is below the slope, but landward of the abyssal plains. Its gradient is intermediate between the slope and the shelf, on the order of 0.5-1°.

a. Continental shelf
b. 1509 Istanbul earthquake
c. 1700 Cascadia earthquake
d. 1703 Genroku earthquake

3. The _____ is the rigid outermost shell of a rocky planet.

In the Earth, the _____ includes the crust and the uppermost mantle, which constitute the hard and rigid outer layer of the planet. The _____ is underlain by the asthenosphere, the weaker, hotter, and deeper part of the upper mantle.

a. Continental drift
b. Juan de Fuca Ridge
c. Lithosphere
d. Gorda Ridge

4. The _____ is a geological signature, usually a thin band, dated to (65.5 ± 0.3) Ma (million years ago). The boundary marks the end of the Mesozoic era and the beginning of the Cenozoic era, and is associated with the Cretaceous-Tertiary extinction event, a mass extinction.

a. 1700 Cascadia earthquake
b. 1509 Istanbul earthquake
c. Shiva crater
d. K-T boundary

5. The _____ is a mid-ocean ridge, a divergent tectonic plate boundary located along the floor of the Atlantic Ocean, and the longest mountain range in the world. It separates the Eurasian Plate and North American Plate in the North Atlantic, and the African Plate from the South American Plate in the South Atlantic. The MAR extends from a junction with the Gakkel Ridge (Mid-Arctic Ridge) northeast of Greenland southward to the Bouvet Triple Junction in the South Atlantic.

a. 1703 Genroku earthquake
b. 1700 Cascadia earthquake
c. 1509 Istanbul earthquake
d. Mid-Atlantic Ridge

6. An _____ or accretionary prism is formed from sediments that are accreted onto the non-subducting tectonic plate at a convergent plate boundary. Most of the material in the _____ consists of marine sediments scraped off from the downgoing slab of oceanic crust but in some cases includes the erosional products of volcanic island arcs formed on the overriding plate.

The internal structure of an _____ is similar to that found in a thin-skinned foreland thrust belt.

Chapter 15. Restless Realm: Oceans and Coasts

a. AL 129-1
b. AASHTO Soil Classification System
c. AL 333
d. Accretionary wedge

7. In geology, a _____ or _____ line is a planar fracture in rock in which the rock on one side of the fracture has moved with respect to the rock on the other side. Large faults within the Earth's crust are the result of differential or shear motion and active _____ zones are the causal locations of most earthquakes. Earthquakes are caused by energy release during rapid slippage along a _____.
   a. Dali
   b. Fault
   c. Stack
   d. Combe

8. A _____ is an underwater mountain range, typically having a valley known as a rift running along its spine, formed by plate tectonics. This type of oceanic ridge is characteristic of what is known as an oceanic spreading center, which is responsible for seafloor spreading. The uplifted sea floor results from convection currents which rise in the mantle as magma at a linear weakness in the oceanic crust, and emerge as lava, creating new crust upon cooling.
   a. Seafloor spreading
   b. Transgression
   c. Permineralization
   d. Mid-ocean ridge

9. The lithosphere is broken up into what are called _____. In the case of Earth, there are eight major and many minor plates The lithospheric plates ride on the asthenosphere. These plates move in relation to one another at one of three types of plate boundaries: convergent, or collisional boundaries; divergent boundaries, also called spreading centers; and transform boundaries.
   a. Gorda Ridge
   b. Tectonic plates
   c. Copperbelt Province
   d. Thrust fault

10. The fault surface of _____ is usually near vertical and the footwall moves either left or right or laterally with very little vertical motion. _____ with left-lateral motion are also known as sinistral faults. Those with right-lateral motion are also known as dextral faults.
    a. Pahoehoe lava
    b. Valley glaciers
    c. Strike-slip faults
    d. Principle of inclusions and components

11. _____ occurs at mid-ocean ridges, where new oceanic crust is formed through volcanic activity and then gradually moves away from the ridge. _____ helps explain continental drift in the theory of plate tectonics.

Earlier theories (e.g., by Alfred Wegener) of continental drift were that continents 'plowed' through the sea. The idea that the seafloor itself moves (and carries the continents with it) as it expands from a central axis was proposed by Harry Hess from Princeton University in the 1960s. The theory is well-accepted now, and the phenomenon is known to be caused by convection currents in the plastic, very weak upper mantle, or asthenosphere.

   a. Saltation
   b. Diagenesis
   c. Deposition
   d. Seafloor spreading

12. The _____, together with its northern extension towards Europe, the North Atlantic Drift, is a powerful, warm, and swift Atlantic ocean current that originates in the Gulf of Mexico, exits through the Strait of Florida, and follows the eastern coastlines of the United States and Newfoundland before crossing the Atlantic Ocean. The process of western intensification causes the _____ to be a northward accelerating current offshore the east coast of North America. At about 30>°W, 40>°N, it splits in two, with the northern stream crossing to northern Europe and the southern stream recirculating off West Africa.
   a. Gulf Stream
   b. 1509 Istanbul earthquake
   c. 1700 Cascadia earthquake
   d. 1703 Genroku earthquake

13. A _____ is a mountain rising from the ocean seafloor that does not reach to the water's surface (sea level), and thus is not an island. These are typically formed from extinct volcanoes, that rise abruptly and are usually found rising from a seafloor of 1,000-4,000 meters depth. They are defined by oceanographers as independent features that rise to at least 1,000 meters above the seafloor.
   a. 1700 Cascadia earthquake
   b. 1509 Istanbul earthquake
   c. Seamount
   d. 1703 Genroku earthquake

14. _____ is a soft, white, porous sedimentary rock, a form of limestone composed of the mineral calcite. It forms under relatively deep marine conditions from the gradual accumulation of minute calcite plates shed from micro-organisms called coccolithophores. It is common to find flint and chert nodules embedded in _____.
   a. 1509 Istanbul earthquake
   b. 1703 Genroku earthquake
   c. Chalk
   d. 1700 Cascadia earthquake

15. An _____ is an oceanographic phenomenon that involves wind-driven motion of dense, cooler, and usually nutrient-rich water towards the ocean surface, replacing the warmer, usually nutrient-depleted surface water. There are at least five types of _____: coastal _____, large-scale wind-driven _____ in the ocean interior, _____ associated with eddies, topographically-associated _____, and broad-diffusive _____ in the ocean interior.

Coastal _____ is the best known type of _____, and the most closely related to human activities as it supports some of the most productive fisheries in the world, like small pelagics (sardines, anchovies, etc.).

   a. AL 333
   b. AL 129-1
   c. AASHTO Soil Classification System
   d. Upwelling

16. _____ describes the large scale motions of Earth's lithosphere. The theory encompasses the older concepts of continental drift, developed during the first decades of the 20th century by Alfred Wegener, and seafloor spreading, understood during the 1960s.

The outermost part of the Earth's interior is made up of two layers: the lithosphere and the asthenosphere.

   a. Thrust fault
   b. Forearc
   c. Plate tectonics
   d. Continental crust

17. A _____ column (or _____) is a column of rising air in the lower altitudes of the Earth's atmosphere. They are created by the uneven heating of the Earth's surface from solar radiation, and an example of convection. The Sun warms the ground, which in turn warms the air directly above it.

a. 1700 Cascadia earthquake
b. 1509 Istanbul earthquake
c. 1703 Genroku earthquake
d. Thermal

18. The term _____ refers to the part of the large-scale ocean circulation that is driven by global density gradients created by surface heat and freshwater fluxes. The adjective thermohaline derives from thermo- referring to temperature and -haline referring to salt content, factors which together determine the density of sea water. Wind-driven surface currents (such as the Gulf Stream) head polewards from the equatorial Atlantic Ocean, cooling all the while and eventually sinking at high latitudes (forming North Atlantic Deep Water.)
   a. 1700 Cascadia earthquake
   b. 1703 Genroku earthquake
   c. 1509 Istanbul earthquake
   d. Thermohaline circulation

19. _____, (Navajo: >Ts>é Bit'a'>í, 'rock with wings' or 'winged rock') is a rock formation rising nearly 1,800 feet (550 m) above the high-desert plain on the Navajo Nation and in San Juan County, New Mexico.

_____ is composed of fractured volcanic breccia and black dikes of igneous rock called 'minette'. It is the erosional remnant of the throat of a volcano, and the volcanic breccia formed in a diatreme. The exposed rock probably was originally formed 2,500-3000 feet (750-1,000 meters) below the earth's surface, but it was exposed after millions of years of erosion. Wall-like sheets of minette, known as dikes, radiate away from the central formation. Radiometric age determinations of the minette establish that these volcanic rocks solidified about 27 million years ago.

   a. 1700 Cascadia earthquake
   b. Shiprock
   c. 1703 Genroku earthquake
   d. 1509 Istanbul earthquake

20. The _____ zone is the area that is exposed to the air at low tide and submerged at high tide, for example, the area between tide marks. This area can include many different types of habitats, including steep rocky cliffs, sandy beaches, or wetlands The area can be a narrow strip, as in Pacific islands that have only a narrow tidal range, or can include many meters of shoreline where shallow beach slope interacts with high tidal excursion.
   a. Overland flow
   b. Eutrophication
   c. AASHTO Soil Classification System
   d. Intertidal

21. In geology, _____ is the process that takes place at convergent boundaries by which one tectonic plate moves under another tectonic plate, sinking into the Earth's mantle, as the plates converge. A _____ zone is an area on Earth where two tectonic plates move towards one another and _____ occurs. Rates of _____ are typically measured in centimeters per year, with the average rate of convergence being approximately 2 to 8 centimeters per year (about the rate a fingernail grows.)
   a. Divergent boundary
   b. Subduction
   c. Motagua Fault
   d. Forearc

22. A _____ is a deep active seismic area in a subduction zone. Differential motion along the zone produces deep-seated earthquakes, the foci of which may be as deep as about 700 kilometres (435 miles.) They develop beneath volcanic island arcs and continental margins above active subduction zones.
   a. Pit crater
   b. Wadati-Benioff zone
   c. Lava
   d. Pyroclastic flow

Chapter 15. Restless Realm: Oceans and Coasts

23. A _____ is a geological phenomenon which includes a wide range of ground movement, such as rock falls, deep failure of slopes and shallow debris flows, which can occur in offshore, coastal and onshore environments. Although the action of gravity is the primary driving force for a _____ to occur, there are other contributing factors affecting the original slope stability. Typically, pre-conditional factors build up specific sub-surface conditions that make the area/slope prone to failure, whereas the actual _____ often requires a trigger before being released.
   a. Mass wasting
   b. Landslide
   c. 1700 Cascadia earthquake
   d. 1509 Istanbul earthquake

24. _____, is the water that washes up on shore after an incoming wave has broken. This action will cause sand and other light particles to be transported up the beach. The direction of the _____ varies with the prevailing wind, whereas the backwash is always perpendicular to the coastline.
   a. Cuspate forelands
   b. 1509 Istanbul earthquake
   c. Longshore drift
   d. Swash

25. The _____ is the maximum depth at which a water wave's passage causes significant water motion. For water depths larger than the _____, bottom sediments are no longer stirred by the wave motion above.

    In deep water, the water particles are moved in a circular orbital motion when a wave passes.

   a. Wave base
   b. 1703 Genroku earthquake
   c. 1509 Istanbul earthquake
   d. 1700 Cascadia earthquake

26. Geologically, a _____ is a long, narrow inlet with steep sides, created in a valley carved by glacial activity.

    The seeds of a _____ are laid when a glacier cuts a U-shaped valley through abrasion of the surrounding bedrock by the sediment it carries. Many such valleys were formed during the recent ice age.

   a. 1509 Istanbul earthquake
   b. 1703 Genroku earthquake
   c. Fjord
   d. 1700 Cascadia earthquake

27. _____ is a sedimentary rock. It is a natural chemical precipitate of carbonate minerals; typically aragonite, but often recrystallized to, or primarily, calcite.

    _____ forms as calcium carbonate is deposited from the water of mineral springs or rivulets that are saturated with dissolved calcium bicarbonate. The spring water from which the calcium carbonate precipitates can be hot, warm or cold. The rate of deposition increases with the temperature of the water, or alternatively, when biotic material accelerates the process of precipitation.

   a. 1509 Istanbul earthquake
   b. 1703 Genroku earthquake
   c. Travertine
   d. 1700 Cascadia earthquake

28. The _____ is a continental transform fault that runs a length of roughly 800 miles (1,300 km) through California in the United States. The fault's motion is right-lateral strike-slip (horizontal motion.) It forms the tectonic boundary between the Pacific Plate and the North American Plate.

a. 1703 Genroku earthquake
b. 1700 Cascadia earthquake
c. 1509 Istanbul earthquake
d. San Andreas Fault

29. _____, sometimes known as shore drift, is a geological process by which sediments such as sand or other materials, move along a beach shore. It uses the process of swash to push the material up the beach and backwash down the beach; until it reaches a groyne or another obstacle.

Where waves approach the coastline at an angle, when they break their swash pushes beach material up the beach at the same angle.

a. Swash
b. Cuspate forelands
c. 1509 Istanbul earthquake
d. Longshore drift

30. _____ is the result of the transformation of an existing rock type, the protolith, in a process called metamorphism, which means 'change in form'. The protolith is subjected to heat and pressure (temperatures greater than 150 to 200 >°C and pressures of 1500 bars) causing profound physical and/or chemical change. The protolith may be sedimentary rock, igneous rock or another older _____.

a. Sedimentary rock
b. Metavolcanic rock
c. Metamorphic rock
d. Migmatite

31. A _____ is any glacially formed accumulation of unconsolidated glacial debris (soil and rock) which can occur in currently glaciated and formerly glaciated regions, such as those areas acted upon by a past ice age. This debris may have been plucked off the valley floor as a glacier advanced or it may have fallen off the valley walls as a result of frost wedging. Moraines may be composed of silt like glacial flour to large boulders.

a. 1509 Istanbul earthquake
b. 1700 Cascadia earthquake
c. 1703 Genroku earthquake
d. Moraine

32. _____ is a naturally occurring granular material composed of finely divided rock and mineral particles.

As the term is used by geologists, _____ particles range in diameter from 0.0625 (or $>^1\!/_{16}$ mm, or 62.5 micrometers) to 2 millimeters. An individual particle in this range size is termed a _____ grain.

a. 1703 Genroku earthquake
b. 1700 Cascadia earthquake
c. 1509 Istanbul earthquake
d. Sand

33. In geology, _____ is transported rock debris overlying the solid bedrock. The term is also sometimes refers to organic debris so-transported. In the largest sense, it refers to the material left behind by retreating continental glaciers.

a. Patterned ground
b. Drift
c. Geodiversity
d. Platform cover

34. A _____, in biogeography, is an isthmus or wider land connection between otherwise separate areas, which allows terrestrial animals and plants to cross over and colonise new lands. They can be created by marine regression, in which sea levels fall, exposing shallow, previously submerged sections of continental shelf; or when new land is created by plate tectonics; or occasionally when the sea floor rises due to post-glacial rebound after an ice age.

Chapter 15. Restless Realm: Oceans and Coasts   161

a. 1703 Genroku earthquake
b. 1509 Istanbul earthquake
c. Land bridge
d. 1700 Cascadia earthquake

35. A _____ or sandbar is a somewhat linear landform within or extending into a body of water, typically composed of sand, silt or small pebbles. A bar is characteristically long and narrow and develops where a stream or ocean current promotes deposition of granular material, resulting in localized shallowing of the water. Bars can appear in the sea, in a lake, or in a river.

The term _____ can be applied to larger geological units that form off a coastline as part of the process of coastal erosion. These include spits and baymouth bars that form across the front of embayments and rias. A tombolo is a bar that forms an isthmus between an island or offshore rock and a mainland shore.

a. 1509 Istanbul earthquake
b. 1700 Cascadia earthquake
c. Shoal
d. 1703 Genroku earthquake

36. An _____ is the result of a sudden release of energy in the Earth's crust that creates seismic waves. They are recorded with a seismometer or the related and mostly obsolete Richter magnitude, with a magnitude 3 or lower _____ being mostly imperceptible and magnitude 7 causing serious damage over large areas.
a. AASHTO Soil Classification System
b. AL 129-1
c. AL 333
d. Earthquake

37. A _____ is a natural formation (or landform) where a rock arch forms, with a natural passageway through underneath. Most natural arches form as a narrow ridge, walled by cliffs, become narrower from erosion, with a softer rock stratum under the cliff-forming stratum gradually eroding out until the rock shelters thus formed meet underneath the ridge, thus forming the arch. They commonly form where cliffs are subject to erosion from the sea, rivers or weathering (sub-aerial processes); the processes 'find' weaknesses in rocks and work on them, making them bigger until they break through.
a. 1509 Istanbul earthquake
b. 1703 Genroku earthquake
c. 1700 Cascadia earthquake
d. Natural arch

38. A _____ is a type of cave formed primarily by the wave action of the sea. The primary process involved is erosion. Sea caves are found throughout the world, actively forming along present coastlines and as relict sea caves on former coastlines.
a. 1509 Istanbul earthquake
b. Sea cave
c. 1700 Cascadia earthquake
d. 1703 Genroku earthquake

39. A _____ is a geological landform consisting of a steep and often vertical column or columns of rock in the sea near a coast. They are formed when part of a headland is eroded by hydraulic action, which is the force of the sea or water crashing against the rock. The force of the water weakens cracks in the headland, causing them to later collapse, forming free-standing stacks and even a small island.
a. Cleavage
b. Melange
c. Stack
d. Dali

40. _____ is any particulate matter that can be transported by fluid flow, and which eventually is deposited.

They are most often transported by water (fluvial processes) transported by wind (aeolian processes) and glaciers. Beach sands and river channel deposits are examples of fluvial transport and deposition, though _____ also often settles out of slow-moving or standing water in lakes and oceans.

a. Brickearth
b. Quicksand
c. Bovey Beds
d. Sediment

41. A _____ or sometimes ayre is a deposition landform in which an island is attached to the mainland by a narrow piece of land such as a spit or bar. They usually form because the island causes wave refraction, depositing sand and shingle moved by longshore drift in each direction around the island where the waves meet. Eustatic sea level rise may also contribute to accretion as material is pushed up with rising sea levels.

a. Tombolo
b. 1509 Istanbul earthquake
c. 1700 Cascadia earthquake
d. 1703 Genroku earthquake

42. _____ is the removal of solids (sediment, soil, rock and other particles) in the natural environment. It usually occurs due to transport by wind, water, or ice; by down-slope creep of soil and other material under the force of gravity; or by living organisms, such as burrowing animals, in the case of bioerosion.

_____ is distinguished from weathering, which is the process of chemical or physical breakdown of the minerals in the rocks, although the two processes may occur concurrently.

a. AL 333
b. AASHTO Soil Classification System
c. Erosion
d. AL 129-1

43. A type of seismic wave, the _____, secondary wave or shear wave (sometimes called an elastic _____) is one of the two main types of elastic body waves, so named because they move through the body of an object, unlike surface waves.

The _____ move as a shear or transverse wave, so motion is perpendicular to the direction of wave propagation: S-waves, like waves in a rope, as opposed to waves moving through a slinky, the P-wave. The wave moves through elastic media, and the main restoring force comes from shear effects.

a. S-wave
b. 1703 Genroku earthquake
c. 1700 Cascadia earthquake
d. 1509 Istanbul earthquake

44. _____ is molten rock expelled by a volcano during eruption. When first expelled from a volcanic vent, it is a liquid at temperatures from 700 >°C to 1,200 >°C (1,300 >°F to 2,200 >°F.) Although _____ is quite viscous, with about 100,000 times the viscosity of water, it can flow great distances before cooling and solidifying, because of both its thixotropic and shear thinning properties.

a. Pit crater
b. Supervolcano
c. Lava
d. Volcanic ash

Chapter 15. Restless Realm: Oceans and Coasts

45. A _____ is an area in which an S-Wave (secondary seismic wave) is not detected due to it not being able to pass through the outer core of the earth due to it being liquid. When an earthquake occurs, seismographs near the epicenter, out to about 90° distance, are able to record both Primary and Secondary waves, but those at a greater distance no longer detect the S-wave. This is because shear waves cannot pass through liquids.
   a. Receiver function
   b. Tornillo event
   c. Maximum magnitude
   d. Shadow zone

46. The _____ is the epoch from 1.8 million to 11550 years BP covering the world's recent period of repeated glaciations. The _____ epoch follows the Pliocene epoch and is followed by the Holocene epoch. The _____ is the third epoch of the Neogene period or 6th epoch of the Cenozoic Era. The end of the _____ corresponds with the retreat of the last continental glacier. It also corresponds with the end of the Paleolithic age used in archaeology.
   a. Pleistocene
   b. Tyrrhenian
   c. Sicilian Stage
   d. Late Pleistocene

47. In geology, a _____ is a location on the Earth's surface that has experienced active volcanism for a long period of time.

J. Tuzo Wilson came up with the idea in 1963 that volcanic chains like the Hawaiian Islands result from the slow movement of a tectonic plate across a 'fixed' _____ deep beneath the surface of the planet.

   a. 1700 Cascadia earthquake
   b. 1509 Istanbul earthquake
   c. 1703 Genroku earthquake
   d. Hotspot

48. The general term '_____' or, more precisely, 'glacial age' denotes a geological period of long-term reduction in the temperature of the Earth's surface and atmosphere, resulting in an expansion of continental ice sheets, polar ice sheets and alpine glaciers. Within a long-term _____, individual pulses of extra cold climate are termed 'glaciations'. Glaciologically, _____ implies the presence of extensive ice sheets in the northern and southern hemispheres; by this definition we are still in an _____
   a. Ice age
   b. AASHTO Soil Classification System
   c. AL 129-1
   d. AL 333

49. A _____ is a chain of volcanic islands or mountains formed by plate tectonics as an oceanic tectonic plate subducts under another tectonic plate and produces magma. There are two types of these: oceanic arcs (commonly called island arcs, a type of archipelago) and continental arcs. In the former, oceanic crust subducts beneath other oceanic crust on an adjacent plate, while in the latter case the oceanic crust subducts beneath continental crust. In some situations, a single subduction zone may show both aspects along its length, as part of a plate subducts beneath a continent and part beneath adjacent oceanic crust.
   a. 1703 Genroku earthquake
   b. 1700 Cascadia earthquake
   c. 1509 Istanbul earthquake
   d. Volcanic arc

50. _____ are structures constructed on coasts as part of coastal defence or to protect an anchorage from the effects of weather and longshore drift.

Offshore _____, also called bulkheads, reduce the intensity of wave action in inshore waters and thereby reduce coastal erosion. They are constructed some distance away from the coast or built with one end linked to the coast.

a. 1700 Cascadia earthquake
b. Breakwaters
c. 1703 Genroku earthquake
d. 1509 Istanbul earthquake

51. The _____ is a geologic period and system, the second of six of the Paleozoic era, and covers the time between 488.3>±1.7 to 443.7>±1.5 million years ago (ICS, 2004.) It follows the Cambrian period and is followed by the Silurian period. The _____ was defined by Charles Lapworth in 1879, to resolve a dispute between followers of Adam Sedgwick and Roderick Murchison, who were placing the same rock beds in northern Wales into the Cambrian and Silurian periods respectively.

a. AL 333
b. AASHTO Soil Classification System
c. AL 129-1
d. Ordovician

52. The _____ is a geologic period and system of the Paleozoic era spanning from >416 to 359.2 million years ago (ICS, 2004.).

During the _____ Period, which occurred in the Paleozoic era, the first fish evolved legsand started to walk on land as tetrapods around 365 Ma.

a. Gogo Formation
b. 1509 Istanbul earthquake
c. Xitun Formation
d. Devonian

53. _____ in geology is a landform sunken or depressed below the surrounding area. Depressions may be formed by various mechanisms, and may be referred to by a variety of technical terms.

- A basin may be any large sediment filled _____. In tectonics, it may refer specifically to a circular, syncline-like _____: a geologic basin; while in sedimentology, it may refer to an area thickly filled with sediment: sedimentary basin.

- A blowout is a _____ created by wind erosion typically in either a desert sand or dry soil (such as a post-glacial loess environment.)

- A graben is a down dropped and typically linear _____ or basin created by rifting in a region under tensional tectonic forces.

- An impact crater is a _____ created by an impact such as a meteorite crater.
- A pit crater is a _____ formed by a sinking, or caving in, of the ground surface lying over a void.
- A kettle is left behind when a piece of ice left behind in glacial deposits melts.

- A _____ may be an area of subsidence caused by the collapse of an underlying structure. Examples include sinkholes above caves in karst topography, or calderas.

a. Depression
b. Diamond Head
c. Cohesion
d. Geothermal

54. _____ is an offshore rise of water associated with a low pressure weather system, typically a tropical cyclone. _____ is caused primarily by high winds pushing on the ocean's surface. The wind causes the water to pile up higher than the ordinary sea level.

a. 1700 Cascadia earthquake
b. Storm surge
c. 1703 Genroku earthquake
d. 1509 Istanbul earthquake

Chapter 16. A Hidden Reserve: Groundwater

1. _____ is water located beneath the ground surface in soil pore spaces and in the fractures of lithologic formations. A unit of rock or an unconsolidated deposit is called an aquifer when it can yield a usable quantity of water. The depth at which soil pore spaces or fractures and voids in rock become completely saturated with water is called the water table.
   a. 1700 Cascadia earthquake
   b. 1509 Istanbul earthquake
   c. Groundwater
   d. Depression focused recharge

2. _____ is a naturally occurring granular material composed of finely divided rock and mineral particles.

As the term is used by geologists, _____ particles range in diameter from 0.0625 (or $>^1\!\!/\!_{16}$ mm, or 62.5 micrometers) to 2 millimeters. An individual particle in this range size is termed a _____ grain.

   a. 1703 Genroku earthquake
   b. Sand
   c. 1509 Istanbul earthquake
   d. 1700 Cascadia earthquake

3. A _____ is a natural depression or hole in the surface topography caused by the removal of soil or bedrock, often both, by water. They may vary in size from less than a meter to several hundred meters both in diameter and depth, and vary in form from soil-lined bowls to bedrock-edged chasms. They may be formed gradually or suddenly, and are found worldwide.
   a. 1703 Genroku earthquake
   b. Sinkhole
   c. 1509 Istanbul earthquake
   d. 1700 Cascadia earthquake

4. The _____ describes the continuous movement of water on, above, and below the surface of the Earth. Since the _____ is truly a 'cycle,' there is no beginning or end. Water can change states among liquid, vapor, and ice at various places in the _____.
   a. Water cycle
   b. Cone of depression
   c. Vadose zone
   d. Hydraulic conductivity

5. _____ is a measure of the void spaces in a material, and is measured as a fraction, between 0-1, or as a percentage between 0-100%. The term is used in multiple fields including ceramics, metallurgy, materials, manufacturing, earth sciences and construction.

Used in geology, hydrogeology, soil science, and building science, the _____ of a porous medium (such as rock or sediment) describes the fraction of void space in the material, where the void may contain, for example, air or water.

   a. Permeability
   b. Saltwater intrusion
   c. Porosity
   d. Phreatic zone

6. _____ is the naturally occurring, unconsolidated or loose covering on the Earth's surface. _____ is composed of particles of broken rock that have been altered by chemical, biological and environmental processes including weathering and erosion. _____ is different from its parent rock(s) source(s), altered by interactions between the lithosphere, hydrosphere, atmosphere, and the biosphere.
   a. Topsoil
   b. Slump
   c. Soil
   d. 1509 Istanbul earthquake

Chapter 16. A Hidden Reserve: Groundwater

7. _____ is a sedimentary rock composed largely of the mineral calcite (calcium carbonate: $CaCO_3$.) The deposition of _____ strata is often a by-product and indicator of biological activity in the geologic record. Calcium (along with nitrogen, phosphorus, and potassium) is a key mineral to plant nutrition: soils overlying _____ bedrock tend to be pre-fertilized with calcium.

   a. 1509 Istanbul earthquake
   b. 1700 Cascadia earthquake
   c. 1703 Genroku earthquake
   d. Limestone

8. The _____ is the earliest of three geologic eras of the Phanerozoic eon. The _____ spanned from roughly 542 to 251 million years ago (ICS, 2004), and is subdivided into six geologic periods; from oldest to youngest they are: the Cambrian, Ordovician, Silurian, Devonian, Carboniferous, and Permian.

   The _____ covers the time from the first appearance of abundant, soft-shelled fossils to the time when the continents were beginning to be dominated by large, relatively sophisticated reptiles and modern plants. The lower (oldest) boundary was classically set at the first appearance of creatures known as trilobites and archeocyathids.

   a. 1703 Genroku earthquake
   b. 1700 Cascadia earthquake
   c. Paleozoic
   d. 1509 Istanbul earthquake

9. A _____ is a deep active seismic area in a subduction zone. Differential motion along the zone produces deep-seated earthquakes, the foci of which may be as deep as about 700 kilometres (435 miles.) They develop beneath volcanic island arcs and continental margins above active subduction zones.

   a. Wadati-Benioff zone
   b. Lava
   c. Pyroclastic flow
   d. Pit crater

10. An _____ is an underground layer of water-bearing permeable rock or unconsolidated materials (gravel, sand, silt, or clay) from which groundwater can be usefully extracted using a water well. The study of water flow in aquifers and the characterization of aquifers is called hydrogeology. Related terms include: an aquitard, which is an impermeable layer along an _____, and an aquiclude (or aquifuge), which is a solid, impermeable area beneath an _____.

    a. Aquifer
    b. AASHTO Soil Classification System
    c. AL 333
    d. AL 129-1

11. _____ are the preserved remains or traces of animals, plants, and other organisms from the remote past. The totality of _____, both discovered and undiscovered, and their placement in fossiliferous rock formations and sedimentary layers (strata) is known as the fossil record. The study of _____ across geological time, how they were formed, and the evolutionary relationships between taxa (phylogeny) are some of the most important functions of the science of paleontology.

    a. 1700 Cascadia earthquake
    b. 1509 Istanbul earthquake
    c. 1703 Genroku earthquake
    d. Fossils

12. _____ in the earth sciences (commonly symbolized as κ a rock or k) is a measure of the ability of a material (typically unconsolidated material) to transmit fluids. It is of great importance in determining the flow characteristics of hydrocarbons in oil and gas reservoirs, and of groundwater in aquifers. It is typically measured in the lab by application of Darcy's law under steady state conditions or, more generally, by application of various solutions to the diffusion equation for unsteady flow conditions.

a. Phreatic zone
c. Permeability
b. Saltwater intrusion
d. Porosity

13. The _____ is the level at which the ground water pressure is equal to atmospheric pressure. It may be conveniently visualized as the 'surface' of the ground water in a given vicinity. It usually coincides with the phreatic surface, but can be many feet above it. As water infiltrates through pore spaces in the soil, it first passes through the zone of aeration, where the soil is unsaturated. At increasing depths water fills in more spaces, until the zone of saturation is reached. The relatively horizontal plane atop this zone constitutes the _____.
    a. Rock bolt
    c. Shaft construction
    b. Crosshole sonic logging
    d. Water table

14. The _____ is the subsurface layer in which groundwater seeps up from a water table by capillary action to fill pores. Pores at the base of the _____ are filled with water due to tension saturation. This saturated portion of the _____ is less than total capillary rise because of the presence of a mix in pore size.
    a. Star dunes
    c. Rockall
    b. Pahoehoe lava
    d. Capillary fringe

15. The _____, also termed the unsaturated zone, is the portion of Earth between the land surface and the phreatic zone or zone of saturation . It extends from the top of the ground surface to the water table. Water in the _____ has a pressure head less than atmospheric pressure, and is retained by a combination of adhesion , and capillary action (capillary groundwater.)
    a. Cone of depression
    c. Stemflow
    b. Hydraulic conductivity
    d. Vadose zone

16. _____ are a type of elastic surface wave that travel on solids. They are produced on the Earth by earthquakes, in which case they are also known as 'ground roll', or by other sources of seismic energy such as an explosion or even a sledgehammer impact. They are also produced in materials by acoustic transducers, and are used in non-destructive testing for detecting defects.
    a. Tornillo event
    c. Seismic waves
    b. Maximum magnitude
    d. Rayleigh waves

17. _____ are a group of rock-forming tectosilicate minerals which make up as much as 60% of the Earth's crust.

    _____ crystallize from magma in both intrusive and extrusive igneous rocks, as veins, and are also present in many types of metamorphic rock. Rock formed entirely of plagioclase feldspar is known as anorthosite.

    a. 1700 Cascadia earthquake
    c. 1509 Istanbul earthquake
    b. 1703 Genroku earthquake
    d. Feldspars

18. _____ or piezometric head is a specific measurement of water pressure above a geodetic datum. It is usually measured as a water surface elevation, expressed in units of length, at the entrance (or bottom) of a piezometer. In an aquifer, it can be calculated from the depth to water in a piezometric well (a specialized water well), and given information of the piezometer's elevation and screen depth.
    a. 1700 Cascadia earthquake
    c. 1703 Genroku earthquake
    b. 1509 Istanbul earthquake
    d. Hydraulic head

Chapter 16. A Hidden Reserve: Groundwater

19. A _____ is any glacially formed accumulation of unconsolidated glacial debris (soil and rock) which can occur in currently glaciated and formerly glaciated regions, such as those areas acted upon by a past ice age. This debris may have been plucked off the valley floor as a glacier advanced or it may have fallen off the valley walls as a result of frost wedging. Moraines may be composed of silt like glacial flour to large boulders.
   a. 1509 Istanbul earthquake
   b. 1700 Cascadia earthquake
   c. Moraine
   d. 1703 Genroku earthquake

20. A _____ occurs in an aquifer when groundwater is pumped from a well. In an unconfined (water table) aquifer, this is an actual depression of the water levels. In confined (artesian) aquifers, the _____ is a reduction in the pressure head surrounding the pumped well.
   a. Specific storage
   b. Water cycle
   c. Stemflow
   d. Cone of depression

21. _____ in geology is a landform sunken or depressed below the surrounding area. Depressions may be formed by various mechanisms, and may be referred to by a variety of technical terms.

   - A basin may be any large sediment filled _____. In tectonics, it may refer specifically to a circular, syncline-like _____: a geologic basin; while in sedimentology, it may refer to an area thickly filled with sediment: sedimentary basin.

   - A blowout is a _____ created by wind erosion typically in either a desert sand or dry soil (such as a post-glacial loess environment.)

   - A graben is a down dropped and typically linear _____ or basin created by rifting in a region under tensional tectonic forces.

   - An impact crater is a _____ created by an impact such as a meteorite crater.
   - A pit crater is a _____ formed by a sinking, or caving in, of the ground surface lying over a void.
   - A kettle is left behind when a piece of ice left behind in glacial deposits melts.

   - A _____ may be an area of subsidence caused by the collapse of an underlying structure. Examples include sinkholes above caves in karst topography, or calderas.

   a. Cohesion
   b. Geothermal
   c. Depression
   d. Diamond Head

22. _____ is molten rock expelled by a volcano during eruption. When first expelled from a volcanic vent, it is a liquid at temperatures from 700 >°C to 1,200 >°C (1,300 >°F to 2,200 >°F.) Although _____ is quite viscous, with about 100,000 times the viscosity of water, it can flow great distances before cooling and solidifying, because of both its thixotropic and shear thinning properties.
   a. Supervolcano
   b. Pit crater
   c. Volcanic ash
   d. Lava

23. The lithosphere is broken up into what are called _____. In the case of Earth, there are eight major and many minor plates The lithospheric plates ride on the asthenosphere. These plates move in relation to one another at one of three types of plate boundaries: convergent, or collisional boundaries; divergent boundaries, also called spreading centers; and transform boundaries.

   a. Copperbelt Province
   b. Thrust fault
   c. Gorda Ridge
   d. Tectonic plates

24. In geology, _____ refers to heat sources within the planet. _____ is technically an adjective (e.g., _____ energy) but in U.S. English the word has attained frequent use as a noun.

The planet's internal heat was originally generated during its accretion, due to gravitational binding energy, and since then additional heat has continued to be generated by decay heat from the radioactive decay of elements.

   a. Dali
   b. Diamond Head
   c. Stratification
   d. Geothermal

25. _____ are type of elastic wave, also called seismic waves, that can travel through gases, elastic solids and liquids, including the Earth. _____ can be produced by earthquakes and recorded by seismometers.

   a. 1509 Istanbul earthquake
   b. P-waves
   c. 1703 Genroku earthquake
   d. 1700 Cascadia earthquake

26. A type of seismic wave, the _____, secondary wave or shear wave (sometimes called an elastic _____) is one of the two main types of elastic body waves, so named because they move through the body of an object, unlike surface waves.

The _____ move as a shear or transverse wave, so motion is perpendicular to the direction of wave propagation: S-waves, like waves in a rope, as opposed to waves moving through a slinky, the P-wave. The wave moves through elastic media, and the main restoring force comes from shear effects.

   a. 1703 Genroku earthquake
   b. 1509 Istanbul earthquake
   c. 1700 Cascadia earthquake
   d. S-wave

27. Geologically, a _____ is a long, narrow inlet with steep sides, created in a valley carved by glacial activity.

The seeds of a _____ are laid when a glacier cuts a U-shaped valley through abrasion of the surrounding bedrock by the sediment it carries. Many such valleys were formed during the recent ice age.

   a. Fjord
   b. 1509 Istanbul earthquake
   c. 1703 Genroku earthquake
   d. 1700 Cascadia earthquake

28. _____ are instruments that measure and record motions of the ground, including those of seismic waves generated by earthquakes, nuclear explosions, and other seismic sources. Records of seismic waves allow seismologists to map the interior of the Earth, and locate and measure the size of these different sources. Seismograph is another Greek term from seismós and γρĺ¬φω, gráphĀ, to draw.

a. Seismometers
b. 1700 Cascadia earthquake
c. 1703 Genroku earthquake
d. 1509 Istanbul earthquake

29. In geology, engineering, and surveying, _____ is the motion of a surface (usually, the Earth's surface) as it shifts downward relative to a datum such as sea-level. The opposite of _____ is uplift, which results in an increase in elevation. There are several types of _____.
   a. 1509 Istanbul earthquake
   b. 1700 Cascadia earthquake
   c. Pothole
   d. Subsidence

30. An _____ is the result of a sudden release of energy in the Earth's crust that creates seismic waves. They are recorded with a seismometer or the related and mostly obsolete Richter magnitude, with a magnitude 3 or lower _____ being mostly imperceptible and magnitude 7 causing serious damage over large areas.
   a. AL 333
   b. Earthquake
   c. AASHTO Soil Classification System
   d. AL 129-1

31. A _____, commonly known as a cave formation, is a secondary mineral deposit formed in a cave. They are typically formed in limestone or dolostone solutional caves.

Water seeping through cracks in a cave's surrounding bedrock may dissolve certain compounds, usually calcite and aragonite, or gypsum (calcium sulfate.)

   a. 1700 Cascadia earthquake
   b. 1703 Genroku earthquake
   c. Speleothem
   d. 1509 Istanbul earthquake

32. A _____ is a type of speleothem (secondary mineral) that hangs from the ceiling or wall of limestone caves. It is sometimes referred to as dripstone.

They are formed by the deposition of calcium carbonate and other minerals, which is precipitated from mineralized water solutions.

   a. Stalactite
   b. 1509 Istanbul earthquake
   c. 1700 Cascadia earthquake
   d. 1703 Genroku earthquake

33. A _____ is a type of speleothem that rises from the floor of a limestone cave due to the dripping of mineralized solutions and the deposition of calcium carbonate.

The corresponding formation on the ceiling of a cave is known as a stalactite. If these formations grow together, the result is known as a column.

   a. 1509 Istanbul earthquake
   b. 1703 Genroku earthquake
   c. Stalagmite
   d. 1700 Cascadia earthquake

34. A _____ is an opening in a planet's surface or crust, which allows hot, molten rock, ash, and gases to escape from below the surface. Volcanic activity involving the extrusion of rock tends to form mountains or features like mountains over a period of time.

a. 1700 Cascadia earthquake
c. Volcano
b. 1509 Istanbul earthquake
d. 1703 Genroku earthquake

35. A _____ is a natural formation (or landform) where a rock arch forms, with a natural passageway through underneath. Most natural arches form as a narrow ridge, walled by cliffs, become narrower from erosion, with a softer rock stratum under the cliff-forming stratum gradually eroding out until the rock shelters thus formed meet underneath the ridge, thus forming the arch. They commonly form where cliffs are subject to erosion from the sea, rivers or weathering (sub-aerial processes); the processes 'find' weaknesses in rocks and work on them, making them bigger until they break through.

a. 1509 Istanbul earthquake
c. 1703 Genroku earthquake
b. 1700 Cascadia earthquake
d. Natural arch

36. The _____ is a geological eon representing a period before the first abundant complex life on Earth. The _____ extended from 2500 Ma to 542.0 >± 1.0 Ma (million years ago), and is the most recent part of the old, informally named 'e;Precambrian'e; time.

The Proterozoic consists of 3 geologic eras, from oldest to youngest:

- Paleoproterozoic
- Mesoproterozoic
- Neoproterozoic

The well-identified events were:

- The transition to an oxygenated atmosphere during the Mesoproterozoic.
- Several glaciations, including the hypothesized Snowball Earth during the Cryogenian period in the late Neoproterozoic.
- The Ediacaran Period (635 to 542 Ma) which is characterized by the evolution of abundant soft-bodied multicellular organisms.

The geoloic record of the Proterozoic is much better than that for the preceding Archean. In contrast to the deep-water deposits of the Archean, the Proterozoic features many strata that were laid down in extensive shallow epicontinental seas; furthermore, many of these rocks are less metamorphosed than Archean-age ones, and plenty are unaltered.

a. 1700 Cascadia earthquake
c. 1509 Istanbul earthquake
b. 1703 Genroku earthquake
d. Proterozoic Eon

Chapter 17. Dry Regions: The Geology of Deserts

1. The _____ is the first geological period of the Phanerozoic eon, lasting from 542 ± 0.3 million years ago to 488.3 ± 1.7 million years ago (ICS, 2004); it is succeeded by the Ordovician. Its subdivisions, and indeed its base, are somewhat in flux. The period was established by Adam Sedgwick, who named it after Cambria, the classical name for Wales, where Britain's _____ rocks are best exposed.

   a. 1700 Cascadia earthquake
   b. 1703 Genroku earthquake
   c. 1509 Istanbul earthquake
   d. Cambrian

2. The _____ or Cambrian radiation was the seemingly rapid appearance of most major groups of complex animals around 530 million years ago, as evidenced by the fossil record. This was accompanied by a major diversification of other organisms, including animals, phytoplankton, and calcimicrobes. Before about 580 million years ago, most organisms were simple, composed of individual cells occasionally organized into colonies.

   a. Conodont Alteration Index
   b. Romer's Gap
   c. Cambrian explosion
   d. Labyrinthodont

3. The _____ Eon is the current eon in the geologic timescale, and the one during which abundant animal life has existed. It covers roughly 545 million years and goes back to the time when diverse hard-shelled animals first appeared.

   a. 1700 Cascadia earthquake
   b. 1703 Genroku earthquake
   c. 1509 Istanbul earthquake
   d. Phanerozoic

4. The _____ is a geological eon representing a period before the first abundant complex life on Earth. The _____ extended from 2500 Ma to 542.0 >± 1.0 Ma (million years ago), and is the most recent part of the old, informally named 'e;Precambrian'e; time.

The Proterozoic consists of 3 geologic eras, from oldest to youngest:

- Paleoproterozoic
- Mesoproterozoic
- Neoproterozoic

The well-identified events were:

- The transition to an oxygenated atmosphere during the Mesoproterozoic.
- Several glaciations, including the hypothesized Snowball Earth during the Cryogenian period in the late Neoproterozoic.
- The Ediacaran Period (635 to 542 Ma) which is characterized by the evolution of abundant soft-bodied multicellular organisms.

The geoloic record of the Proterozoic is much better than that for the preceding Archean. In contrast to the deep-water deposits of the Archean, the Proterozoic features many strata that were laid down in extensive shallow epicontinental seas; furthermore, many of these rocks are less metamorphosed than Archean-age ones, and plenty are unaltered.

   a. 1509 Istanbul earthquake
   b. 1700 Cascadia earthquake
   c. 1703 Genroku earthquake
   d. Proterozoic Eon

5. A _____ is the shadow a rain drop has before it lands on the ground, with respect to prevailing wind direction. In a more geographical sense, a _____ is an area of land that has suffered desertification from proximity to mountain ranges. The mountains block the passage of rain-producing weather systems, casting a 'shadow' of dryness behind them.
   a. 1700 Cascadia earthquake
   b. 1509 Istanbul earthquake
   c. 1703 Genroku earthquake
   d. Rain shadow

6. The _____ is a geological signature, usually a thin band, dated to (65.5 ± 0.3) Ma (million years ago). The boundary marks the end of the Mesozoic era and the beginning of the Cenozoic era, and is associated with the Cretaceous-Tertiary extinction event, a mass extinction.
   a. 1509 Istanbul earthquake
   b. 1700 Cascadia earthquake
   c. Shiva crater
   d. K-T boundary

7. _____ is the naturally occurring, unconsolidated or loose covering on the Earth's surface. _____ is composed of particles of broken rock that have been altered by chemical, biological and environmental processes including weathering and erosion. _____ is different from its parent rock(s) source(s), altered by interactions between the lithosphere, hydrosphere, atmosphere, and the biosphere.
   a. Soil
   b. 1509 Istanbul earthquake
   c. Topsoil
   d. Slump

8. _____ is the process by which soil is created. It is the major topic of the science of pedology, whose other aspects include the soil morphology, classification (taxonomy) of soils, and their distribution in nature, present and past (soil geography and paleopedology).
   a. Laterite
   b. Soil structure
   c. Podsol
   d. Pedogenesis

9. _____ is the decomposition of Earth rocks, soils and their minerals through direct contact with the planet's atmosphere. _____ occurs in situ, or 'with no movement', and thus should not be confused with erosion, which involves the movement of rocks and minerals by agents such as water, ice, wind and gravity.

Two important classifications of _____ processes exist -- physical and chemical _____.

   a. Physical weathering
   b. Frost disintegration
   c. 1509 Istanbul earthquake
   d. Weathering

10. A _____ is a deep active seismic area in a subduction zone. Differential motion along the zone produces deep-seated earthquakes, the foci of which may be as deep as about 700 kilometres (435 miles.) They develop beneath volcanic island arcs and continental margins above active subduction zones.
    a. Pyroclastic flow
    b. Pit crater
    c. Lava
    d. Wadati-Benioff zone

11. _____ is the removal of solids (sediment, soil, rock and other particles) in the natural environment. It usually occurs due to transport by wind, water, or ice; by down-slope creep of soil and other material under the force of gravity; or by living organisms, such as burrowing animals, in the case of bioerosion.

_____ is distinguished from weathering, which is the process of chemical or physical breakdown of the minerals in the rocks, although the two processes may occur concurrently.

a. AL 333
b. AL 129-1
c. AASHTO Soil Classification System
d. Erosion

12. In geology, _____ is a specific type of particle transport by fluids such as wind, or the denser fluid water. It occurs when loose material is removed from a bed and carried by the fluid, before being transported back to the surface. Examples include pebble transport by rivers, sand drift over desert surfaces, soil blowing over fields, or even snow drift over smooth surfaces such as those in the Arctic or Canadian Prairies.
   a. Permineralization
   b. Transgression
   c. Hydrothermal circulation
   d. Saltation

13. _____ is the term for the fine particles that are light enough to be carried in a stream without touching the stream bed. These particles are generally of the fine sand, silt and clay size, although they can be larger, especially in cases of high discharge, such as during floods. This is in contrast to bed load which is carried along the bottom of the stream.
   a. Strike-slip faults
   b. Valley glaciers
   c. Tertiary
   d. Suspended load

14. _____ pertain to the activity of the winds and more specifically, to the winds' ability to shape the surface of the Earth and other planets. Winds may erode, transport, and deposit materials, and are effective agents in regions with sparse vegetation and a large supply of unconsolidated sediments. Although water is much more powerful than wind, _____ are important in arid environments such as deserts.
   a. AASHTO Soil Classification System
   b. AL 129-1
   c. AL 333
   d. Aeolian processes

15. A _____ is a desert surface that is covered with closely packed, interlocking angular or rounded rock fragments of pebble and cobble size.

Several theories have been proposed for their formation. The more common theory is that they form by the gradual removal of the sand, dust and other fine grained material by the wind and intermittent rain leaving only the larger fragments behind.

   a. 1700 Cascadia earthquake
   b. 1509 Istanbul earthquake
   c. 1703 Genroku earthquake
   d. Desert pavement

16. _____ are rocks that have been abraded, pitted, etched, grooved, or polished by wind-driven sand or ice crystals. These geomorphic features are most typically found in arid environments where there is little vegetation to interfere with aeolian particle transport, where there are frequently strong winds, and where there is a steady but not overwhelming supply of sand.

_____ can be abraded to eye-catching natural sculptures.

   a. Fault breccia
   b. Coprolite
   c. 1509 Istanbul earthquake
   d. Ventifacts

17. The _____ or Appalachian orogeny is one of the geological mountain-forming events (orogeny) that formed the Appalachian Mountains and Allegheny Mountains. The term and spelling 'Alleghany Orogeny' (sic) originally proposed by H.P. Woodward (1957, 1958) is preferred usage. Approximately 350 million to 300 million years ago, in the Carboniferous period, the combined continents of Europe and Africa (Gondwana) collided with North America to form the supercontinent of Pangaea.
   a. Alpine orogeny
   b. Alice Springs Orogeny
   c. Antler orogeny
   d. Alleghenian orogeny

18. An _____ is a fan-shaped deposit formed where a fast flowing stream flattens, slows, and spreads typically at the exit of a canyon onto a flatter plain. A convergence of neighboring fans into a single apron of deposits against a slope is called a bajada, or compound _____.
   a. AASHTO Soil Classification System
   b. Alluvial fan
   c. AL 129-1
   d. AL 333

19. _____ are sandy depressions in a sand dune ecosystem (psammosere) caused by the removal of sediments by wind.

   _____ occur in partially vegetated dunefields or sandhills. _____ form when a patch of protective vegetation is lost, allowing strong winds to 'blow out' sand and form a depression.

   a. 1700 Cascadia earthquake
   b. Pothole
   c. 1509 Istanbul earthquake
   d. Blowouts

20. _____ refers to natural mountain building, and may be studied as a tectonic structural event, (b) as a geographical event, and (c) a chronological event. Orogenic events (a) cause distinctive structural phenomena and related tectonic activity, (b) affect certain regions of rocks and crust, and (c) happen within a specific period of time.
   a. Antler orogeny
   b. Alice Springs Orogeny
   c. Orogeny
   d. Orogenesis

21. _____ is a term given to an accumulation of broken rock fragments at the base of crags, mountain cliffs, or valley shoulders. Landforms associated with these materials are sometimes called _____ slopes or talus piles. These deposits typically have a concave upwards form, while the maximum inclination of such deposits corresponds to the angle of repose of the mean debris size.
   a. 1700 Cascadia earthquake
   b. 1703 Genroku earthquake
   c. 1509 Istanbul earthquake
   d. Scree

22. _____ or dolomite rock is a sedimentary carbonate rock that contains a high percentage of the mineral dolomite. In old U.S.G.S. publications it was referred to as magnesian limestone. Most _____ formed as a magnesium replacement of limestone or lime mud prior to lithification.
   a. Dolostone
   b. Lithification
   c. Jasperoid
   d. Pelagic sediments

Chapter 17. Dry Regions: The Geology of Deserts

23. The general term '_____' or, more precisely, 'glacial age' denotes a geological period of long-term reduction in the temperature of the Earth's surface and atmosphere, resulting in an expansion of continental ice sheets, polar ice sheets and alpine glaciers. Within a long-term _____, individual pulses of extra cold climate are termed 'glaciations'. Glaciologically, _____ implies the presence of extensive ice sheets in the northern and southern hemispheres; by this definition we are still in an _____
   a. AL 333
   b. Ice age
   c. AL 129-1
   d. AASHTO Soil Classification System

24. _____ is a homogeneous, typically nonstratified, porous, friable, slightly coherent, often calcareous, fine-grained, silty, pale yellow or buff, windblown (aeolian) sediment. It generally occurs as a widespread blanket deposit that covers areas of hundreds of square kilometers and tens of meters thick. _____ often stands in either steep or vertical faces.
   a. 1509 Istanbul earthquake
   b. Loess
   c. 1703 Genroku earthquake
   d. 1700 Cascadia earthquake

25. The _____ Formation is one of the world's most celebrated fossil localities, and is famous for the exceptional preservation of the fossils found within it, in which the soft parts are preserved. It is 505 million years (Middle Cambrian) in age, making it one of the earliest fossil beds to preserve the soft parts of animals. The pre-Cambrian fossil record of animals is sparse and ambiguous.
   a. 1703 Genroku earthquake
   b. 1509 Istanbul earthquake
   c. Burgess Shale
   d. 1700 Cascadia earthquake

26. _____ is a region of the Colorado Plateau characterized by a cluster of vast and iconic sandstone buttes, the largest reaching 1,000 ft (300 m) above the valley floor. It is located on the southern border of Utah with northern Arizona (around >>36>°59>'N 110>°6>'W'#20;/'#20;>36.983>°N 110.1>°W>'#20;/'#20;36.983; -110.1), near the Four Corners area. The valley lies within the range of the Navajo Nation Reservation, and is accessible from U.S. Highway 163.
   a. Thirtynine Mile volcanic field
   b. Rano Kau
   c. 1509 Istanbul earthquake
   d. Monument Valley

27. _____ is a fine-grained sedimentary rock whose original constituents were clay minerals or muds. It is characterized by thin laminae breaking with an irregular curving fracture, often splintery and usually parallel to the often-indistinguishable bedding plane. This property is called fissility.
   a. Mudstone
   b. Shale
   c. Pelagic sediments
   d. Metasediment

28. _____ are the preserved remains or traces of animals, plants, and other organisms from the remote past. The totality of _____, both discovered and undiscovered, and their placement in fossiliferous rock formations and sedimentary layers (strata) is known as the fossil record. The study of _____ across geological time, how they were formed, and the evolutionary relationships between taxa (phylogeny) are some of the most important functions of the science of paleontology.
   a. 1700 Cascadia earthquake
   b. 1703 Genroku earthquake
   c. 1509 Istanbul earthquake
   d. Fossils

29. A _____ is a tall thin spire of rock that protrudes from the bottom of an arid drainage basin or badland. Hoodoos are composed of soft sedimentary rock and are topped by a piece of harder, less easily-eroded stone that protects the column from the elements.

178 Chapter 17. Dry Regions: The Geology of Deserts

They are mainly located in the desert in dry, hot areas.

a. Hoodoo
b. 1703 Genroku earthquake
c. 1700 Cascadia earthquake
d. 1509 Istanbul earthquake

30. The _____ are a 159 square mile (412 km^2) salt flat in northwestern Utah. The depth of the salt has been recorded at 6 feet (1.8 m) in many areas. A remnant of the ancient Lake Bonneville of glacial times, the salt flats are now public land managed by the Bureau of Land Management.
a. 1703 Genroku earthquake
b. 1700 Cascadia earthquake
c. 1509 Istanbul earthquake
d. Bonneville Salt Flats

31. An _____ is the result of a sudden release of energy in the Earth's crust that creates seismic waves. They are recorded with a seismometer or the related and mostly obsolete Richter magnitude, with a magnitude 3 or lower _____ being mostly imperceptible and magnitude 7 causing serious damage over large areas.
a. AL 333
b. AL 129-1
c. Earthquake
d. AASHTO Soil Classification System

32. A _____ or inselberg is an isolated rock hill, knob, ridge, or small mountain that rises abruptly from a gently sloping or virtually level surrounding plain. The term '_____' is usually used in the United States, whereas 'inselberg' is the more common international term. In southern and southern-central Africa, a similar formation of granite is known as a kopje (in fact a Dutch word) from the Afrikaans word: koppie.

_____ is an originally Native American term for an isolated hill or a lone mountain that has risen above the surrounding area, typically by surviving erosion.

a. 1509 Istanbul earthquake
b. Rogen moraine
c. Sandur
d. Monadnock

33. A _____ is a geological phenomenon which includes a wide range of ground movement, such as rock falls, deep failure of slopes and shallow debris flows, which can occur in offshore, coastal and onshore environments. Although the action of gravity is the primary driving force for a _____ to occur, there are other contributing factors affecting the original slope stability. Typically, pre-conditional factors build up specific sub-surface conditions that make the area/slope prone to failure, whereas the actual _____ often requires a trigger before being released.
a. Mass wasting
b. 1509 Istanbul earthquake
c. Landslide
d. 1700 Cascadia earthquake

34. A _____ is a natural formation (or landform) where a rock arch forms, with a natural passageway through underneath. Most natural arches form as a narrow ridge, walled by cliffs, become narrower from erosion, with a softer rock stratum under the cliff-forming stratum gradually eroding out until the rock shelters thus formed meet underneath the ridge, thus forming the arch. They commonly form where cliffs are subject to erosion from the sea, rivers or weathering (sub-aerial processes); the processes 'find' weaknesses in rocks and work on them, making them bigger until they break through.
a. 1509 Istanbul earthquake
b. Natural arch
c. 1703 Genroku earthquake
d. 1700 Cascadia earthquake

Chapter 17. Dry Regions: The Geology of Deserts

35. _____ is a geologic term for a type of topography characterized by a series of separate and parallel mountain ranges with broad valleys interposed, extending over a more or less wide area. It is typified by the topography found in the Great Basin in the western United States, which is part of a larger regional topography known as the _____ Province. _____ topography results from crustal extension.
   a. Rill
   b. Tidal scour
   c. Zechstein
   d. Basin and Range

36. The _____ is a large geologic province which includes parts of the southwestern United States and northwestern Mexico, typified by basin and range topography.

The topography of the _____ is a result of crustal extension within this part of the North American Plate. The cause of this extension is as yet not fully understood, although several hypotheses have been offered. The crust here has been stretched up to 100% of its original width. In fact, the crust underneath the _____, especially under the Great Basin, is some of the thinnest in the world.

   a. Quaternary
   b. Canadian Shield
   c. Yilgarn Craton
   d. Basin and Range Province

37. The _____ is a physiographic region of the Intermontane Plateaus, roughly centered on the Four Corners region of the southwestern United States. The province covers an area of 337,000 km^2 within western Colorado, northwestern New Mexico, southern and eastern Utah, and northern Arizona. About 90% of the area is drained by the Colorado River and its main tributaries; the Green, San Juan and Little Colorado.

Development of the province has in large part been influenced by structural features in its oldest rocks. Part of the Wasatch Line and its various faults form the western edge of the province. Faults that run parallel to the Wasatch Fault that lies along the Wasatch Range form the boundaries between the plateaus in the High Plateaus Section. The Uinta Basin, Uncompahgre Uplift, and the Paradox Basin were also created by movement along structural weaknesses in the region's oldest rock.

   a. Colorado Plateau
   b. 1509 Istanbul earthquake
   c. 1700 Cascadia earthquake
   d. 1703 Genroku earthquake

38. A _____ is a mountain rising from the ocean seafloor that does not reach to the water's surface (sea level), and thus is not an island. These are typically formed from extinct volcanoes, that rise abruptly and are usually found rising from a seafloor of 1,000-4,000 meters depth. They are defined by oceanographers as independent features that rise to at least 1,000 meters above the seafloor.
   a. 1703 Genroku earthquake
   b. 1700 Cascadia earthquake
   c. Seamount
   d. 1509 Istanbul earthquake

39. A _____ dune is an arc-shaped sand ridge, comprising well-sorted sand. This type of dune possesses two 'horns' that face downwind, with the slip face (the downwind slope) at the angle of repose, or approximately 32 degrees. The upwind side is packed by the wind, and stands at about 15 degrees. Simple _____ dunes may stretch from meters to a hundred meters or so between the tips of the horns.
   a. 1509 Istanbul earthquake
   b. 1703 Genroku earthquake
   c. Barchan
   d. 1700 Cascadia earthquake

Chapter 17. Dry Regions: The Geology of Deserts

40. In geology a _____ is the smallest division of a geologic formation or stratigraphic rock series marked by well-defined divisional planes (bedding planes) separating it from layers above and below. A _____ is the smallest lithostratigraphic unit, usually ranging in thickness from a centimeter to several meters and distinguishable from beds above and below it. Beds can be differentiated in various ways, including rock or mineral type and particle size.
    a. Sequence stratigraphy
    b. Biozones
    c. Cyclostratigraphy
    d. Bed

41. A _____ is any glacially formed accumulation of unconsolidated glacial debris (soil and rock) which can occur in currently glaciated and formerly glaciated regions, such as those areas acted upon by a past ice age. This debris may have been plucked off the valley floor as a glacier advanced or it may have fallen off the valley walls as a result of frost wedging. Moraines may be composed of silt like glacial flour to large boulders.
    a. Moraine
    b. 1509 Istanbul earthquake
    c. 1703 Genroku earthquake
    d. 1700 Cascadia earthquake

42. Radially symmetrical, _____ are pyramidal sand mounds with slipfaces on three or more arms that radiate from the high center of the mound. They tend to accumulate in areas with multidirectional wind regimes. _____ grow upward rather than laterally. They dominate the Grand Erg Oriental of the Sahara. In other deserts, they occur around the margins of the sand seas, particularly near topographic barriers. In the southeast Badain Jaran Desert of China, the _____ are up to 500 meters tall and may be the tallest dunes on Earth.
    a. Pahoehoe lava
    b. Loihi Seamount
    c. Principle of inclusions and components
    d. Star dunes

43. _____ is a fluvial process of erosion that lengthens a stream, a valley or a gully at its head and also enlarges its drainage basin. The stream erodes away at the rock and soil at its headwaters in the opposite direction that it flows. Once a stream has begun to cut back, the erosion is sped up by the steep gradient the water is flowing down. As water erodes a path from its headwaters to its mouth at a standing body of water, it tries to cut an ever-shallower path. This leads to increased erosion at the steepest parts, which is _____.
    a. Mid-ocean ridge
    b. Saltation
    c. Transgression
    d. Headward erosion

44. A _____ is a gently inclined erosional surface carved into bedrock. It is thinly covered with Fluvial gravel that has developed at the foot of mountains. It develops when running water erodes most of the mass of the mountain. It is typically a concave surface gently sloping away from mountainous desert areas.
    a. Geodiversity
    b. Platform cover
    c. Pediment
    d. Karst fenster

45. In geology, a _____ or _____ line is a planar fracture in rock in which the rock on one side of the fracture has moved with respect to the rock on the other side. Large faults within the Earth's crust are the result of differential or shear motion and active _____ zones are the causal locations of most earthquakes. Earthquakes are caused by energy release during rapid slippage along a _____.
    a. Combe
    b. Stack
    c. Dali
    d. Fault

46. The _____ is a continental transform fault that runs a length of roughly 800 miles (1,300 km) through California in the United States. The fault's motion is right-lateral strike-slip (horizontal motion.) It forms the tectonic boundary between the Pacific Plate and the North American Plate.

Chapter 17. Dry Regions: The Geology of Deserts   181

   a. 1703 Genroku earthquake
   b. 1700 Cascadia earthquake
   c. 1509 Istanbul earthquake
   d. San Andreas Fault

47. The lithosphere is broken up into what are called _____. In the case of Earth, there are eight major and many minor plates The lithospheric plates ride on the asthenosphere. These plates move in relation to one another at one of three types of plate boundaries: convergent, or collisional boundaries; divergent boundaries, also called spreading centers; and transform boundaries.
   a. Thrust fault
   b. Copperbelt Province
   c. Gorda Ridge
   d. Tectonic plates

48. _____ is a naturally occurring granular material composed of finely divided rock and mineral particles.

As the term is used by geologists, _____ particles range in diameter from 0.0625 (or $>^1\!/_{16}$ mm, or 62.5 micrometers) to 2 millimeters. An individual particle in this range size is termed a _____ grain.

   a. 1703 Genroku earthquake
   b. Sand
   c. 1700 Cascadia earthquake
   d. 1509 Istanbul earthquake

49. The _____ is an engineering property of granular materials. The _____ is the maximum angle of a stable slope determined by friction, cohesion and the shapes of the particles.

When bulk granular materials are poured onto a horizontal surface, a conical pile will form. The internal angle between the surface of the pile and the horizontal surface is known as the _____ and is related to the density, surface area, and coefficient of friction of the material.

   a. AL 333
   b. AASHTO Soil Classification System
   c. Angle of repose
   d. AL 129-1

50. _____ is a sedimentary rock composed mainly of sand-size mineral or rock grains. Most _____ is composed of quartz and/or feldspar because these are the most common minerals in the Earth's crust. Like sand, _____ may be any color, but the most common colors are tan, brown, yellow, red, gray and white.
   a. Lithification
   b. Sandstone
   c. Porcellanite
   d. Dolostone

51. The _____ or the Dirty Thirties was a period of severe dust storms causing major ecological and agricultural damage to American and Canadian prairie lands from 1930 to 1936 (in some areas until 1940.) The phenomenon was caused by severe drought coupled with decades of extensive farming without crop rotation or other techniques to prevent erosion. Deep plowing of the virgin topsoil of the Great Plains had killed the natural grasses that normally kept the soil in place and trapped moisture even during periods of drought and high winds.
   a. 1509 Istanbul earthquake
   b. Dust Bowl
   c. 1700 Cascadia earthquake
   d. 1703 Genroku earthquake

52. A _____ is a large, slow-moving mass of ice, formed from compacted layers of snow, that slowly deforms and flows in response to gravity and high pressure.

_____ ice is the largest reservoir of fresh water on Earth, and second only to oceans as the largest reservoir of total water.

a. Little Ice Age
b. Glacier
c. Keeling Curve
d. Pacific Decadal Oscillation

Chapter 18. Amazing Ice: Glaciers and Ice Ages

1. A _____ is a piece of rock that differs from the size and type of rock native to the area in which it rests. They are carried by glacial ice, often over distances of hundreds of kilometres and can range in size from pebbles to large boulders such as Big Rock (16,500 tons) in Alberta.
   a. 1700 Cascadia earthquake
   b. 1703 Genroku earthquake
   c. 1509 Istanbul earthquake
   d. Glacial erratic

2. A _____ is a large, slow-moving mass of ice, formed from compacted layers of snow, that slowly deforms and flows in response to gravity and high pressure.

   _____ ice is the largest reservoir of fresh water on Earth, and second only to oceans as the largest reservoir of total water.

   a. Glacier
   b. Pacific Decadal Oscillation
   c. Little Ice Age
   d. Keeling Curve

3. The _____ was an ocean that existed in the Neoproterozoic and Paleozoic eras of the geologic timescale (between 600 and 400 million years ago.) The _____ was situated in the southern hemisphere, between the paleocontinents of Laurentia, Baltica and Avalonia. The ocean disappeared with the Caledonian, Taconic and Acadian orogenies, when these three continents joined to form one big landmass called Laurussia.
   a. AL 129-1
   b. AASHTO Soil Classification System
   c. AL 333
   d. Iapetus Ocean

4. The _____ is a geological signature, usually a thin band, dated to (65.5 ± 0.3) Ma (million years ago). The boundary marks the end of the Mesozoic era and the beginning of the Cenozoic era, and is associated with the Cretaceous-Tertiary extinction event, a mass extinction.
   a. 1509 Istanbul earthquake
   b. Shiva crater
   c. K-T boundary
   d. 1700 Cascadia earthquake

5. The general term '_____' or, more precisely, 'glacial age' denotes a geological period of long-term reduction in the temperature of the Earth's surface and atmosphere, resulting in an expansion of continental ice sheets, polar ice sheets and alpine glaciers. Within a long-term _____, individual pulses of extra cold climate are termed 'glaciations'. Glaciologically, _____ implies the presence of extensive ice sheets in the northern and southern hemispheres; by this definition we are still in an _____.
   a. AASHTO Soil Classification System
   b. AL 333
   c. Ice age
   d. AL 129-1

6. Alpine glaciers form high on the mountain slopes and are niche, slope or cirque glaciers. As a mountain glacier increases in size it can begin to flow down valley, and are referred to as _____.
   a. Tertiary
   b. Valley glaciers
   c. Pahoehoe lava
   d. Star dunes

7. A _____ is an amphitheatre-like valley formed at the head of a glacier by erosion. A _____ is also known as a coombe or coomb in England, a combe or comb in America, a corrie in Scotland and Ireland, and a cwm in Wales, although these terms apply to a specific feature of which several may be found in a _____. The term 'comb' is often found at the end of placenames such as Newcomb and Maycomb, where it is pronounced /kÉ™m/.

Chapter 18. Amazing Ice: Glaciers and Ice Ages

a. 1509 Istanbul earthquake
b. 1700 Cascadia earthquake
c. 1703 Genroku earthquake
d. Cirque

8. A _____ is formed in a cirque, bowl-shaped depressions on the side of mountains. Snow and ice accumulation in corries often occurs as the result of avalanching from higher surrounding slopes.

In these depressions, snow persists through summer months, and becomes glacier ice.

a. Cordilleran Ice Sheet
b. Snowball Earth
c. Pastonian Stage
d. Cirque glacier

9. An _____ is an ice mass that covers less than 50 000 km² of land area (usually covering a highland area.) Masses of ice covering more than 50 000 km² are termed an ice sheet.

They are not constrained by topographical features (i.e., they will lie over the top of mountains) but their dome is usually centred on the highest point of a massif.

a. AL 129-1
b. AL 333
c. AASHTO Soil Classification System
d. Ice cap

10. The _____ is a geological eon representing a period before the first abundant complex life on Earth. The _____ extended from 2500 Ma to 542.0 >± 1.0 Ma (million years ago), and is the most recent part of the old, informally named 'e;Precambrian'e; time.

The Proterozoic consists of 3 geologic eras, from oldest to youngest:

- Paleoproterozoic
- Mesoproterozoic
- Neoproterozoic

The well-identified events were:

- The transition to an oxygenated atmosphere during the Mesoproterozoic.
- Several glaciations, including the hypothesized Snowball Earth during the Cryogenian period in the late Neoproterozoic.
- The Ediacaran Period (635 to 542 Ma) which is characterized by the evolution of abundant soft-bodied multicellular organisms.

The geoloic record of the Proterozoic is much better than that for the preceding Archean. In contrast to the deep-water deposits of the Archean, the Proterozoic features many strata that were laid down in extensive shallow epicontinental seas; furthermore, many of these rocks are less metamorphosed than Archean-age ones, and plenty are unaltered.

a. 1703 Genroku earthquake
c. 1509 Istanbul earthquake
b. 1700 Cascadia earthquake
d. Proterozoic Eon

11. _____ is the act of a glacier sliding over the bed before it due to meltwater under the ice acting as a lubricant. This movement very much depends on the temperature of the area, the slope of the glacier, the bed's sediment size, the amount of meltwater from the glacier, and the glacier's size.

The movement that happens to these glaciers as they slide is that of a jerky motion where any seismic events, especially at the base of glacier, can cause movement.

a. Bull Lake glaciation
c. Terminal moraine
b. Bramertonian Stage
d. Basal sliding

12. A _____ is a huge crack formed by two glaciers colliding. Accelerations in glacier speed cause extension and can initiate a _____. Crevasses often have vertical or near-vertical walls, which can then melt and create seracs, arches, etc.; these walls sometimes expose layers that represent the glacier's stratigraphy.

a. Geohazard
c. Crevasse
b. Sturzstrom
d. Predator trap

13. In mineralogy and crystallography, a _____ is a unique arrangement of atoms in a crystal. A _____ is composed of a motif, a set of atoms arranged in a particular way, and a lattice. Motifs are located upon the points of a lattice, which is an array of points repeating periodically in three dimensions.

a. 1703 Genroku earthquake
c. 1700 Cascadia earthquake
b. 1509 Istanbul earthquake
d. Crystal structure

14. _____ is partially-compacted n>év>é, a type of snow that has been left over from past seasons and has been recrystallized into a substance denser than n>év>é. It is ice that is at an intermediate stage between snow and glacial ice. _____ has the appearance of wet sugar, but has a hardness that makes it extremely resistant to shovelling. It generally has a density greater than 550 kg/mÂ³ and is often found underneath the snow that accumulates at the head of a glacier.

a. Bramertonian Stage
c. Firn
b. Bull Lake glaciation
d. Glaciolacustrine deposits

15. On a glacier, the _____, zone of ablation or zone of wastage is the area in which annual loss of snow through melting, evaporation, iceberg calving and sublimation exceeds annual gain of snow and ice on the surface. Of these, melting is most important in most glaciers, but the others, especially iceberg calving, can be significant. Spatially, the zone of ablation can be identified as the part of the glacier below the snowline.

a. AL 333
c. AASHTO Soil Classification System
b. AL 129-1
d. Ablation zone

16. The _____ is the epoch from 1.8 million to 11550 years BP covering the world's recent period of repeated glaciations. The _____ epoch follows the Pliocene epoch and is followed by the Holocene epoch. The _____ is the third epoch of the Neogene period or 6th epoch of the Cenozoic Era. The end of the _____ corresponds with the retreat of the last continental glacier. It also corresponds with the end of the Paleolithic age used in archaeology.

a. Sicilian Stage
c. Pleistocene
b. Tyrrhenian
d. Late Pleistocene

Chapter 18. Amazing Ice: Glaciers and Ice Ages

17. Geologically, a _____ is a long, narrow inlet with steep sides, created in a valley carved by glacial activity.

The seeds of a _____ are laid when a glacier cuts a U-shaped valley through abrasion of the surrounding bedrock by the sediment it carries. Many such valleys were formed during the recent ice age.

a. 1509 Istanbul earthquake
b. 1703 Genroku earthquake
c. Fjord
d. 1700 Cascadia earthquake

18. _____ are the largest glaciers, enormous masses of ice that are not visibly affected by the landscape and that cover the entire surface beneath them, except possibly on the margins where they are thinnest. Antarctica and Greenland are the only places where continental _____ currently exist. These regions contain vast quantities of fresh water.

a. AL 333
b. AL 129-1
c. AASHTO Soil Classification System
d. Ice sheets

19. A _____ is a mountain rising from the ocean seafloor that does not reach to the water's surface (sea level), and thus is not an island. These are typically formed from extinct volcanoes, that rise abruptly and are usually found rising from a seafloor of 1,000-4,000 meters depth. They are defined by oceanographers as independent features that rise to at least 1,000 meters above the seafloor.

a. 1703 Genroku earthquake
b. 1509 Istanbul earthquake
c. 1700 Cascadia earthquake
d. Seamount

20. _____ is mechanical scraping of a rock surface by friction between rocks and moving particles during their transport in wind, glacier, waves, gravity or running water, after friction, the moving particles dislodge loose and weak debris from the side of the rock, these particles can be dissolved in the water source.

The intensity of _____ depends on the hardness, concentration, velocity and mass of moving particles.

A virtually smooth marine platform cut by the ocean waves at a coastline.

a. AL 333
b. AASHTO Soil Classification System
c. Abrasion
d. AL 129-1

21. A _____ is an elongated whale-shaped hill formed by glacial action. Its long axis is parallel with the movement of the ice, with the blunter end facing into the glacial movement. They may be more than 45 m (150 ft) high and more than 0.8 km (1/2 mile) long, and are often in _____ fields of similarly shaped, sized and oriented hills. They usually have layers indicating that the material was repeatedly added to a core, which may be of rock or glacial till.

a. 1509 Istanbul earthquake
b. Monadnock
c. Drumlin
d. Sandur

22. An _____ is the result of a sudden release of energy in the Earth's crust that creates seismic waves. They are recorded with a seismometer or the related and mostly obsolete Richter magnitude, with a magnitude 3 or lower _____ being mostly imperceptible and magnitude 7 causing serious damage over large areas.

a. AL 129-1
b. AASHTO Soil Classification System
c. AL 333
d. Earthquake

Chapter 18. Amazing Ice: Glaciers and Ice Ages

23. _____ is the removal of solids (sediment, soil, rock and other particles) in the natural environment. It usually occurs due to transport by wind, water, or ice; by down-slope creep of soil and other material under the force of gravity; or by living organisms, such as burrowing animals, in the case of bioerosion.

_____ is distinguished from weathering, which is the process of chemical or physical breakdown of the minerals in the rocks, although the two processes may occur concurrently.

   a. Erosion
   b. AASHTO Soil Classification System
   c. AL 129-1
   d. AL 333

24. _____ is caused by movement of ice, typically as glaciers. Glaciers erode predominantly by three different processes: abrasion/scouring, plucking, and ice thrusting. In an abrasion process, debris in the basal ice scrapes along the bed, polishing and gouging the underlying rocks, similar to sandpaper on wood. Glaciers can also cause pieces of bedrock to crack off in the process of plucking. In ice thrusting, the glacier freezes to its bed, then as it surges forward, it moves large sheets of frozen sediment at the base along with the glacier. This method produced some of the many thousands of lake basins that dot the edge of the Canadian Shield. These processes, combined with erosion and transport by the water network beneath the glacier, leave moraines, drumlins, eskers, ground moraine (till), kames, kame deltas, moulins, and glacial erratics in their wake, typically at the terminus or during glacier retreat.
   a. Ice erosion
   b. AL 129-1
   c. AASHTO Soil Classification System
   d. AL 333

25. _____ consists of clay-sized particles of rock, generated by glacial erosion or by artificial grinding to a similar size. Because the material is very small, it becomes suspended in river water making the water appear cloudy.

If the river flows into a glacial lake, the lake may appear turquoise in color as a result.

   a. Glacial period
   b. Cirque glacier
   c. Cordilleran Ice Sheet
   d. Rock flour

26. A _____ is a mountain lake or pool, formed in a cirque excavated by a glacier. A moraine may form a natural dam below a _____. A corrie may be called a cirque.
   a. Fault
   b. Platform
   c. Combe
   d. Tarn

27. A _____ is a deep active seismic area in a subduction zone. Differential motion along the zone produces deep-seated earthquakes, the foci of which may be as deep as about 700 kilometres (435 miles.) They develop beneath volcanic island arcs and continental margins above active subduction zones.
   a. Wadati-Benioff zone
   b. Pyroclastic flow
   c. Pit crater
   d. Lava

28. A _____ is a tributary valley with the floor at a higher relief than the main channel into which it flows. They are most commonly associated with U-shaped valleys when a tributary glacier flows into a glacier of larger volume. The main glacier erodes a deep U-shaped valley with nearly vertical sides while the tributary glacier, with a smaller volume of ice, makes a shallower U-shaped valley.

Chapter 18. Amazing Ice: Glaciers and Ice Ages

a. Hanging valley
b. 1703 Genroku earthquake
c. 1509 Istanbul earthquake
d. 1700 Cascadia earthquake

29. _____ is the geological process by which material is added to a landform or land mass. Fluids such as wind and water, as well as sediment gravity flows, transport previously eroded sediment, which, at the loss of enough kinetic energy in the fluid, is deposited, building up layers of sediment.

_____ occurs when the forces responsible for sediment transportation are no longer sufficient to overcome the forces of particle weight and friction, which resist motion.

a. Deposition
b. Headward erosion
c. Downcutting
d. Diagenesis

30. In geology, _____ is transported rock debris overlying the solid bedrock. The term is also sometimes refers to organic debris so-transported. In the largest sense, it refers to the material left behind by retreating continental glaciers.

a. Platform cover
b. Patterned ground
c. Geodiversity
d. Drift

31. _____ is any particulate matter that can be transported by fluid flow, and which eventually is deposited.

They are most often transported by water (fluvial processes) transported by wind (aeolian processes) and glaciers. Beach sands and river channel deposits are examples of fluvial transport and deposition, though _____ also often settles out of slow-moving or standing water in lakes and oceans.

a. Quicksand
b. Sediment
c. Brickearth
d. Bovey Beds

32. _____ or dolomite rock is a sedimentary carbonate rock that contains a high percentage of the mineral dolomite. In old U.S.G.S. publications it was referred to as magnesian limestone. Most _____ formed as a magnesium replacement of limestone or lime mud prior to lithification.

a. Dolostone
b. Lithification
c. Pelagic sediments
d. Jasperoid

33. _____ is the largest volcano on earth in terms of area covered and one of five volcanoes that form the Island of Hawaii in the U.S. state of Hawai>Ê»i in the Pacific Ocean. It is an active shield volcano, with a volume estimated at approximately 18,000 cubic miles (75,000 kmÂ³), although its peak is about 120 feet (37 m) lower than that of its neighbor, Mauna Kea. The Hawaiian name '_____' means 'Long Mountain'.

a. 1509 Istanbul earthquake
b. Mauna Loa
c. 1703 Genroku earthquake
d. 1700 Cascadia earthquake

34. A _____ is an opening in a planet's surface or crust, which allows hot, molten rock, ash, and gases to escape from below the surface. Volcanic activity involving the extrusion of rock tends to form mountains or features like mountains over a period of time.

a. 1703 Genroku earthquake
b. 1509 Istanbul earthquake
c. 1700 Cascadia earthquake
d. Volcano

Chapter 18. Amazing Ice: Glaciers and Ice Ages

35. A _____ is a moraine that forms at the end of the glacier called the snout.

They mark the maximum advance of the glacier. An end moraine is at the present boundary of the glacier. They are one of the most prominent types of moraines in the Arctic. One famous _____ is the Giant's Wall in Norway.

   a. Bull Lake glaciation
   b. Bramertonian Stage
   c. Firn
   d. Terminal moraine

36. Two important classifications of weathering processes exist -- _____ and chemical weathering. Mechanical or _____ involves the breakdown of rocks and soils through direct contact with atmospheric conditions, such as heat, water, ice and pressure. The second classification, chemical weathering, involves the direct effect of atmospheric chemicals or biologically produced chemicals (also known as biological weathering) in the breakdown of rocks, soils and minerals.
   a. 1509 Istanbul earthquake
   b. Physical weathering
   c. Frost disintegration
   d. Weathering

37. A _____ is any glacially formed accumulation of unconsolidated glacial debris (soil and rock) which can occur in currently glaciated and formerly glaciated regions, such as those areas acted upon by a past ice age. This debris may have been plucked off the valley floor as a glacier advanced or it may have fallen off the valley walls as a result of frost wedging. Moraines may be composed of silt like glacial flour to large boulders.
   a. 1703 Genroku earthquake
   b. 1700 Cascadia earthquake
   c. 1509 Istanbul earthquake
   d. Moraine

38. A _____ is a glacial outwash plain formed of sediments deposited by meltwater at the terminus of a glacier.

_____ are found in glaciated areas, such as Svalbard, Kerguelen Islands, and Iceland. Glaciers and icecaps contain large amounts of silt and sediment, picked up as they erode the underlying rocks when they move slowly downhill, and at the snout of the glacier, meltwater can carry this sediment away from the glacier and deposit it on a broad plain.

   a. Monadnock
   b. Rogen moraine
   c. 1509 Istanbul earthquake
   d. Sandur

39. A _____ is an annual layer of sediment or sedimentary rock. Initially, _____ was used to describe the separate components of annual layers in glacial lake sediments, but at the 1910 Geological Congress, the Swedish geologist Gerard De Geer (1858-1943) proposed a new formal definition where _____ described the whole of any annual sedimentary layer.
   a. 1509 Istanbul earthquake
   b. 1700 Cascadia earthquake
   c. 1703 Genroku earthquake
   d. Varve

40. _____ is the decomposition of Earth rocks, soils and their minerals through direct contact with the planet's atmosphere. _____ occurs in situ, or 'with no movement', and thus should not be confused with erosion, which involves the movement of rocks and minerals by agents such as water, ice, wind and gravity.

Two important classifications of _____ processes exist -- physical and chemical _____.

a. 1509 Istanbul earthquake
b. Frost disintegration
c. Physical weathering
d. Weathering

41. _____ are a type of elastic surface wave that travel on solids. They are produced on the Earth by earthquakes, in which case they are also known as 'ground roll', or by other sources of seismic energy such as an explosion or even a sledgehammer impact. They are also produced in materials by acoustic transducers, and are used in non-destructive testing for detecting defects.
   a. Seismic waves
   b. Maximum magnitude
   c. Rayleigh waves
   d. Tornillo event

42. _____ is unsorted glacial sediment. Glacial drift is a general term for the coarsely graded and extremely heterogeneous sediments of glacial origin. Glacial _____ is that part of glacial drift which was deposited directly by the glacier. In cases where _____ has been indurated or lithified by subsequent burial into solid rock, it is known as the sedimentary rock tillite.
   a. Till
   b. 1509 Istanbul earthquake
   c. 1703 Genroku earthquake
   d. 1700 Cascadia earthquake

43. An _____ is a long winding ridge of stratified sand and gravel, examples of which occur in glaciated and formerly glaciated regions of Europe and North America. They are frequently several miles long and, because of their peculiar uniform shape, are somewhat like railroad embankments.

Most are believed to form in ice-walled tunnels by streams which flowed within (englacial) and under (subglacial) glaciers.

   a. AASHTO Soil Classification System
   b. AL 129-1
   c. AL 333
   d. Esker

44. The _____ describes the continuous movement of water on, above, and below the surface of the Earth. Since the _____ is truly a 'cycle,' there is no beginning or end. Water can change states among liquid, vapor, and ice at various places in the _____.
   a. Cone of depression
   b. Hydraulic conductivity
   c. Vadose zone
   d. Water cycle

45. A _____, in biogeography, is an isthmus or wider land connection between otherwise separate areas, which allows terrestrial animals and plants to cross over and colonise new lands. They can be created by marine regression, in which sea levels fall, exposing shallow, previously submerged sections of continental shelf; or when new land is created by plate tectonics; or occasionally when the sea floor rises due to post-glacial rebound after an ice age.
   a. 1509 Istanbul earthquake
   b. Land bridge
   c. 1703 Genroku earthquake
   d. 1700 Cascadia earthquake

46. _____ is a geologic term for a type of topography characterized by a series of separate and parallel mountain ranges with broad valleys interposed, extending over a more or less wide area. It is typified by the topography found in the Great Basin in the western United States, which is part of a larger regional topography known as the _____ Province. _____ topography results from crustal extension.

a. Rill
b. Tidal scour
c. Basin and Range
d. Zechstein

47. The _____ is a large geologic province which includes parts of the southwestern United States and northwestern Mexico, typified by basin and range topography.

The topography of the _____ is a result of crustal extension within this part of the North American Plate. The cause of this extension is as yet not fully understood, although several hypotheses have been offered. The crust here has been stretched up to 100% of its original width. In fact, the crust underneath the _____, especially under the Great Basin, is some of the thinnest in the world.

a. Yilgarn Craton
b. Quaternary
c. Canadian Shield
d. Basin and Range Province

48. _____ was a prehistoric pluvial lake that covered much of North America's Great Basin region. Most of the territory it covered was in present-day Utah, though parts of the lake extended into present-day Idaho and Nevada. Formed about 32,000 years ago, it existed until about 16,800 years ago, when a large portion of the lake was released through the Red Rock Pass in Idaho.

Like most, if not all, of the ice age pluvial lakes of the American West, _____ was a result of the combination of lower temperatures, decreased evaporation, and higher precipitation that then prevailed in the region, perhaps due to a more southerly jet stream than today's. The lake was probably not a singular entity either; geologic evidence suggests that it may have evaporated and reformed as many as 28 times in the last 3 million years.

a. Lake Bonneville
b. 1703 Genroku earthquake
c. 1509 Istanbul earthquake
d. 1700 Cascadia earthquake

49. _____ is a term used to describe the distinct, and often symmetrical geometric shapes formed by ground material in periglacial regions. Typically found in remote regions of the Arctic, Antarctica, and the Australian outback, but also found anywhere that freezing and thawing of soil alternate, the geometric shapes and patterns associated with _____ are often mistaken as artistic human creations. The nature of _____ puzzled scientists for ages.

a. Patterned ground
b. Geopetal
c. Reading Prong
d. Haloclasty

50. In geology, _____ or _____ soil is soil at or below the freezing point of water (0 >°C or 32 >°F) for two or more years. Ice is not always present, as may be in the case of nonporous bedrock, but it frequently occurs and it may be in amounts exceeding the potential hydraulic saturation of the ground material. Most _____ is located in high latitudes (i.e. land in close proximity to the North and South poles), but alpine _____ may exist at high altitudes in much lower latitudes.

a. 1509 Istanbul earthquake
b. 1703 Genroku earthquake
c. Permafrost
d. 1700 Cascadia earthquake

51. In geology and climatology, a _____ was an extended period of abundant rainfall lasting many thousands of years. The term is especially applied to such periods during the Pleistocene Epoch. A minor, short _____ may be termed a 'subpluvial'.

Chapter 18. Amazing Ice: Glaciers and Ice Ages

a. 1700 Cascadia earthquake
c. Pluvial

b. 1509 Istanbul earthquake
d. 1703 Genroku earthquake

52. A _____ is a lake that experiences significant increase in depth and extent as a result of increased precipitation and reduced evaporation. Such lakes are likely to be endorheic.

They represent changes in the hydrological cycle -- wet cycles generate large lakes, whereas dry cycles cause the lakes to dry up leaving large flat plains.

a. 1700 Cascadia earthquake
c. 1509 Istanbul earthquake

b. 1703 Genroku earthquake
d. Pluvial lake

53. The _____ was a massive sheet of ice that covered hundreds of thousands of square miles, including most of Canada and a large portion of the northern United States, between c. 95,000 and c. 20,000 years before the present day.

a. 1509 Istanbul earthquake
c. Laurentide ice sheet

b. 1703 Genroku earthquake
d. 1700 Cascadia earthquake

54. The _____ is the earliest of three geologic eras of the Phanerozoic eon. The _____ spanned from roughly 542 to 251 million years ago (ICS, 2004), and is subdivided into six geologic periods; from oldest to youngest they are: the Cambrian, Ordovician, Silurian, Devonian, Carboniferous, and Permian.

The _____ covers the time from the first appearance of abundant, soft-shelled fossils to the time when the continents were beginning to be dominated by large, relatively sophisticated reptiles and modern plants. The lower (oldest) boundary was classically set at the first appearance of creatures known as trilobites and archeocyathids.

a. 1703 Genroku earthquake
c. 1509 Istanbul earthquake

b. 1700 Cascadia earthquake
d. Paleozoic

55. The _____ was a major ice sheet that covered, during glacial periods of the Quaternary, a large area of North America. This included the following areas:

- Western Montana
- The Idaho Panhandle
- Northern Washington state down to about Seattle and Spokane, Washington
- All of British Columbia
- The southwestern third or so of Yukon territory
- All of the Alaska Panhandle
- South Central Alaska
- The Alaska Peninsula
- Almost all of the continental shelf north of the Strait of Juan de Fuca

The ice sheet covered up to two and a half million square kilometres at the Last Glacial Maximum and probably more than that in some previous periods, when it may have extended into the northeast extremity of Oregon and the Salmon River Mountains in Idaho. It is probable, though, that its northern margin also migrated south due to the influence of starvation caused by very low levels of precipitation.

Chapter 18. Amazing Ice: Glaciers and Ice Ages

At its eastern end the _____ merged with the Laurentide ice sheet at the Continental Divide, forming an area of ice that contained one and a half times as much water as the Antarctic ice sheet does today.

a. Rock flour
b. Snowball Earth
c. Wolstonian Stage
d. Cordilleran ice sheet

56. The _____ is a geological epoch which began approximately 11,700 years ago (10,000 ^{14}C years ago). According to traditional geological thinking, the _____ continues to the present. The _____ is part of the Neogene and Quaternary periods.

a. 1700 Cascadia earthquake
b. 1509 Istanbul earthquake
c. Neoglaciation
d. Holocene

57. The _____ is an oceanic tectonic plate beneath the Pacific Ocean.

To the north the easterly side is a divergent boundary with the Explorer Plate, the Juan de Fuca Plate and the Gorda Plate forming respectively the Explorer Ridge, the Juan de Fuca Ridge and the Gorda Ridge. In the middle the easterly side is a transform boundary with the North American Plate along the San Andreas Fault and a boundary with the Cocos Plate.

a. Pacific Plate
b. Somali Plate
c. Conway Reef Plate
d. Gorda Plate

58. An _____ is a geological interval of warmer global average temperature that separates glacial periods within an ice age. The current Holocene _____ has persisted since the Pleistocene, about 11,400 years ago.

During the 2.5 million year span of the Pleistocene, numerous glacials, or significant advances of continental ice sheets in North America and Europe have occurred at intervals of approximately 40,000 to 100,000 years.

a. AL 129-1
b. AASHTO Soil Classification System
c. AL 333
d. Interglacial

59. In the geosciences, _____ can have two meanings. The first meaning, common in geology and paleontology, refers to a former soil preserved by burial underneath either sediments (alluvium or loess) or volcanic deposits (Volcanic ash), which in case of older deposits have lithified into rock. In Quaternary geology, sedimentology, paleoclimatology, and geology in general, it is the typical and accepted practice to use the term '_____' to designate such 'fossil' soils found buried within either sedimentary or volcanic deposits exposed in all continents as illustrated by Rettallack (2001), Kraus (1999), and innumerable other published papers and books.

a. Paleosol
b. Soil horizon
c. Soil structure
d. Mollisols

Chapter 18. Amazing Ice: Glaciers and Ice Ages

60. _____, originally Gondwanaland, is the name given to a southern precursor-supercontinent and then as a remnant separated from Laurasia 180-200 million years ago during the breakup of the Pangaea supercontinent that existed about 500 to 200 Ma ago into two large segments. While the corresponding northern hemisphere continent Laurasia moved further north, the nearly equal in area _____ included most of the landmasses in today's southern hemisphere, including Antarctica, South America, Africa, Madagascar, Australia-New Guinea, and New Zealand, as well as Arabia and the Indian subcontinent, which have now moved into the Northern Hemisphere.
   a. Gondwana
   b. Laurasia
   c. 1700 Cascadia earthquake
   d. 1509 Istanbul earthquake

61. _____ was the supercontinent that is theorized to have existed during the Paleozoic and Mesozoic eras about 250 million years ago, before the component continents were separated into their current configuration.

The name was first used by the German originator of the continental drift theory, Alfred Wegener, in the 1920 edition of his book The Origin of Continents and Oceans, in which a postulated supercontinent _____ played a key role.

The single enormous ocean which surrounded Pangaea is known as Panthalassa.

   a. 1700 Cascadia earthquake
   b. 1703 Genroku earthquake
   c. Pangea
   d. 1509 Istanbul earthquake

62. The terms _____ and icehouse Earth refer to the prevailing global climate on a timescale of millions of years.

During a _____ Earth period, the planet's atmosphere contains sufficient _____ gases such as carbon dioxide and methane for ice to be entirely absent from the planet's surface.

During icehouse periods, glaciers are present in fluctuating amounts; variations in the Earth's orbit may result in many ice ages, glacials, and interglacials.

   a. 1700 Cascadia earthquake
   b. 1509 Istanbul earthquake
   c. 1703 Genroku earthquake
   d. Greenhouse

63. _____ refers to hypotheses regarding paleoclimatic global-scale glaciation, claiming that the Earth's surface was nearly or entirely frozen at some points in its past. The occurrence of _____ remains controversial. Proponents claim it best explains sedimentary deposits generally regarded as of glacial origin at tropical latitudes and other enigmatic features of the geological record.
   a. Snowball Earth
   b. Pastonian Stage
   c. Cirque glacier
   d. Pre-Pastonian Stage

64. The _____ of an object is the extent to which it diffusely reflects light from the Sun. It is therefore a more specific form of the term reflectivity. _____ is defined as the ratio of diffusely reflected to incident electromagnetic radiation.
   a. AASHTO Soil Classification System
   b. AL 129-1
   c. AL 333
   d. Albedo

Chapter 18. Amazing Ice: Glaciers and Ice Ages

65. The _____ is the mechanically weak ductily-deforming region of the upper mantle of the Earth. It lies below the lithosphere, at depths between 100 and 200 km (~ 62 and 124 miles) below the surface, but perhaps extending as deep as 400 km (~ 249 miles.)

The _____ is a portion of the upper mantle just below the lithosphere that is involved in plate movements and isostatic adjustments. In spite of its heat, pressures keep it plastic, and it has a relatively low density. Seismic waves pass relatively slowly through the _____, compared to the overlying lithospheric mantle, thus it has been called the low-velocity zone. This was the observation that originally alerted seismologists to its presence and gave some information about its physical properties, as the speed of seismic waves decreases with decreasing rigidity.

   a. AL 129-1
   c. AL 333
   b. AASHTO Soil Classification System
   d. Asthenosphere

66. The _____ is the rigid outermost shell of a rocky planet.

In the Earth, the _____ includes the crust and the uppermost mantle, which constitute the hard and rigid outer layer of the planet. The _____ is underlain by the asthenosphere, the weaker, hotter, and deeper part of the upper mantle.

   a. Juan de Fuca Ridge
   c. Gorda Ridge
   b. Continental drift
   d. Lithosphere

67. _____ describes the large scale motions of Earth's lithosphere. The theory encompasses the older concepts of continental drift, developed during the first decades of the 20th century by Alfred Wegener, and seafloor spreading, understood during the 1960s.

The outermost part of the Earth's interior is made up of two layers: the lithosphere and the asthenosphere.

   a. Plate tectonics
   c. Thrust fault
   b. Forearc
   d. Continental crust

68. A _____ column (or _____) is a column of rising air in the lower altitudes of the Earth's atmosphere. They are created by the uneven heating of the Earth's surface from solar radiation, and an example of convection. The Sun warms the ground, which in turn warms the air directly above it.
   a. 1700 Cascadia earthquake
   c. 1703 Genroku earthquake
   b. 1509 Istanbul earthquake
   d. Thermal

69. The term _____ refers to the part of the large-scale ocean circulation that is driven by global density gradients created by surface heat and freshwater fluxes. The adjective thermohaline derives from thermo- referring to temperature and -haline referring to salt content, factors which together determine the density of sea water. Wind-driven surface currents (such as the Gulf Stream) head polewards from the equatorial Atlantic Ocean, cooling all the while and eventually sinking at high latitudes (forming North Atlantic Deep Water.)
   a. 1509 Istanbul earthquake
   c. 1700 Cascadia earthquake
   b. 1703 Genroku earthquake
   d. Thermohaline circulation

Chapter 18. Amazing Ice: Glaciers and Ice Ages

70. The _____ was a period of cooling occurring after a warmer North Atlantic era known as the Medieval Warm Period. While not a true ice age, the term was introduced into scientific literature by Fran>çois E. Matthes in 1939. Climatologists and historians working with local records no longer expect to agree on either the start or end dates of this period, which varied according to local conditions.
   a. Geologic temperature record
   b. Pacific Decadal Oscillation
   c. Little ice age
   d. Glacier

71. _____ is a tidewater glacier in the U.S. state of Alaska and the Yukon Territory of Canada. From its source in the Yukon, the glacier stretches 122 km (76 mi) to the sea at Yakutat Bay and Disenchantment Bay. It is the longest tidewater glacier in Alaska, with an open calving face over ten kilometers (6 mi) wide.
   a. 1703 Genroku earthquake
   b. 1509 Istanbul earthquake
   c. 1700 Cascadia earthquake
   d. Hubbard glacier

Chapter 19. Global Change in the Earth System

1. _____ is a common extrusive volcanic rock. It is usually grey to black and fine-grained due to rapid cooling of lava at the surface of a planet. It may be porphyritic containing larger crystals in a fine matrix, or vesicular, or frothy scoria.
   - a. 1509 Istanbul earthquake
   - b. 1703 Genroku earthquake
   - c. Basalt
   - d. 1700 Cascadia earthquake

2. In mineralogy and crystallography, a _____ is a unique arrangement of atoms in a crystal. A _____ is composed of a motif, a set of atoms arranged in a particular way, and a lattice. Motifs are located upon the points of a lattice, which is an array of points repeating periodically in three dimensions.
   - a. 1703 Genroku earthquake
   - b. Crystal structure
   - c. 1509 Istanbul earthquake
   - d. 1700 Cascadia earthquake

3. _____ is the removal of solids (sediment, soil, rock and other particles) in the natural environment. It usually occurs due to transport by wind, water, or ice; by down-slope creep of soil and other material under the force of gravity; or by living organisms, such as burrowing animals, in the case of bioerosion.

   _____ is distinguished from weathering, which is the process of chemical or physical breakdown of the minerals in the rocks, although the two processes may occur concurrently.

   - a. Erosion
   - b. AASHTO Soil Classification System
   - c. AL 333
   - d. AL 129-1

4. The _____ is a chronologic schema (or idealized model) relating stratigraphy to time that is used by geologists, paleontologists and other earth scientists to describe the timing and relationships between events that have occurred during the history of the Earth. The table of geologic time spans presented here agrees with the dates and nomenclature proposed by the International Commission on Stratigraphy, and uses the standard color codes of the United States Geological Survey.

   Evidence from radiometric dating indicates that the Earth is about 4.570 billion years old.

   - a. 1509 Istanbul earthquake
   - b. 1703 Genroku earthquake
   - c. 1700 Cascadia earthquake
   - d. Geologic time scale

5. _____ are the largest glaciers, enormous masses of ice that are not visibly affected by the landscape and that cover the entire surface beneath them, except possibly on the margins where they are thinnest. Antarctica and Greenland are the only places where continental _____ currently exist. These regions contain vast quantities of fresh water.
   - a. AASHTO Soil Classification System
   - b. AL 129-1
   - c. AL 333
   - d. Ice sheets

6. _____ is a sedimentary rock. It is a natural chemical precipitate of carbonate minerals; typically aragonite, but often recrystallized to, or primarily, calcite.

   _____ forms as calcium carbonate is deposited from the water of mineral springs or rivulets that are saturated with dissolved calcium bicarbonate. The spring water from which the calcium carbonate precipitates can be hot, warm or cold. The rate of deposition increases with the temperature of the water, or alternatively, when biotic material accelerates the process of precipitation.

Chapter 19. Global Change in the Earth System

a. 1700 Cascadia earthquake
b. 1509 Istanbul earthquake
c. 1703 Genroku earthquake
d. Travertine

7. The _____ was a major ice sheet that covered, during glacial periods of the Quaternary, a large area of North America. This included the following areas:

- Western Montana
- The Idaho Panhandle
- Northern Washington state down to about Seattle and Spokane, Washington
- All of British Columbia
- The southwestern third or so of Yukon territory
- All of the Alaska Panhandle
- South Central Alaska
- The Alaska Peninsula
- Almost all of the continental shelf north of the Strait of Juan de Fuca

The ice sheet covered up to two and a half million square kilometres at the Last Glacial Maximum and probably more than that in some previous periods, when it may have extended into the northeast extremity of Oregon and the Salmon River Mountains in Idaho. It is probable, though, that its northern margin also migrated south due to the influence of starvation caused by very low levels of precipitation.

At its eastern end the _____ merged with the Laurentide ice sheet at the Continental Divide, forming an area of ice that contained one and a half times as much water as the Antarctic ice sheet does today.

a. Wolstonian Stage
b. Snowball Earth
c. Rock flour
d. Cordilleran ice sheet

8. A _____ is a deep active seismic area in a subduction zone. Differential motion along the zone produces deep-seated earthquakes, the foci of which may be as deep as about 700 kilometres (435 miles.) They develop beneath volcanic island arcs and continental margins above active subduction zones.

a. Lava
b. Pyroclastic flow
c. Pit crater
d. Wadati-Benioff zone

9. A _____ is a geological phenomenon which includes a wide range of ground movement, such as rock falls, deep failure of slopes and shallow debris flows, which can occur in offshore, coastal and onshore environments. Although the action of gravity is the primary driving force for a _____ to occur, there are other contributing factors affecting the original slope stability. Typically, pre-conditional factors build up specific sub-surface conditions that make the area/slope prone to failure, whereas the actual _____ often requires a trigger before being released.

a. 1700 Cascadia earthquake
b. 1509 Istanbul earthquake
c. Landslide
d. Mass wasting

10. The _____ is the level at which the ground water pressure is equal to atmospheric pressure. It may be conveniently visualized as the 'surface' of the ground water in a given vicinity. It usually coincides with the phreatic surface, but can be many feet above it. As water infiltrates through pore spaces in the soil, it first passes through the zone of aeration, where the soil is unsaturated. At increasing depths water fills in more spaces, until the zone of saturation is reached. The relatively horizontal plane atop this zone constitutes the _____.

a. Shaft construction	b. Water table
c. Rock bolt	d. Crosshole sonic logging

11. A _____ is a large, slow-moving mass of ice, formed from compacted layers of snow, that slowly deforms and flows in response to gravity and high pressure.

_____ ice is the largest reservoir of fresh water on Earth, and second only to oceans as the largest reservoir of total water.

a. Little Ice Age	b. Keeling Curve
c. Pacific Decadal Oscillation	d. Glacier

12. _____ was the supercontinent that is theorized to have existed during the Paleozoic and Mesozoic eras about 250 million years ago, before the component continents were separated into their current configuration.

The name was first used by the German originator of the continental drift theory, Alfred Wegener, in the 1920 edition of his book The Origin of Continents and Oceans , in which a postulated supercontinent _____ played a key role.

The single enormous ocean which surrounded Pangaea is known as Panthalassa.

a. 1509 Istanbul earthquake	b. 1700 Cascadia earthquake
c. 1703 Genroku earthquake	d. Pangea

13. The _____ is the epoch from 1.8 million to 11550 years BP covering the world's recent period of repeated glaciations. The _____ epoch follows the Pliocene epoch and is followed by the Holocene epoch. The _____ is the third epoch of the Neogene period or 6th epoch of the Cenozoic Era. The end of the _____ corresponds with the retreat of the last continental glacier. It also corresponds with the end of the Paleolithic age used in archaeology.

a. Late Pleistocene	b. Sicilian Stage
c. Tyrrhenian	d. Pleistocene

14. A _____ is an elongated whale-shaped hill formed by glacial action. Its long axis is parallel with the movement of the ice, with the blunter end facing into the glacial movement. They may be more than 45 m (150 ft) high and more than 0.8 km (1/2 mile) long, and are often in _____ fields of similarly shaped, sized and oriented hills. They usually have layers indicating that the material was repeatedly added to a core, which may be of rock or glacial till.

a. Monadnock	b. 1509 Istanbul earthquake
c. Drumlin	d. Sandur

15. The _____ is a fundamental concept in geology that describes the dynamic transitions through geologic time among the three main rock types: sedimentary, metamorphic, and igneous. Each type of rock is altered or destroyed when it is forced out of its equilibrium conditions. An igneous rock such as basalt may break down and dissolve when exposed to the atmosphere, or melt as it is subducted under a continent.

a. Petrology	b. Laccolith
c. Volcanic rock	d. Rock cycle

16. In geology, a _____ is a landmass comprising more than one continental core, or craton. The assembly of cratons and accreted terranes that form Eurasia qualifies as a _____ today.

Most commonly, paleogeographers employ the term _____ to refer to a single landmass consisting of all the modern continents.

   a. 1700 Cascadia earthquake
   b. 1703 Genroku earthquake
   c. 1509 Istanbul earthquake
   d. Supercontinent

17. The _____ is a geological signature, usually a thin band, dated to (65.5 ± 0.3) Ma (million years ago). The boundary marks the end of the Mesozoic era and the beginning of the Cenozoic era, and is associated with the Cretaceous-Tertiary extinction event, a mass extinction.
   a. 1700 Cascadia earthquake
   b. 1509 Istanbul earthquake
   c. Shiva crater
   d. K-T boundary

18. The _____ is the biogeochemical cycle by which carbon is exchanged among the biosphere, pedosphere, geosphere, hydrosphere, and atmosphere of the Earth.

The _____ is usually thought of as four major reservoirs of carbon interconnected by pathways of exchange. These reservoirs are:

   • The plants
   • The terrestrial biosphere, which is usually defined to include fresh water systems and non-living organic material, such as soil carbon.
   • The oceans, including dissolved inorganic carbon and living and non-living marine biota,
   • The sediments including fossil fuels.

The annual movements of carbon, the carbon exchanges between reservoirs, occur because of various chemical, physical, geological, and biological processes. The ocean contains the largest active pool of carbon near the surface of the Earth, but the deep ocean part of this pool does not rapidly exchange with the atmosphere.

   a. Carbon cycle
   b. Nanogeoscience
   c. Cosmogenic isotopes
   d. 1509 Istanbul earthquake

19. _____ are the preserved remains or traces of animals, plants, and other organisms from the remote past. The totality of _____, both discovered and undiscovered, and their placement in fossiliferous rock formations and sedimentary layers (strata) is known as the fossil record. The study of _____ across geological time, how they were formed, and the evolutionary relationships between taxa (phylogeny) are some of the most important functions of the science of paleontology.
   a. 1509 Istanbul earthquake
   b. Fossils
   c. 1703 Genroku earthquake
   d. 1700 Cascadia earthquake

20. The _____ describes the continuous movement of water on, above, and below the surface of the Earth. Since the _____ is truly a 'cycle,' there is no beginning or end. Water can change states among liquid, vapor, and ice at various places in the _____.

a. Vadose zone	b. Hydraulic conductivity
c. Cone of depression	d. Water cycle

21. _____ is the solid-state recrystallization of pre-existing rocks due to changes in physical and chemical conditions, primarily heat, pressure, and the introduction of chemically active fluids. Both mineralogical, chemical and crystallographic changes can occur during this process.

Three types of _____ exist: dynamic, contact and regional.

a. Detritus	b. Reading Prong
c. Compression	d. Metamorphism

22. A _____ is a natural depression or hole in the surface topography caused by the removal of soil or bedrock, often both, by water. They may vary in size from less than a meter to several hundred meters both in diameter and depth, and vary in form from soil-lined bowls to bedrock-edged chasms. They may be formed gradually or suddenly, and are found worldwide.

a. 1700 Cascadia earthquake	b. 1509 Istanbul earthquake
c. 1703 Genroku earthquake	d. Sinkhole

23. The _____ is an oceanic tectonic plate beneath the Pacific Ocean.

To the north the easterly side is a divergent boundary with the Explorer Plate, the Juan de Fuca Plate and the Gorda Plate forming respectively the Explorer Ridge, the Juan de Fuca Ridge and the Gorda Ridge. In the middle the easterly side is a transform boundary with the North American Plate along the San Andreas Fault and a boundary with the Cocos Plate.

a. Conway Reef Plate	b. Gorda Plate
c. Somali Plate	d. Pacific Plate

24. The _____ is a geological eon representing a period before the first abundant complex life on Earth. The _____ extended from 2500 Ma to 542.0 >± 1.0 Ma (million years ago), and is the most recent part of the old, informally named 'e;Precambrian'e; time.

The Proterozoic consists of 3 geologic eras, from oldest to youngest:

- Paleoproterozoic
- Mesoproterozoic
- Neoproterozoic

The well-identified events were:

- The transition to an oxygenated atmosphere during the Mesoproterozoic.
- Several glaciations, including the hypothesized Snowball Earth during the Cryogenian period in the late Neoproterozoic.
- The Ediacaran Period (635 to 542 Ma) which is characterized by the evolution of abundant soft-bodied multicellular organisms.

The geoloic record of the Proterozoic is much better than that for the preceding Archean. In contrast to the deep-water deposits of the Archean, the Proterozoic features many strata that were laid down in extensive shallow epicontinental seas; furthermore, many of these rocks are less metamorphosed than Archean-age ones, and plenty are unaltered.

a. 1700 Cascadia earthquake
b. 1509 Istanbul earthquake
c. 1703 Genroku earthquake
d. Proterozoic Eon

25. The terms _____ and icehouse Earth refer to the prevailing global climate on a timescale of millions of years.

During a _____ Earth period, the planet's atmosphere contains sufficient _____ gases such as carbon dioxide and methane for ice to be entirely absent from the planet's surface.

During icehouse periods, glaciers are present in fluctuating amounts; variations in the Earth's orbit may result in many ice ages, glacials, and interglacials.

a. 1703 Genroku earthquake
b. Greenhouse
c. 1509 Istanbul earthquake
d. 1700 Cascadia earthquake

26. The lithosphere is broken up into what are called _____. In the case of Earth, there are eight major and many minor plates The lithospheric plates ride on the asthenosphere. These plates move in relation to one another at one of three types of plate boundaries: convergent, or collisional boundaries; divergent boundaries, also called spreading centers; and transform boundaries.

a. Gorda Ridge
b. Thrust fault
c. Copperbelt Province
d. Tectonic plates

27. The general term '_____' or, more precisely, 'glacial age' denotes a geological period of long-term reduction in the temperature of the Earth's surface and atmosphere, resulting in an expansion of continental ice sheets, polar ice sheets and alpine glaciers. Within a long-term _____, individual pulses of extra cold climate are termed 'glaciations'. Glaciologically, _____ implies the presence of extensive ice sheets in the northern and southern hemispheres; by this definition we are still in an _____.

a. AL 129-1
b. AL 333
c. AASHTO Soil Classification System
d. Ice age

28. The _____ is a geological epoch which began approximately 11‰700 years ago (10‰000 ^{14}C years ago). According to traditional geological thinking, the _____ continues to the present. The _____ is part of the Neogene and Quaternary periods.
   a. 1509 Istanbul earthquake
   b. Holocene
   c. Neoglaciation
   d. 1700 Cascadia earthquake

29. The _____ or Medieval Climate Optimum was a time of warm climate in the North Atlantic region, lasting from about the tenth century to about the fourteenth century. It was followed by the a cooler period in the North Atlantic termed as the Little Ice Age. The _____ is often invoked in discussions of global warming.
   a. Maunder Minimum
   b. Middle Bronze Age Cold Epoch
   c. Paleocene-Eocene Thermal Maximum
   d. Medieval warm period

30. An _____ is the result of a sudden release of energy in the Earth's crust that creates seismic waves. They are recorded with a seismometer or the related and mostly obsolete Richter magnitude, with a magnitude 3 or lower _____ being mostly imperceptible and magnitude 7 causing serious damage over large areas.
   a. AL 129-1
   b. AASHTO Soil Classification System
   c. AL 333
   d. Earthquake

31. The _____ is the rigid outermost shell of a rocky planet.

In the Earth, the _____ includes the crust and the uppermost mantle, which constitute the hard and rigid outer layer of the planet. The _____ is underlain by the asthenosphere, the weaker, hotter, and deeper part of the upper mantle.

   a. Juan de Fuca Ridge
   b. Gorda Ridge
   c. Continental drift
   d. Lithosphere

32. The _____ was a period of cooling occurring after a warmer North Atlantic era known as the Medieval Warm Period. While not a true ice age, the term was introduced into scientific literature by Fran>çois E. Matthes in 1939. Climatologists and historians working with local records no longer expect to agree on either the start or end dates of this period, which varied according to local conditions.
   a. Little ice age
   b. Pacific Decadal Oscillation
   c. Geologic temperature record
   d. Glacier

33. _____ describes the large scale motions of Earth's lithosphere. The theory encompasses the older concepts of continental drift, developed during the first decades of the 20th century by Alfred Wegener, and seafloor spreading, understood during the 1960s.

The outermost part of the Earth's interior is made up of two layers: the lithosphere and the asthenosphere.

   a. Continental crust
   b. Forearc
   c. Thrust fault
   d. Plate tectonics

34. Geologically, a _____ is a long, narrow inlet with steep sides, created in a valley carved by glacial activity.

Chapter 19. Global Change in the Earth System

The seeds of a _____ are laid when a glacier cuts a U-shaped valley through abrasion of the surrounding bedrock by the sediment it carries. Many such valleys were formed during the recent ice age.

a. 1700 Cascadia earthquake
b. 1703 Genroku earthquake
c. 1509 Istanbul earthquake
d. Fjord

35. The _____ is a geologic period and system, the second of six of the Paleozoic era, and covers the time between 488.3>±1.7 to 443.7>±1.5 million years ago (ICS, 2004.) It follows the Cambrian period and is followed by the Silurian period. The _____ was defined by Charles Lapworth in 1879, to resolve a dispute between followers of Adam Sedgwick and Roderick Murchison, who were placing the same rock beds in northern Wales into the Cambrian and Silurian periods respectively.

a. Ordovician
b. AASHTO Soil Classification System
c. AL 333
d. AL 129-1

36. A _____ column (or _____) is a column of rising air in the lower altitudes of the Earth's atmosphere. They are created by the uneven heating of the Earth's surface from solar radiation, and an example of convection. The Sun warms the ground, which in turn warms the air directly above it.

a. 1700 Cascadia earthquake
b. 1703 Genroku earthquake
c. 1509 Istanbul earthquake
d. Thermal

37. The term _____ refers to the part of the large-scale ocean circulation that is driven by global density gradients created by surface heat and freshwater fluxes. The adjective thermohaline derives from thermo- referring to temperature and -haline referring to salt content, factors which together determine the density of sea water. Wind-driven surface currents (such as the Gulf Stream) head polewards from the equatorial Atlantic Ocean, cooling all the while and eventually sinking at high latitudes (forming North Atlantic Deep Water.)

a. 1509 Istanbul earthquake
b. 1703 Genroku earthquake
c. 1700 Cascadia earthquake
d. Thermohaline circulation

ANSWER KEY

Chapter 1
1. d	2. d	3. d	4. d	5. b	6. d	7. c	8. d	9. d	10. d
11. d	12. d	13. d	14. d	15. d	16. c	17. d	18. a	19. a	20. d
21. d	22. b	23. d	24. d	25. d	26. b	27. a	28. d	29. d	30. b
31. a	32. d	33. b	34. b	35. d	36. c	37. d	38. d	39. d	40. c
41. d	42. d	43. c	44. c	45. b	46. c	47. c	48. b	49. a	50. b
51. b	52. d	53. c	54. a						

Chapter 2
1. d	2. a	3. d	4. c	5. d	6. a	7. b	8. d	9. d	10. d
11. c	12. b	13. a	14. b	15. d	16. d	17. a	18. b	19. a	20. d
21. d	22. d	23. b	24. a	25. a	26. a	27. d	28. d	29. d	30. d
31. b	32. d	33. a	34. b	35. b	36. a	37. d	38. d	39. d	40. d
41. d	42. b	43. d	44. c	45. b	46. a	47. b	48. d	49. d	50. c

Chapter 3
1. d	2. d	3. d	4. d	5. d	6. b	7. c	8. a	9. d	10. c
11. b	12. b	13. c	14. d	15. c	16. c	17. a	18. a	19. a	20. c
21. d	22. a	23. b	24. d	25. d	26. d	27. b	28. d	29. d	30. d
31. d	32. b	33. d	34. d	35. b	36. d	37. d	38. a	39. d	40. b
41. a	42. d	43. b	44. d	45. d	46. d	47. d	48. d	49. a	50. d
51. b	52. b	53. d	54. d	55. b	56. d	57. d	58. c	59. c	60. b
61. a	62. c	63. a							

Chapter 4
1. b	2. a	3. d	4. a	5. d	6. a	7. d	8. b	9. b	10. b
11. d	12. d	13. a	14. d	15. a	16. d	17. b	18. b	19. c	20. c
21. d	22. b	23. d	24. a	25. c	26. a	27. a	28. c	29. d	30. c
31. d	32. d	33. d	34. d	35. d	36. c	37. a	38. b	39. c	40. d
41. c	42. d	43. d	44. a	45. c	46. c	47. d	48. a	49. d	

Chapter 5
1. a	2. b	3. d	4. d	5. c	6. d	7. d	8. d	9. a	10. a
11. d	12. b	13. d	14. d	15. d	16. d	17. d	18. d	19. d	20. a
21. a	22. a	23. d	24. d	25. c	26. c	27. d	28. d	29. c	30. a
31. c	32. d	33. d	34. d	35. d	36. d	37. c	38. d	39. c	40. c
41. b	42. d	43. a	44. d	45. d	46. a	47. d	48. d	49. a	50. d
51. d	52. a	53. c	54. c	55. a	56. d	57. a	58. a	59. a	60. d
61. d	62. c	63. d	64. d	65. d	66. b	67. b	68. d	69. d	70. d
71. d	72. b	73. d	74. d	75. d	76. d	77. b	78. b		

Chapter 6

1. d	2. c	3. c	4. c	5. d	6. d	7. d	8. d	9. a	10. c
11. d	12. a	13. c	14. c	15. b	16. c	17. a	18. d	19. d	20. d
21. d	22. c	23. d	24. b	25. d	26. a	27. c	28. b	29. a	30. d
31. d	32. d	33. c	34. a	35. d	36. b	37. b	38. d	39. a	40. d
41. d	42. d	43. a	44. d	45. b	46. b	47. b	48. b	49. d	50. a
51. c	52. b	53. d	54. b	55. d	56. b	57. d	58. a	59. c	60. d
61. d	62. b	63. d	64. d	65. c	66. a	67. d	68. a		

Chapter 7

1. d	2. a	3. a	4. d	5. c	6. d	7. a	8. d	9. b	10. b
11. b	12. d	13. d	14. d	15. d	16. b	17. d	18. d	19. b	20. a
21. d	22. d	23. c	24. d	25. d	26. a	27. c	28. d	29. d	30. b
31. d	32. c	33. a	34. d	35. d	36. d	37. a	38. c	39. a	40. d
41. a	42. c	43. d	44. c	45. d	46. d	47. d	48. d	49. c	50. d
51. d	52. d	53. d	54. d	55. b	56. d	57. a	58. d	59. b	60. d

Chapter 8

1. a	2. c	3. b	4. d	5. d	6. c	7. d	8. a	9. d	10. b
11. a	12. d	13. b	14. b	15. d	16. d	17. d	18. a	19. c	20. d
21. c	22. d	23. a	24. d	25. d	26. c	27. c	28. a	29. b	30. d
31. c	32. d	33. c	34. c	35. d	36. a	37. d	38. d	39. d	40. d
41. d	42. a	43. d	44. d	45. d	46. d	47. d	48. d	49. d	50. b
51. b	52. d	53. c	54. d	55. a	56. d	57. b	58. d	59. d	60. b
61. d	62. d	63. c	64. a	65. a	66. d				

Chapter 9

1. d	2. a	3. a	4. a	5. d	6. d	7. d	8. a	9. c	10. c
11. a	12. a	13. b	14. d	15. b	16. d	17. c	18. a	19. d	20. b
21. c	22. b	23. d	24. c	25. a	26. a	27. d	28. d	29. c	30. b
31. d	32. d	33. a	34. b	35. d	36. d	37. d	38. b	39. b	40. a
41. a	42. c	43. a	44. b	45. d	46. d	47. a	48. d	49. b	50. b
51. d	52. b	53. d	54. a	55. d	56. d	57. c	58. a	59. b	60. b
61. c	62. d	63. d	64. d	65. d	66. b	67. b	68. d	69. d	70. b
71. b	72. c								

Chapter 10

1. b	2. d	3. d	4. a	5. d	6. d	7. c	8. c	9. d	10. c
11. d	12. d	13. d	14. b	15. d	16. c	17. d	18. d	19. d	20. a
21. c	22. d	23. b	24. d	25. c	26. d	27. d	28. d	29. d	30. d
31. c	32. d								

Chapter 11

1. d	2. c	3. d	4. b	5. d	6. d	7. b	8. a	9. d	10. a
11. d	12. b	13. d	14. a	15. b	16. d	17. b	18. d	19. c	20. d
21. d	22. c	23. b	24. b	25. b	26. d	27. d	28. d	29. d	30. d
31. d	32. d	33. b	34. d	35. d	36. d	37. d	38. d	39. d	40. d
41. d	42. d	43. a	44. d	45. a	46. d	47. a	48. c	49. a	50. b
51. d	52. c	53. a	54. b	55. b	56. b	57. d	58. d	59. b	60. b
61. d	62. d	63. a	64. d	65. c	66. a	67. d	68. b	69. d	70. a

Chapter 12

1. d	2. b	3. a	4. d	5. c	6. d	7. c	8. d	9. d	10. d
11. b	12. d	13. c	14. a	15. d	16. c	17. d	18. b	19. c	20. a
21. b	22. b	23. d	24. b	25. d	26. b	27. a	28. c	29. d	30. c
31. b	32. b	33. c	34. d	35. b	36. a	37. a	38. d	39. b	40. b
41. d	42. d	43. d	44. a	45. d	46. a	47. a	48. d	49. a	50. c
51. c	52. d	53. a	54. d	55. d	56. c	57. d	58. a	59. d	60. a
61. b	62. a	63. d	64. d						

Chapter 13

1. b	2. b	3. d	4. c	5. b	6. c	7. d	8. a	9. c	10. c
11. d	12. a	13. d	14. a	15. a	16. a	17. d	18. b	19. d	20. d
21. d	22. d	23. d	24. d	25. a	26. b	27. d	28. b	29. a	30. b
31. a	32. c	33. b							

Chapter 14

1. b	2. c	3. b	4. b	5. c	6. d	7. c	8. a	9. d	10. d
11. d	12. d	13. a	14. c	15. d	16. d	17. c	18. b	19. d	20. d
21. b	22. c	23. d	24. d	25. c	26. d	27. d	28. d	29. d	30. a
31. a	32. a	33. c	34. c	35. d	36. d	37. d	38. a	39. d	40. d
41. b	42. a	43. c							

Chapter 15

1. b	2. a	3. c	4. d	5. d	6. d	7. b	8. d	9. b	10. c
11. d	12. a	13. c	14. c	15. d	16. c	17. d	18. d	19. b	20. d
21. b	22. b	23. b	24. d	25. a	26. c	27. c	28. d	29. d	30. c
31. d	32. d	33. b	34. c	35. c	36. d	37. d	38. b	39. c	40. d
41. a	42. c	43. a	44. c	45. d	46. a	47. d	48. a	49. d	50. b
51. d	52. d	53. a	54. b						

Chapter 16

1. c	2. b	3. b	4. a	5. c	6. c	7. d	8. c	9. a	10. a
11. d	12. c	13. d	14. d	15. d	16. d	17. d	18. d	19. c	20. d
21. c	22. d	23. d	24. d	25. b	26. d	27. a	28. a	29. d	30. b
31. c	32. a	33. c	34. c	35. d	36. d				

Chapter 17

1. d	2. c	3. d	4. d	5. d	6. d	7. a	8. d	9. d	10. d
11. d	12. d	13. d	14. d	15. d	16. d	17. d	18. b	19. d	20. c
21. d	22. a	23. b	24. b	25. c	26. d	27. b	28. d	29. a	30. d
31. c	32. d	33. c	34. b	35. d	36. d	37. a	38. c	39. c	40. d
41. a	42. d	43. d	44. c	45. d	46. d	47. d	48. b	49. c	50. b
51. b	52. b								

Chapter 18

1. d	2. a	3. d	4. c	5. c	6. b	7. d	8. d	9. d	10. d
11. d	12. c	13. d	14. c	15. d	16. c	17. c	18. d	19. d	20. c
21. c	22. d	23. a	24. a	25. d	26. d	27. a	28. a	29. a	30. d
31. b	32. a	33. b	34. d	35. d	36. b	37. d	38. d	39. d	40. d
41. c	42. a	43. d	44. d	45. b	46. c	47. d	48. a	49. a	50. c
51. c	52. d	53. c	54. d	55. d	56. d	57. a	58. d	59. a	60. a
61. c	62. d	63. a	64. d	65. d	66. d	67. a	68. d	69. d	70. c
71. d									

Chapter 19

1. c	2. b	3. a	4. d	5. d	6. d	7. d	8. d	9. c	10. b
11. d	12. d	13. d	14. c	15. d	16. d	17. d	18. a	19. b	20. d
21. d	22. d	23. d	24. d	25. b	26. d	27. d	28. b	29. d	30. d
31. d	32. a	33. d	34. d	35. a	36. d	37. d			

www.ingramcontent.com/pod-product-compliance
Lightning Source LLC
Chambersburg PA
CBHW081351230426
43667CB00017B/2798